# FAILURE
## — THE —
# BACKDOOR
## — TO —
# SUCCESS

# FAILURE
## THE
## BACKDOOR
## TO
## SUCCESS

## ERWIN W. LUTZER

**MOODY PRESS**
CHICAGO

© 1975 by
THE MOODY BIBLE INSTITUTE
OF CHICAGO

All Scripture quotations, unless noted otherwise, are from the *New American Standard Bible*, © 1960, 1962, 1963, 1968, 1971, 1972, 1973, 1975, and 1977 by The Lockman Foundation, and are used by permission.

Library of Congress Cataloging in Publication Data
Lutzer, Erwin W
    Failure, the back door to success.
    1. Success.      2. Failure (Psychology)
3. Psychology, Religious.    I. Title.
BF637.S8L87      158'.1      75-16177
ISBN 0-8024-2593-3

7 9 10 8 6

*Printed in the United States of America*

*To Harry Verploegh, who persistently reminded me that nothing—not even our supposed failures or successes—is as important as learning to worship the Lord our God*

# Contents

# Foreword

Failure is one of the uglies of life. We deny it, run away from it, or, upon being overtaken, fall into permanent paralyzing fear. Probably because of our reluctance to face it, not much is written about the anatomy of failure. As Christians we wave our visionary banners proclaiming, "Victory in Christ," refusing often even to admit that the path to ultimate victory may include intermediate bloody noses.

Accidents on the road to success are, of course, often blamed on the heavy traffic in which we travel. Pastor Lutzer's no-fault insurance plan advises the victim not to criticize other people's or even his own reckless driving so much as to evaluate his collision and move on. The author's route up out of the ditch is paved with common sense, logical reasoning, and biblical authority. Anyone who himself has been stuck in the slough of despond will gratefully respond to this simple escape plan. It bears the stamp of authenticity.

Not only the return road to success but the path to fulfillment is mapped out. Of his own success, Dr. Lutzer says, "I was so busy I scarcely had time to ask God to rubber-stamp my plans!" Success without satisfaction is little reward; learning to follow God's directions adds the mission dimension. It is this component of the book that makes it more than a mere manual for staying inside the solid white line.

Solving problems assumes we ask and answer the right questions: Why failure? How can one change a poor self-image? What happens when a Christian steps out of God's will? Is it ever too late? What does God want most from His children? Through twelve chapters Lutzer delves into the why's of the loser syndrome.

With disarming honesty, this writer, weathered in the college classroom and the pastorate, heaves an initial sigh of boredom and frustration with the current spate of success manuals and proceeds with sensitive understanding to show why and how we are so often checkmated. Some of his real-life vignettes stumble right on down to final defeat—just like it happens in experience. The reader instinctively picks up the vibes that this man knows what failure is about.

For the new believer, beset by the many chuckholes of the Christian life, this book is a valuable guide for the journey. For the more experienced Christian, who has as much as sprained his spiritual ankle, it is a welcome support and encouragement. Happily, I think, this writer had avoided the buck-up-and-look-on-the-bright-side counsel. With a masterful finesse that belies his youth, he has in effect—like a wise old grandfather—said, "Now, son, let's take a look at what's wrong here. Yep, you're right. It's not so good. But you can get out of that booby trap with some know-how. There's a foolproof way. You listen here."

This book is sorely needed in our overanalyzed, undermotivated, and guilt-ridden Christian society. It can be a life changer to anyone tired of the old one-step-forward-and-two-backward routine.

HOWARD G. HENDRICKS

# Preface

Perhaps you have been as frustrated as I at the many books available on the topic of how to be a success. Many of these books are written for people who simply lack initiative or who haven't established worthy goals for their lives. But there are scores of Christians whose lives are so characterized by perpetual failure that simply applying some novel "secret" of success smacks of mockery.

What about those whose lives are filled with regret? What about those who have committed gross sins? Or those who have been trapped into a meaningless marriage? Where do such people begin in their quest for peace and fulfillment?

My conviction is that failure of some kind is common to us all. And since God had people like us in mind when Christ died, God's grace is adequate to make the best of any situation. Successful people are those who apply God's remedy for failure.

This does not mean that we must fail miserably before we can be a success; it does mean that we cannot be successful in God's sight until we see our own sinfulness—our potential for failure. Only those who see themselves as utterly destitute can fully appreciate the grace of God.

Although personal failure is not a requirement for being a success, our failures can be used as stepping-stones to a more meaningful relationship with God. Having failed, we can yet be successful in God's sight because of the incredible generosity of God's forgiveness and acceptance.

This book has been written with the earnest prayer that it might be an encouragement to us as Christians. As I shall explain later, some people who believe they are successes may actually be failures; others who have failed may really be quite successful. For all, there is hope! Salvation was designed for people who have made mistakes, failed, and sinned. Despite our past, all of us can say, "I delight to do thy will, O my God" (Psalms 40:8, KJV*).

*King James Version.

# 1

# Failure Is for Real

I didn't know whether to laugh or cry; so I laughed, then I cried.

Discouragement was etched indelibly on Jim's face. He spoke with urgency and only occasionally showed the trace of a smile. "Living for Christ is fine if you are on the top of the pile," he surmised with conviction, "but it's a different story when you are at the bottom."

Two years before this, I had met Jim (not his real name) when he was in high school. He had recently accepted Christ as his Savior. I'll never forget his impromptu prayers. "Lord, it's me again," he'd say. "Remember old Duncan Bell? Well, You know I don't like him, so I need all the help You can give me."

After high school Jim was accepted for Royal Canadian Mounted Police training in Canada. From the first day, he sincerely tried to be a witness to his comrades. He read his Bible, refused to share sordid jokes, and would not participate in sensual amusements. In short, he "lived for Christ," as most preachers urge us to do.

And that was the beginning of his troubles. Friends dubbed him "the religious nut." Some scorned his piety. Others schemed to have him blamed for activities he did not do. He was ousted (often literally) from the games and social events of his companions.

Perhaps this is what Christians should expect. Are not the godly promised persecution? Did Christ not say that we should rejoice when we are reviled, because our reward would be great in heaven? Yes.

But one fact troubled him. In any group, one person is always first, but by necessity, one must also be last. Jim had that distinction.

He got the lowest score on examinations and barely passed in practical achievements. He was not a leader, neither did he have a winsome personality. Worse yet, he commanded little or no respect.

As we talked together, he stared aimlessly into space. "My friends are rejecting Christ," he commented, "but maybe it's just because they don't want to be like me, and on that score I don't blame them. Who'd want to be like me?" He forced a smile to hold back the tears. "I'm a failure, and I know it."

My mind raced over all those sermons I have heard about how we should do well at school or at our vocations to be a "testimony." But that advice couldn't apply to Jim. God had not given him the ability to gain the respect of others by intellectual or physical accomplishments.

So I explained to Jim—or at least I tried to explain—that maybe God didn't expect as much from him as He did from others. Maybe he should accept his limitations and learn to be satisfied with his role in life. But my explanation was either deficient or unconvincing, or both.

A year later Jim committed suicide.

Shocking? Yes. I did not suspect that Jim had become that discouraged. It was the last desperate act of a Christian who believed that success was forever beyond his grasp.

Since that time I've come to know many who are like Jim. They read the how-to-be-a-success books, they try positive thinking, and yet they are hounded by the suspicion that they are failures.

Most of us have unclear (usually false) notions of success. We hear testimonies of converted movie stars, professional singers, or those who are "successful" in some vocation.

Unconsciously, we assume that all Christians should be like them.

Perhaps we have forgotten that not many wise, noble, and mighty are chosen by God. We judge ourselves and others by a false standard.

A *few* noble, wise, and gifted are called. But they are exceptions. God usually chooses the weak, the ordinary, and the despised. Why, then, do so many of us believe we are failures? Perhaps we have a totally *false notion of success.* More of that later.

Many Christians feel trapped because of ugly circumstances. Some have made wrong choices or have been discouraged because they are "out of God's will."

Consider Beth. She accepted Christ at the age of ten. A dozen years later, she fell in love with a promising young executive. She blissfully entered marriage without a single reservation about her serious-minded husband. *Of course* God would bless their marriage. *Of course* they'd live happily. But optimism does not guarantee success.

For more than twenty years she has lived with a hot-tempered, egotistical, and irrational husband. He rashly punished the children for misdeeds he falsely supposed they committed. He even now demeans his wife in public and is insensitive to her needs. The children are floundering in rebellion, trying to adjust to the world.

Before her marriage Beth sang, played the piano, and displayed other artistic abilities. But these gifts were quickly squelched under the iron-handed rule of a jealous husband. Now most of her life is behind her. She is broken in spirit and weary of life itself. She belatedly asks, "Was my marriage in the will of God? If not, can God ever bless me again? Where does someone begin when it's too late to begin from the beginning?" Is any type of success still open to someone who has been trapped in a senseless marriage?

Such questions can only be resolved by a correct understanding of the will of God. Often we assume that God is unable to work in spite of our weaknesses, mistakes, and sins.

We forget that God is a specialist; He is well able to work our failures into His plans.

Finally, there is Brian. He and his wife were accepted for missionary work in Africa. Evidently they had misjudged their ability to adapt to the diverse culture of a primitive tribe. Soon after they arrived in Africa they began to resent their new role. They felt it was unfair for them to sacrifice promising careers for people who did not appreciate them. They felt isolated, resentful, cheated.

Had God called them to Africa? It seemed so. They would not have been there if they had not believed that God had led them to missionary work.

That sense of calling had now disappeared. Or, at least, it *seemed* to them that God was not keeping His side of the bargain. They promised to go if He would bless. They went, but there was no blessing.

In order to save face and to give themselves the satisfaction of knowing they were not quitters, they stayed to the end of the four-year term. By that time the conflicts with fellow missionaries and the pressure of the foreign culture had left this young couple emotionally scarred.

When they returned home, their friends anticipated glowing reports about their missionary endeavors. Could they return home and with a bit of exaggeration, give the reports the people expected? That was one possibility. But how could they explain why they would not be returning to Africa? Would that not belie their glowing reports? No, they preferred to become a statistic, "a missionary casualty." They relocated in a large American city and simply informed their friends that they would not be returning to Africa for "health reasons."

Such an adjustment was both easy and difficult: easy because Brian was able to get a job readily; difficult because they were hounded by the realization that they were failures. Permanently.

No success in America could erase the gnawing fact that they had not been able to survive spiritually in the fierce struggles of cross-cultural adaptation. One thought lodged in their minds: *they were now doomed to be second-class citizens of the kingdom of heaven.*

Furthermore, they found it awkward to pray for God's blessing. If they were called to Africa and were now out of God's will, could they *sincerely* expect God to bless them? Can God bless those who skirt the hard road and substitute an easy one?

There are thousands of Jims, Beths, and Brians. Some have been forced into marriage by pregnancy; others have faced bankruptcy. Many parents have had to watch their children rebel against Christianity. Countless others are defeated, pessimistic, and guilt-ridden. They are convinced that they will be second-class citizens in the kingdom.

There is another class of failures: those who mistakenly believe they are successes. They may earn an honest living and be fine supporters of the church. They unconsciously (or sometimes all too consciously) consider themselves examples for others to follow. Yet they do not realize that from God's perspective they are failures. One man put it this way: "I climbed the ladder of success only to discover that my ladder was leaning against the wrong wall!"

Heaven will be filled with surprises. Many "successful" Christians will be nobodies, and some whose lives were strewn with the wreckage of one failure after another will be great in the kingdom.

This book is written *for those who believe they are failures and for those who falsely believe they aren't!* It is a message of hope for those who are filled with regret; it is a message designed to disturb those who mistakenly feel they have "made it" in life.

The pages that follow are a modest attempt to rid us of worldly notions of success and humbly return us to God's perspective.

By what standard does God measure success? What happens when we are disobedient? What can we do when it is too late to begin again?

# 2

## Choosing Your Yardstick

A co-ed wrote the following letter to her parents:

> Dear Mom and Dad,
>
> Just thought I'd drop you a note to clue you in on my plans. I've fallen in love with a guy called Jim. He quit high school after grade eleven to get married. About a year ago he got a divorce.
>
> We've been going steady for two months and plan to get married this fall. Until then, I've decided to move into his apartment (I think I might be pregnant).
>
> At any rate, I dropped out of school last week, although I'd like to finish college sometime in the future.

On the next page, the letter continued,

> Mom and Dad, I just want to know that everything I've written so far in this letter is false. NONE of it is true.
>
> But, Mom and Dad, it IS true that I got a C- in French and flunked my Math. . . . It IS true that I'm going to need some more money for my tuition payments.

This girl made her point! Even bad news can sound like good news if it is seen from a different perspective. Success and failure are relative: their meaning depends on the standard of comparison we use.

Unfortunately, we often judge ourselves and others by inadequate yardsticks. We are quick to compare ourselves with a superficial standard. On this basis, we either conclude that we have "made it" in life, or else we assume the opposite, that we have failed miserably and are beyond hope.

Neither conclusion may be correct. Remember, it's the standard that counts. Let's consider a few common notions of success, all of them distortions that we have borrowed from the world.

### Comparing Our Abilities

Have you ever overheard students discussing the results of their exams? One says, "I got an A"; the other sulks, "He gave me an F."

Human nature? Yes. We tend to blame others for our failures and take credit for our success. Also, we usually use our friends as a basis of comparison.

This is not all wrong, of course. A student should strive for high grades; a Christian businessman ought to succeed financially (and honestly). But often a spirit of comparison breeds envy and discontent.

Consider the man who will not become involved in the church because he feels inadequate. He even might disguise his pride (which lies at the root of all such attitudes) and call it humility. He will convince himself that this feeling of inferiority shows that he is truly humble. Actually, he is so concerned that people think well of him that he will not expose himself to any situation where he can fail. He plays it safe and does nothing.

Parents are often guilty of making their children targets of unfavorable comparison. "Why can't you be like Freddie!" they shout with disgust. They forget that no child is *the* standard by which others are to be judged.

God did not make us like General Motors makes Buicks (the only difference is the color and serial number). God did not give everyone the same ability, intelligence, or aptitude. And if we wish to make everyone the same, we are discrediting the wisdom of God. Our abilities (or lack of them) are not an accurate barometer of success or failure.

Comparing Bankbooks

Listen to a conversation in a barber shop or at a lunch counter. You will soon learn that the most popular basis of comparison is *money*. You would think that the chief end of man is to earn money and enjoy it forever!

A wife who compares herself with her friends is tempted to become dissatisfied with her husband's income. She feels cheated because she cannot buy the clothes or furniture her wealthy friends enjoy. She is in bondage to the social status of her neighbors.

If money is a basis of judging success or failure, it is obvious that Jesus Christ was a failure! Consider this: when He had to pay taxes, He asked Peter to find a coin in a fish's mouth. Why? He didn't have a coin of His own.

Christ was born under the shelter of a stable's roof. Most of us would be appalled if our children could not be born in a modern hospital! When He died, the soldiers cast lots for His garment. *That* was all He owned of this world's goods. He died naked, in the presence of gawking bystanders.

Was Christ a failure? Yes, if money is the standard by which He is judged. The foxes have holes, the birds of the air have nests, but the Son of Man did not have a place He could call home.

Of course, earning money (and even saving some) is both legitimate and necessary. But the amount we earn is not a barometer of God's blessing. The sun rises on the righteous as well as the wicked. In fact, it is usually the wicked who prosper and God's children who are often penniless.

Yet, even Christians (who above all people of the earth should know better) still think they are better (or worse) than others because of the amount they earn! Money does not commend us to God.

Remember the parable of the rich man and Lazarus? Lazarus was a beggar whose body was covered with sores. He and the dogs shared the crumbs that fell from the rich man's table. Later, both Lazarus and the rich man died.

Lazarus was taken to Abraham's bosom; the rich man was confined to Hades. Abraham's rebuke was, "Child, remember that during your life you received your good things, and likewise Lazarus bad things; but now he is being comforted here, and you are in agony" (Luke 16:25). Money is *not* a valid basis for judging success.

COMPARING FRIENDS

Have you ever met a name-dropper? You will recognize him when you do. He is the man who casually informs you that he met the president of the United States at a luncheon and that he is closely acquainted with outstanding athletes. He calls celebrities by their first name. If he could write a book, he'd entitle it, *Ten Famous Men Who Met Me.*

More seriously, we often like to be associated with the "right" people. Our pride is nurtured if we can dine with the famous and be entertained by the wealthy. The fact that God has chosen the poor of this world to be rich in faith and heirs of the kingdom often does not dampen our enthusiasm for celebrities.

However, knowing the greatest men and women does not elevate us one centimeter in the sight of God. The best of men are still sinners. If we take pride in the "greats" of this world, we have a warped view of God's values. He chooses the base, the lowly, and the unknown.

James (the author of the epistle of James) was Christ's half brother. They grew up in the same home, played together, laughed together, and worked together. After Jesus began his public ministry, neither James nor his other brothers could believe that Jesus was the Messiah. Later, the dramatic events of the crucifixion and resurrection convinced them that they had indeed grown up with the Messiah, the King of Israel.

What an opportunity for James to tell his friends, "I knew Him when . . ." But he never did. Neither in his speech in Acts 15 nor in his letter does James ever allude to the fact that Jesus was his half brother.

The reasons are simple. Being related to *anyone* (including Christ in the flesh) does not improve one's relationship with God. Furthermore, when James did accept Christ as the Messiah he did not inherit any special privileges that are not available to all who believe. Before God, every individual is either accepted or rejected on *the same basis*.

God is not impressed with celebrities or those who would like to be. He is impressed by only one man—Christ. And only those who accept Christ by faith receive God's approval.

The point? No person is a success because he (or she) is acquainted with the famous of today; conversely, no one is a failure in the kingdom because his friends were not well known.

In the book of James, worldliness is specifically described as an attitude of personal favoritism. It is seeking the friendship of the rich (and, we might add, the famous) and ignoring the poor (James 2:1-10).

The conclusion? "If you show partiality, you are committing sin and are convicted by the law as transgressors" (James 2:9). Your social status has nothing to do with God's standard of success.

## COMPARING RESULTS

A friend of mine who pastored a small church told me how depressing it was for him to attend pastors' conferences. There he would suffer through the reports of the wonderful success of other churches. It seemed that all churches had either doubled in their membership or tripled their income during the preceding year.

His church, on the other hand, was small and had a history of difficulties. It had problems with bitterness, complaining, and factions. On some occasions the pastor was publicly humiliated by irate members. His story (which could be the subject of an entire book) reminds us that carnal Christians can be just as obstinate as worldly pagans.

What did the pastor do? He lived with the abuse. He preached Scripture and taught doctrine. Eventually, a few individuals began to show signs of spiritual growth. In the lives of a handful, there was fruit. But most of the seed fell by the wayside; it was choked by thorns of worldly anxiety or drowned in the slough of resentment.

When I heard the full story, I said, "Roy, I would not have stayed there for a month!" His reply was a rebuke: "I've always wondered if I had love for people. God put me in the most trying situation I could endure. He wanted to teach me how to show love in a place where there was none."

Was he a success? Not if nickles and noses are the measuring sticks! Results *can* be a barometer of God's blessing —but not necessarily.

There is at least one instance in Scripture where God called a man to be a failure—according to human standards. After Isaiah responded to God's call by saying, "Here am I. Send me" (Isaiah 6:8), God gave him a discouraging assignment:

> Go, and tell this people: "Keep on listening, but do not perceive; keep on looking, but do not understand." Render the hearts of this people insensitive, their ears dull, and their eyes dim, lest they see with their eyes, hear with their ears, understand with their hearts, and return and be healed. (Isaiah 6:9-10)

Isaiah was told *in advance* that the people would *not* respond to his ministry. He was to preach only to provide a further reason for God's coming judgment! Obviously, you can't always evaluate a preacher by the number that come forward when he gives the invitation.

I don't mean to imply that statistics are totally irrelevant to success. Those who vehemently object to "numbers" are often the ones who have no numbers to count! In the book of Acts, statistics were a part of the record: three thousand were converted on the Day of Pentecost and another five thousand later. But statistics are not the whole story. Results (even *scriptural* results) are not necessarily a proof of God's blessing.

Remember the Israelites at the water of Meribah? They were impatient with Moses. They had repeatedly accused him of bringing them into the desert to let them die. He had brought them out of Egypt, but he couldn't take them into Canaan. Tempers flared. The people felt cheated.

God told Moses to speak to the rock. He, in a fit of anger, hit the rock instead. Yet water flowed! The children and cattle had cool, clear water.

Perhaps a small minority said, "Moses disobeyed. He will be punished." Yet possibly the majority responded, "Why complain? Aren't you glad that we have water? Who cares how it got here. At least we will not die of thirst!"

Water flowed. The people were jubilant. Was Moses a success? *Yes, in the eyes of men. No, in the eyes of God.* His disobedience brought water, but it also brought punishment.

Results in themselves are not a proof that God is pleased. It is possible to win attendance contests and disseminate the gospel and see results; all these activities can be done without pleasing God! Such results can be achieved by deceptive gimmicks or for purely personal satisfaction. It is not enough to do God's work; it must be done in His way and for His credit.

Was Jeremiah a success? Was John the Baptist? Christ? Not by purely human standards. If these men had turned in annual reports, they would not have received achievement awards.

Are *you* achieving results? If so, thank God. If not take heart! You might not be as great a failure as you think.

When Christ was on earth He predicted that someday Peter would have his hands stretched out and someone else would clothe him and carry him where he did not wish to go, that is, to his martyrdom. When Peter heard this, he was distressed. He wondered what would happen to his friend John. Would he live until Christ returned, or would he die a horrible death, too? Peter asked, "Lord, and what about this man?"

Christ replied, "If I want him to remain until I come, what is that to you? You follow me!" (John 21:21-22).

If God wishes to bless others more than us, if they are famous and we are unknown, if they are wealthy and we are poor, if they are gifted and we are mediocre—what is that to *us*? Christ says to us individually, "*You follow Me!*"

A spirit of comparison is worldly, carnal, and devilish. Read carefully Paul's words: "For we are not bold to class or compare ourselves with some of those who commend themselves; but when they measure themselves by themselves, and compare themselves with themselves, they are without understanding" (2 Corinthians 10:12).

As Christ would say, "*You follow Me!*"

## The Single Eye

What made Moses a great servant of God? Maybe it was his faith. Perhaps it was patience. I'd like to suggest that it was his humility. When God told him he could not enter the land and Joshua would replace him, Moses showed no trace of jealousy. We might have expected him to say, "Why should this young upstart do in three days what I couldn't do in forty years?" But he didn't. Instead he prayed for God's blessing on his young successor.

Why was Moses not jealous? Because he did not compare his *career with someone else's*. If God wanted to use Joshua in a spectacular way, fine.

Think of this: Christ left the eternal glory of the Father to suffer the ultimate humiliation of a shameful *human* death. Yet He never complained because He had to abandon the glory that the other two members of the Trinity retained. If He had compared His role in redemption with those of the Father and the Holy Spirit, He might have felt cheated. Why should He—equal with the other two members—be the one to become the scum of the earth?

If Christ had compared Himself with other men (remember, He was fully human), He might have thought that He should be the greatest of them. Yet (incredibly) He became the lowest of them. When the disciples were wondering who would perform the duties of a household servant, Christ took a towel and basin of water and washed their feet!

How could the One who was so high stoop so low? One reason is that He did not compare Himself with others but *cared only about meeting the standard that the Father had ordained.* "I delight to do thy will, O my God" (Psalms 40:8, KJV). That's all that mattered.

Is it realistic for us to follow His example? John the Baptist came close to it. Large crowds had gathered to hear John speak. He generated so much excitement that a special synagogue delegation came to ask him who he was. Some thought he was the Messiah. John was not flattered.

Later, the large crowds left John and began to follow Christ. John's disciples were concerned about their leader's reputation. They did not want their teacher left in the cold.

John was not concerned. He responded, "A man can receive nothing, unless it has been given him from heaven" (John 3:27). When one person is more effective than another, it is because God has ordained it so! All abilities and talents are gifts of God. Jealousy in the Body of Christ is an ugly sore, a malignant tumor.

John continued (v. 28), "You yourselves bear me witness, that I said, 'I am not the Christ,' but, 'I have been sent before Him.'" John evaluated his ministry from a proper perspective. He did not say that he was useless (as those with a false humility are apt to assert). He realized that He was sent before the Messiah but that he himself was not the Messiah. He had a realistic self-image.

In the Middle East, it was customary for the friend of the bridegroom (today we call him the best man) to be sure that no one went into the room of the bride except the proper lover, that is, the bridegroom. The friend of the bridegroom stood by the door so that only the bridegroom could enter. Therefore, the bridegroom would have to identify himself, usually by speaking a few words.

John, using this imagery, told his disciples, "The friend of the bridegroom, who stands and hears him, rejoices greatly because of the bridegroom's voice. And so this joy of mine has been made full" (John 3:29). John said that his responsibility was merely to introduce the bride to the bridegroom, that is, to introduce Israel to Christ.

John's joy was not found in the crowds. He was not elated because some people mistook him for the Messiah. His satisfaction was found in knowing Christ. And *any* part he could have in introducing people to Christ was neither too great nor too small.

His reputation was not threatened when his ministry was eclipsed by someone greater than he. He could watch his popularity plummet in the wake of another's ministry; there was no jealousy, only joy. In his words, "He must increase, but I must decrease" (John 3:30).

Is such humility unrealistic? John the Baptist was a great man; he could afford to be humble! Christ said that among those born of women there had not arisen anyone greater than John the Baptist. Perhaps if *we* were that great, we would also be that godly. Perhaps if we had known Christ personally as John did, we could accept the end of our career!

Would you like to be as great as John the Baptist? You *can* be. Regarding John, Christ added, "Yet he who is least in the kingdom of God is greater than he" (Luke 7:28). How do we become great (so secure that we need not compare ourselves with others)? By becoming so small that comparison becomes ridiculous! The least is the greatest; the last shall be first.

Are you ready for the implications of this?

# 3

# We're All Chips off the Same Block

Most of us would agree that success and failure are poles apart. What could be more obvious than the fact that some people "make it" in life and others don't?

After all, the differences among people are striking: there are the rich and the poor, the beautiful and the ugly, the winsome and the boring.

But God isn't impressed with such distinctions. His ways are not our ways; He does not see us as others do.

For this reason we cannot as Christians easily classify ourselves (or others) as either a success or failure. There is a mixture of *both* in us all. In fact, it is only as we understand failure and accept it that we discover the secret of success.

Often the doorway to success is entered through the hallway of failure. Our sins are a forcible reminder of our need for God's grace; our weaknesses make us appreciate God's strength. An understanding of our frailty is the basis for a dynamic relationship with God.

That is why the distinction between success and failure is so slight: the line that divides the two is incredibly fine—so fine that we cannot even recognize it unless we know what we are looking for. More of that later.

Let's back up for a moment and see ourselves as God sees us. Whether this flatters us or not, His X-ray shows the following results: *there is not much difference between us.* We are all chips off the same block—Adam. In one sense we are all the same. Let me explain.

### OUR NATURES ARE IDENTICAL

Who is the most wicked man that ever lived? Hitler? Eichmann? Judas? Take your choice. His nature at birth was no more wicked than yours. We are *all* the children of wrath (Ephesians 2:3); we are *all* conceived in sin. There is none righteous, *no, not one.*

Read carefully the words of Christ: "For from within, out of the heart of men, proceed the evil thoughts and fornications, thefts, murders, adulteries, deeds of coveting and wickedness, as well as deceit, sensuality, envy, slander, pride and foolishness" (Mark 7:21-22). This description does not merely apply to your neighbor. Christ was speaking about *you.* The potential for every imaginable evil lies within us all.

If that isn't startling, listen to this: "The heart is more deceitful than all else and is desperately sick; Who can understand it?" (Jeremiah 17:9). In what way is the heart deceitful above all else? It is deceitful because we convince ourselves that we are not really wicked! We tell ourselves that we, by nature, are better than murderers and adulterers. But God knows better. Some people commit greater sins than others; but, by seeing the heart, God knows that the differences between us are negligible. Our sinful natures are essentially the same.

### OUR NEW NATURES ARE IDENTICAL

What happens when we believe in Christ? We become a new creation; we receive a new nature. The sinful nature remains, but the new nature is now also within us. All who believe in Christ receive the same nature and the same Holy Spirit. On that score we are identical.

Since we have *both* natures within us, conflict is inevitable. "For the flesh sets its desire against the Spirit, and the Spirit against the flesh; for these are in opposition to one another, so that you may not do the things that you please" (Galatians 5:17). As Christians, we now find that there are spiritual victories—freedom from sins; and also spiritual failures—the times when we lapse back into our former ways. All Christians know this conflict to some degree. We have all experienced a mixture of failure and victory.

Have you heard the story of the two men trying to jump across a thirty-foot river? One jumps ten feet and the other jumps twenty. One does better than the other, but *neither* makes it to the other shore.

This story is usually told to illustrate that only small differences exist between unsaved men. Some are better than others, but everyone is condemned because all come short of God's standards. But this story applies to Christians with equal force.

We have the same sinful nature; we have the same Holy Spirit. We all experience failure of one kind or another. God knows our frame; He remembers that everyone of us is dust.

In fact, even those who are considered outstanding Christians and those who are considered failures may not be as far apart in God's eyes as we think.

Let's find out why.

### ONLY GOD KNOWS FOR SURE

Our judgments are often superficial. We look at some Christians and are convinced that they are successful in their relationship with God. They have a kind spirit, appear to be happy, and trouble no one. They are generous with their money and do not mind helping fellow believers. Then we look at others who are discouraged or emotionally crippled. Perhaps they are pessimistic and defeated. We are tempted to suggest that the former group is a success and the latter is a failure.

Are such judgments valid? Perhaps yes. More often, no.

Consider this: *the reason some people are more noticeably a success than others is that they have not had a chance to fail!* For example, I have never had to return home defeated from missionary work in a foreign country. But perhaps the reason is that I have never *gone* as a missionary to a foreign country! Can I honestly understand the loneliness, culture shock, and adjustments some missionaries have had to make?

It is cowardly to judge others when they fail to reach goals that we have never tried to achieve ourselves. Spectators find it easy (and enjoyable) to boo a football player for misjudging a play. But what if those spectators had to play? How would they measure up against the skills of that "despicable" quarterback? There is one sure way of never missing a touchdown pass: *just never play the game.*

Think of those who have experienced emotional or mental trauma. Can we honestly understand the pressures they have had to face? Often such Christians have been reared in broken homes, rejected by their parents. Others have had to cope with mental limitations or physical handicaps. Perhaps they do find it difficult to trust God; perhaps they have not yet worked through the resentment which has been nurtured by the harsh environment of a hate-filled family. Are they successful? Let God judge. I, for one, believe that under similar conditions I would have fared no better than they.

Similarly, there are those who have been guilty of overt moral sins. Others have lived in sexual purity. But might it not be that some have not committed adultery because they have not been confronted with explicit moral temptation? Some Christians have been sheltered from the enticement of a Potiphar's wife. Others have grown up in a generation with less moral perversion and fewer temptations.

This is not to suggest (as some might erroneously conclude) that we are not responsible for our sins or that we can simply blame our circumstances if we commit sin. Far from it! Paul did not condone any form of sexual impurity in the church at Corinth, even though such sins were rampant in the city. The Scriptures are filled with warnings, exhortations, and condemnations for those who practice evil.

The fact that circumstances need not force us into sin is vividly illustrated by the story of Joseph. He had every opportunity to commit adultery and get away with it, but he refused to do "this great evil, and sin against God" (Genesis 39:9). One of the most powerful indicators of God's power is that He is able to preserve believers from the sins of an adulterous and sinful society.

My point is simply that when we judge others (and it is legitimate to reprove those who have been overcome with a fault or need church discipline), we must do so realizing that we ourselves could easily be guilty of the same sins. If we are free from guilt, it is because of God's grace; it is not because we are inherently better than others. He that believes he is standing should take heed lest he fall! *You and I are capable of indescribable evil. The potential for every sin lies within us.*

Some others never dabble in the lusts of the world because they don't have the nerve! They appear to be successful, but they are not. What keeps them in line is fearing that failure would ruin their reputation.

Remember the elder brother in the story of the prodigal son? Although he is usually ignored (the prodigal receives all the attention), we shall consider the elder brother the focal point of the story. In many ways, he was an example for others to follow. He was a hard worker and lived a "separated" life. While his young brother was enjoying the far country, the elder brother was faithful at home.

Yet, for all this, the elder brother did not please his father. One reason is that the father delighted in giving, and the elder brother refused to accept the father's wealth. Not once did the boy ask for a young goat so that he could enjoy a party with his friends. He refused to accept his inheritance.

A second reason the elder brother did not please the father is that his heart was not in the father's work. His mind was in the far country. He told his father, "When this son of yours came, who has devoured your wealth with harlots, you killed the fattened calf for him" (Luke 15:30). How did he know his brother had wasted money on prostitutes? He didn't. But the elder brother knew what *he* would be doing if he had a chance to leave the farm! His work was on the farm; his heart was in the far country.

Here was a man busy in the father's work yet out of harmony with the father's heart. This nice boy stayed home only because he didn't have the nerve to leave! His reputation was at stake.

Does this story ring a bell? Unfortunately, many Christians (who appear successful) envy those who enjoy worldly pleasures. They are faithful in church, not because their heart is in it but because they are expected to be involved. The "work of the Lord" is not a delight: it is drudgery. But they know they should not enjoy the world, so they play it safe. They are not failures in their works, but they are failures in their hearts. And the tragedy is that they believe they are fine Christians!

Remember Christ's words? To look at a woman in lust is adultery, and to hate your brother is to be a murderer. And if you *love* the world (even if you do not do worldly things), the love of the Father is not in you.

Of course, overt acts of sin have greater consequences than sins of the heart. In that sense, all sins are not equal. If David had only lusted after Bathsheba instead of committing the act of adultery, the consequences that followed his sins would not have occurred. But *legally* and *judicially* sins of the mind and overt acts are the same in God's sight.

The reason we think there are great differences between Christians is that we compare our lives with those of other believers. When we compare ourselves with God, those differences are negligible. One molehill is nearly the height of another, if you measure them all against the Himalayas.

When God judges us He takes everything into account. He knows our personal struggles, pressures, and background. He knows all of our failures—public and private. Against the backdrop of God's holiness, we all come far short of God's standard.

Consequently, some Christians who are publicly active in God's work only appear successful *to us*. God judges the heart. Remember, the differences between us are smaller than we care to admit!

Perhaps you think of yourself as a success, or maybe you believe you have failed miserably. Regardless of your opinion, here is good news: God can turn your failures into success if you learn to apply His remedy.

But, before we consider God's plan in detail, we must analyze failure more specifically. What is failure, anyway? What is its cause?

We'll discuss these questions in the next chapter.

# 4

# A Profile of Failure

Intelligent, gifted, well adjusted—all of these descriptions applied to a young man who began his career with every advantage imaginable. He did not have the physical and moral defects that inflict so many of us. He could blame neither his heredity nor his environment if he made unwise decisions. Yet, for all this, there was one other word that described him: *failure*.

This man, more than any other, provides a case study on failure. With virtually all the cards stacked in his favor, he blew an unprecedented opportunity. He could have gone down in history as a hero; but he is remembered primarily for a gigantic mistake: he opened the door for every failure imaginable. Generations of his descendants—in fact, all of us—felt the repercussions of his sin. This man's failure became the basis for our failure; a study of his experience is basically a study of ourselves. The effect of his foolish choice gives the clue to two questions that plague us: What is failure? and, Why do we fail?

The man's name is Adam. He was created perfect by a direct act of God. He was put in a beautiful garden and given a wife. He, for one, did not have to question whether he had married "the right one." At least *that* marriage was made in heaven. Furthermore, he had direct communication with God.

There was no static on the line when he spoke with the Almighty. But Adam failed.

Notice this: Adam was created to have three relationships.

First, he was made in the image of God, so that he would be able to know God (Genesis 1:27). This also involved ruling the earth under God's direction (Genesis 1:26). He would get his orders from God and spend time in fellowship with Him. In this way, Adam would be fulfilling the chief purpose of his existence. It was a great relationship.

Second, Adam was given a wife. He was essentially a social being and needed companionship. The desire for marriage and the need for friends are inherent in us all. A relationship with God does not vitiate our need for one another. God did not create Adam without desires. Since he needed companionship, God saw that he got it.

Third, Adam was adjusted to the world. He was given a garden to cultivate and keep (Genesis 2:15). Taking care of this responsibility was one way of showing his appreciation to God.

Let's suppose that a rich man asked you to oversee his estate. You'd want to be sure that you carried out his orders carefully. You'd also know that everything you cared for was not your own. If it did belong to you, you could do as you wished. But you are responsible to him, because it is his. Similarly, Adam was to take care of God's garden, trees, and animals. He was to submit to God's authority over all creation.

Imagine! Adam was given a job with explicit instructions; he could discuss his work with God; he had a wife that was custom-made. But he failed. He and his wife disobeyed God's direct command that they should not eat of the tree of "the knowledge of good and evil" (Genesis 2:17).

The result? Failure was no longer a mere possibility; it was now a damning reality.

## THE COMPONENTS OF FAILURE

What happened when Adam and Eve sinned? The relationships created in the Garden of Eden were destroyed or at best perverted. The three basic drives were still there, but their expression became debased. Now the three legitimate desires were inverted and warped.

We have inherited the consequences of Adam's disobedience. Of course, we also add our own sins to his; by nature we choose to turn away from God. But Adam's sin shattered man's original relationships, and we have been trying to fit the pieces together ever since.

The Bible specifies what the symptoms of these consequences are. John wrote, "For all that is in the world, the lust of the flesh and the lust of the eyes and the boastful pride of life, is not from the Father, but is from the world" (1 John 2:16). These three expressions describe our perverted drives. Let's consider them one at a time.

First, there is the *pride of life*—self-exaltation. Instead of obeying God, we by nature want to be our own god. Adam chose to eat of the forbidden fruit precisely because he wanted to be like God; he wanted to be his own god. Whenever we substitute our own desires for God we are guilty of pride.

Visualize a young executive as he nervously paces the floor while waiting for an elevator. He is dressed well and knows it. He is secretly pleased with himself. He considers himself superior to others and is determined to force others to admit that "obvious" truth. He is so consumed with ambition that he is almost oblivious to coworkers who walk by. At any given moment he might be filled with resentment toward another man in his company who tried to "cross him." Before he eventually falls asleep at night, he schemes to get even with his rival. In the morning he enjoys a replay of the malicious thoughts of the night before. He can hardly wait to execute his plans.

At home his wife may be starving for companionship. Yet he is so preoccupied with himself (he would say with his *business*) that he runs roughshod over the feelings of his family. He is insensitive to the needs under his own roof. He honestly sees nothing wrong with his life-style. Doesn't he provide for his family? Doesn't one have to earn a living? His pride blinds him to the deep emotional and spiritual needs of others.

His wife may be controlled by a different form of pride. Her life-style is different from his, and she may even resent her husband's conceit. But she too may be the victim of pride —pride that has become complex; it will often turn inward and become an inferiority complex. The symptom of such a psychological attitude is usually depression.

Let me explain. When we withdraw from others, it is usually because of the fear of failure. We often don't want to risk friendship lest someone find out what we are really like. In order to keep our reputation intact, we are tempted to spend our time on the sidelines. Our excuse is inferiority, but the root of it is pride.

Or, let us suppose that we cannot accept ourselves for what we are. The resentment we feel toward others often becomes directed toward ourselves. "Why can't I be like _____? Why do I have so many handicaps? I was born stupid!" All such attitudes lead to depression, but beneath it all is pride. We are envious of others and angry for not getting the recognition we crave.

Pride in all of its forms is probably the most obvious reason for failure. One person may not be able to work with others because of his stubborn desire to maintain his "rights." Another may resent his colleague's superior ability. Still another may refuse to become involved because of feelings of inferiority. Insensitivity, resentment, and anger—these are symptoms of the "boastful pride of life." All of this started when Adam chose to be his own god.

Second, there is the *lust of the flesh*—the craving for sensual desire. God had given Adam a wife; this relationship defined the prescribed limits of sexual conduct. But, in every age, God's restrictions have been largely ignored. Our own day is characterized by hedonism—the love of pleasure. The sexual revolution has made sexual purity a rarity, if not an oddity. Since "everybody is doing it," the temptation to capitulate to sexual looseness is powerful. Yet, of all sins, sexual immorality is one of the most serious.

Many people—Christians as well as non-Christians— have succumbed to illicit sexual relationships. Many have had their reputations ruined; some have had their marriages destroyed. As I shall point out later, even in such cases all is not lost. Fellowship with the living God is still always a possibility. But, if pride is the most universal cause of failure, surely sensuality has the most devastating consequences.

The lives of David and Samson in the Old Testament point to this fact: sexual sins have far-reaching repercussions.

Finally, there is the *lust of the eyes*—covetousness. Adam was supposed to work in the garden while recognizing that it belonged to God. God was the owner of all things. If God gave Adam a job to do, he was to be merely a steward. Adam was accountable because he owned nothing.

Today we covet the things of this world—things that belong to God alone. Covetousness is the hallmark of the sales industry. To be content with what we have is a cardinal sin; if we are satisfied with our present car, we will not get a new one. So we are bombarded with advertisements designed to make us dissatisfied with our black-and-white TV, our outdated lapels, and our favorite mouthwash.

Many people have an inner compulsion to possess everything they see. If their relatives have better stereos, newer cars, or more expensive homes, they are dissatisfied with their lot in life. Such people are failures because they have invested in the bank of the world—a bank that is already in the red.

What causes failure? What makes a man come to the end of his life and admit he lived in vain? What motivates a man to commit suicide because he is not as gifted as others? What makes a missionary return from Africa because he felt his abilities were unappreciated? What causes a man to jeopardize his Christian testimony and have an affair with his neighbor's wife? The answer: sin—specifically pride, covetousness, or sensual desire.

Of course, there are failures quite unrelated to sinful motivations: a student might fail in school, or a man might make an unwise investment. Many people have failed at their jobs or simply fallen short of their goals. We shouldn't minimize this type of failure, but in the long run it is not as serious as spiritual failure. God does not expect everyone to have a college education; He did not create us with the capacity to successfully tackle every situation. All of us have at some time set unrealistic goals for ourselves or attempted projects beyond our abilities. These failures usually don't happen because of sin per se but are the result of our lack of ability. Human frailty is ever with us.

However, God often uses this kind of failure to remind us how desperately we need Him. I know of a man who, as a non-Christian, cried to God for help only after his business went bankrupt. A student who flunked college was forced to accept his limitations, and he learned to find his personal fulfillment in God.

My point is this: God is adequate for all kinds of failure. Some failures may not be our fault, but they serve as reminders that we must live with eternal priorities in mind. Other failures are directly the result of our own sinful choices.

This book is primarily concerned with spiritual and moral failure for one reason: these kinds of failure have the most devastating consequences. Flunking school or losing a job is minor in comparison to being controlled by pride, covetousness, or sensual desire. Failures that result from human frailty have no eternal consequences (unless we respond to them in the wrong way). Spiritual and moral failures often permanently affect our children, our friends, and, of course, ourselves. These crushing experiences bring guilt, defeat, and depression. If we know how to apply God's remedy to these spiritual problems, we will find it much easier to accept other kinds of failure.

Did God provide a remedy for the most ugly kind of failure? The answer is yes. He has the wisdom to take the messes we have made and straighten them out. No one has failed too greatly or too often for God. Remember, He had sinners like us in mind when He initiated His redemptive plans.

## A PREVIEW OF GOD'S REMEDY FOR FAILURE

God is well aware of the pitfalls along our path. Sin did not take Him by surprise. Long before Adam and Eve were created, God planned to turn our failure into success. With a detailed knowledge of all the facts, God provided a remedy that would not fail—if it was seriously applied.

God's plan is to strike at the root of our problem. He did not decide merely to help us adjust to our misery; we needed something more drastic. Furthermore, his remedy had to be inclusive; it had to be broad enough to cover every eventuality.

If His plan could work only for those with many natural abilities, it would hardly meet the deepest needs of the majority of us. If only those who had committed small sins were eligible to receive the benefits of God's remedy, then God's foresight could be questioned.

Only a God who knows all things and who has infinite wisdom could draft a plan that would anticipate virtually every situation, every sin, every failure. God has done just that.

The focal point of the plan is Christ's death on the cross. That sacrifice made forgiveness for all sins a possibility. Thus, broken communication between us and God can be repaired. God can again be loved, obeyed, and worshiped. Forgiveness in its fullest sense can be a reality.

Furthermore, God intends to change our basic motivations. We need not be controlled by pride, covetousness, or lust. Christ's death did not only make forgiveness possible; it also opened the door to a life of personal freedom from the sins that plague us. But, before we can enjoy such a new relationship, we have to face our sin squarely. Many people who ask for God's help are disappointed. The reason? They should begin by asking for God's forgiveness. Asking for God's strength before we have confessed our weaknesses (sins) is like trying to cure a headache with a Band-Aid. God wants to go to the root of our problem. Once we understand how sinful we are, we will appreciate God's grace.

My purpose in the succeeding chapters is to concentrate on how God can take our failures, forgive them, and then incorporate us back into His plan. Even those who are entangled in a web of sin can still find acceptance and fulfillment with God.

What is failure? It is living with perverted values. It is being hooked on one or more of the three worldly motivations.

What is success? It is learning to apply the grace of God. It is understanding how we can be accepted by God despite our bitter experiences in the past.

### God's Definition of Success

Some people please God, and others do not. We cannot judge, for our knowledge is superficial. Our basis of judgment is often wrong. We are "outward" oriented; God is "inward" oriented.

If success is learning to apply God's grace, how do we do this? The first step is to stop trusting ourselves and to trust Christ alone for our acceptance before God. Then, God declares us righteous despite our personal failures. The implications of this will be discussed later. The key question you should face now is whether you are depending on your own goodness or trusting the forgiveness God offers in Christ.

Christ illustrated this point with a parable:

> Two men went up into the temple to pray, one a Pharisee, and the other a tax-gatherer. The Pharisee stood and was praying thus to himself, "God, I thank Thee that I am not like other people: swindlers, unjust, adulterers, or even like this tax-gatherer. I fast twice a week; I pay tithes of all that I get." But the tax-gatherer, standing some distance away, was even unwilling to lift up his eyes to heaven, but was beating his breast, saying, "God, be merciful to me, the sinner!" (Luke 18:10-13)

Christ's conclusion was, "I tell you, this man went down to his house justified rather than the other; for every one who exalts himself shall be humbled, but he who humbles himself shall be exalted" (Luke 18:14).

The Pharisee depended on his own works to gain approval before God. But notice carefully: his works were *good*, furthermore, *he thanked God* that he was not like other men. Perhaps this Pharisee did *not* take the credit for his works; he realized that his ability to do good was a gift of God. Yet, even such an attitude doesn't make us acceptable to God!

The tax-gatherer never listed his achievements. Perhaps it was because he never had any; perhaps he realized that even if he did have accomplishments, they could never be acceptable to God.

Therefore, he prayed, "God be merciful to me, the sinner." The word *merciful* is more accurately translated "propitious." He prays that God's wrath would be mercifully turned away. As we know, that was later done by the sacrifice of Christ.

The one man went home justified, that is, acceptable to God, the other did not. What made the difference? One realized that his acceptance before God depended solely on God's grace (made available by an offering for sin); the other believed it depended on himself. And *that* separates the successful from the unsuccessful in God's sight.

Notice how clearly the Scriptures teach that our works cannot make us righteous in God's sight. "By the works of the Law no flesh will be justified in His sight; for through the Law comes the knowledge of sin" (Romans 3:20). And again, "For by grace you have been saved through faith; and that not of yourselves, it is the gift of God; not as a result of works, that no one should boast" (Ephesians 2:8-9). Do you want to have God's approval? You must stop trusting yourself and consciously transfer your trust to Christ. God's standard is so high that only Christ can meet it. So we cannot depend on ourselves but must depend on Christ, who met God's requirement for us. When we decide to trust Christ,

God declares us righteous. We are acquitted of our guilt and have God's approval.

But there is a second step to learning to apply God's grace: personal experience. Although our faith in Christ makes us members of God's family, we can dishonor our relationship. The prodigal son had all the rights of sonship; but, when living in a pig sty, he was hardly a credit to his father!

Believing on Christ makes us joint heirs with Him, but we can still choose to live selfish, worldly lives. Legally, we have an incredible spiritual inheritance at our disposal, and our acceptance is secure; but we can fail to accept what God wants to do for us.

So, although as Christians we are all successful in the sense that we have God's unconditional acceptance, we may be *un*successful in experiencing the implications of that acceptance. Consequently, failure—serious failure—is a possibility for us all. Even the apostle Paul feared that, after he had run the race of life and preached to others, he himself should be disqualified (1 Corinthians 9:27).

God wants us to be successful in applying His remedy to our sinful, human condition. This means much more than simply going to church, praying, reading the Bible occasionally, and staying out of trouble. Aren't these things commendable? Yes, even necessary. But an atheist could do as much!

It is wrong to assume that every act of service automatically pleases God. Some Christians refer with smug satisfaction to many years of "faithful service" to the Lord. They are quite sure that they will receive a great reward at the judgment seat of Christ—and, candidly, they believe they deserve it. Obviously, they have not understood the words of Christ that the first shall be last and the last shall be first. Surprises lie ahead!

What then makes our works pleasing to God? It is when they are spiritual sacrifices acceptable to God by Jesus Christ (1 Peter 2:5). That means that even the works of Christians do not inherently please God. Works are pleasing to God only when they are done with the motivation and strength that Christ can give. They are acceptable *by Jesus Christ.*

We've already seen that many appear successful only because they have lived "normal" lives. Some have never had a chance to fail. They have lived respectful and decent lives. Such are often admired in the Christian community, but in God's sight they are failures: their works will go up in smoke. Why? They lived decently but not supernaturally. They did not have the humility to see how desperately they needed God. Perhaps they thought that their good works gave them special status with God. They did not realize that only Christ has special status with God. We, therefore, are pleasing to God to the extent that we apply God's grace to every experience of our lives.

On the other hand, many who have failed miserably are usually good candidates for appreciating God's grace and power, the most successful discovery a sinner can make. It is not necessary to fail before we succeed, but God often uses our failures to make us more sensitive to our need of Him.

Remember the story of the harlot who brought an alabaster vial of perfume and anointed Christ's feet and then wiped His feet with her hair? As she displayed her love, her tears mingled with the perfume on Christ's feet. When Simon objected, Christ replied,

> "Do you see this woman? I entered your house, you gave Me no water for My feet, but she has wet My feet with her tears, and wiped them with her hair. You gave Me no kiss; but she, since the time I came in, has not ceased to kiss My feet. You did not anoint My head with oil, but she anointed My feet with perfume. For this reason I say to you, her sins, which are many, have been forgiven, for she loved much; but he who is forgiven little, loves little." (Luke 7:44-47)

The one who is forgiven much loves much; the one who is forgiven little loves little. The secret of loving Christ—and serving Him acceptably—is to appreciate His forgiveness. It is to live in constant appreciation of God's grace.

No, we don't have to commit gross sins to appreciate God's grace; any sin is vile enough, if we see it in perspective. But many of us are blinded by self-righteousness. We love little, because we *think* we have been forgiven little! The greatest obstacle to applying God's grace is satisfaction in our own accomplishments. A person satisfied with himself never learns to lean on God.

Christ repeatedly taught His disciples this general principle: the last shall be first, the first last. The one who is least realizes that he has nothing to offer God; he comes solely on the basis of God's mercy. He who wishes to be first in the kingdom betrays his belief that he is inherently better than someone else, and because of that deception he will be last!

The result? The humble (who see clearly their need for mercy) are exalted; the proud (who believe they have a slight edge on others) will be brought down.

What then is success? On one level it is receiving Christ as Savior and thereby having His righteousness attributed to us. However, on the level of personal experience, it is living supernaturally; it is living in dependence on Christ. It is being motivated to serve Christ out of sheer gratitude. It is dying to our personal ambitions and letting Christ be in control. To such, Christ will say, "Well done."

The point? From God's perspective, a successful person is one who *knows how to accept God's remedy for failure.* Since we are essentially the same, only an application of God's grace distinguishes us. Let's consider that now.

# 5

# How Much Can God Forgive?

"I can't come to God about *that* sin again," sighed the disillusioned young man. "God is weary of hearing me ask forgiveness for the same thing over and over. I've decided to let everything slide until I know I can hold out." His story is one that in principle has happened a thousand times. He accepted Christ as Savior at about the age of twelve. After the novelty wore off, his relationship with God took a nosedive. During his teen years, he rebelled against his parents' restrictions. He soon learned to swear, drink, and read pornography on the sly. He often asked God's forgiveness and vowed that he would not repeat the endless cycle of personal failure, but for some reason he never made a clean break.

As he grew older, he felt so discouraged that he often would go for days or weeks without praying. Sometimes he determined to do better. He felt sure that if he read the Bible more regularly and spent time in prayer, God would give him the victory he desired.

So he tried. He got out of bed a half hour earlier, read a few verses, and prayed. Nothing happened. Nothing, that is, except that he felt more exhausted during the day. If only he knew for certain that he was forgiven. If only he could have "whatever it takes" to live in fellowship with God.

I am convinced that the greatest single cause of spiritual defeat is a guilty conscience. We know we have sinned and are weary of it; yet we don't know how to be free from a sense of failure. In fact, most of us have experienced the same futile cycle. We sin, we feel guilty, we try to confess our sins, and still our past fills our minds. We then try to do something good to offset our guilt; but the harder we try the more useless it becomes. The result? Discouragement and the suspicion that we have blown it. So we commit the same sins again.

C. S. Lewis, in *Screwtape Letters*, vividly describes Satan's strategy: he gets Christians to become preoccupied with their failures; from then on, the battle is won.

One minister, who has spent many hours counseling people with psychological and spiritual problems, believes that demons are often directly responsible for discouragement and a sense of failure. He has rebuked the demons, and, in many instances, depression has vanished. The caption on the desk of one Christian worker is accurate. It reads: "Discouragement is of the devil."

The greatest blunder of Christians is not their failure when trying to live for Christ; a greater mistake is that they do not understand God's provision for sin, defeat, and guilt. We are successful to the extent that we understand God's remedy for failure! Read the next few pages carefully: they are an attempt to explain God's cure for the guilt syndrome.

First, Christ's death on the cross included a sacrifice for *all* our sins—past, present, and future. Every sin that you will ever commit has already been paid for. All of our sins were future when Christ died two thousand years ago. Therefore, He made one payment for *all* sins past and future. There is no sin that you will ever commit that has not *already* been included in Christ's death (Colossians 2:13).

God does not find it difficult to forgive us. It is not as though He must regretfully give us a second chance. The price of forgiveness has already been paid, and God wants us to accept it freely.

Christ "is the propitiation for our sins; and not for ours only, but also for those of the whole world" (1 John 2:2). That means He satisfied God for all sins that can *possibly be committed.* Let me repeat, God has been propitiated (satisfied) for any imaginable evil you might commit.

An atheist asked Billy Graham, "If Hitler had received Christ on his deathbed, would he have gone to heaven, whereas someone who lived a good life but rejected Christ would go to hell?" That is a trick question. It was asked in such a way as to make the gospel appear ridiculous. But the answer is yes. If Hitler accepted Christ, God could forgive him completely, because Christ's death included all of Hitler's sins! God values Christ so much that He can accept Hitler with Christ's merit. Visualize the worst sin imaginable —possibly it is nailing Christ to the cross—Christ died for *that* sin, too.

When Christ cried, "It is finished," the expression is but one word in Greek, *tetelestai,* a word used for business transactions. When this word was written across a bill, it meant "paid in full." You need never try to "make up" for your sins on your own. Christ's death paid for our sins *in full.*

Second, God cannot punish us for our sins. All of the punishment for sin has already been given to Christ. As Isaiah predicted, "The Lord was pleased to crush [Christ], putting Him to grief; if He would render Himself as a guilt offering, He will see His offspring, He will prolong His days, and the good pleasure of the Lord will prosper in His hand" (Isaiah 53:10). God bruised Christ; Christ received God's anger for sin. As William Cowper put it,

> Death and the curse were in our cup
> O, Christ, 'twas full for Thee,
> But Thou hast drained the last dark drop—
> 'Tis empty now for me!
> Jehovah bade His sword awake,
> O, Christ, it woke 'gainst Thee,
> Thy blood the flaming blade must slake,
> Thy heart its sheath must be
> All for my sake—my peace to make,
> Now sleeps that sword for me.

God disciplines us, but He does not punish us. He can never be angry with us anymore: His justice was satisfied at the cross. Some Christians interpret all calamities as God trying to get even with them. A sick child, an accident, financial problems, all of these are sometimes falsely believed to be God punishing us for sins.

In fact, some people try to punish *themselves* for their sins. They often brood over their mistakes and even injure themselves physically to try to satisfy God. All such attempts to pay for our sin are diabolical. Satan does not want us to understand that Christ paid it all!

Many years ago, a father and his daughter were walking through the grass on the Canadian prairie. In the distance, they saw a prairie fire; eventually, they realized, it would engulf them. The father knew there was only one way of escape: they would quickly begin a fire right where they were and burn a large patch of grass. When the huge fire drew near, they then would stand on the section that had already burned. When the fire actually did approach them, the girl was terrified by the raging flames. But her father assured her, "The flames can't get to us. We are standing *where the fire has already been.*"

Are you afraid of God's judgment? If you have trusted Christ as Savior, you can never come under His wrath. When we depend on Him, we are secure; we are where the wrath of God already has been.

Third, although we may become weary of confessing the same sins, God does not become weary of hearing our confession. If we say to God, "I am coming to confess the same sin," God's reply is, "What sin?" Any previous sins that have been confessed *have already been blotted out* forever! "I have wiped out your transgressions like a thick cloud," God told His people (Isaiah 44:22). David reminds us, "As far as the east is from the west, so far has He removed our transgressions from us" (Psalms 103:12).

When God forgives us, our sins are blotted out so completely that He does not "remember" them (i.e., He never holds them against us again). The sins you confessed yesterday will never again be a barrier between you and God, unless you refuse to accept God's forgiveness and doubt the value of Christ's sacrifice.

Perhaps you have seen an electronic computer, used to calculate mathematical problems. What happens if you get your information confused or make an error? You can press the "cancel" button. Automatically, all of the information is eliminated from the apparatus. You can begin your calculation again without trying to sort out previous mistakes. In fact, there is no record of the previous information; it is lost forever! That's what happens to our sins when God forgives us. The *consequences* often remain, but the guilt (the legal condemnation for the offense) is gone. If we have a clear conscience toward others (which is brought about by personal confession) we can always have a clear conscience before God.

One of Satan's most popular deceptions is to make us believe that we should not confess our sins until some future time when we are living more "victoriously." Since Satan deceives by feelings as well as words, he gets us to "feel" we are unforgiven; he makes us believe that God is not pleased with our performance, and therefore, we should stop bothering Him about forgiveness!

In order to defend themselves against this attack, Christians often resort to trying to find some sign that God is not displeased with them. They think, "I've received such a blessing from reading my Bible today, surely God must be pleased with me." Or perhaps they have been extra kind or patient. On this basis, they hope to meet Satan's attack. They hope to please God by being victorious, thinking that should give them a more meaningful relationship with the Almighty.

The result? Endless despair and more failure. We are never made acceptable to God by our faithful reading of Scripture or by disciplined prayer (though both are needed). We don't receive God's approval because we witness to others or are faithful at church. God does not even accept us because we do works that He gives us the ability to do! As we shall see later, God is pleased with the good works of His children because of what they signify—love and gratefulness. But the works per se are not the basis of our acceptance.

Our basis for pleasing God? It is standing by faith on the sacrifice of Christ, a sacrifice that satisfied the Father completely. We are accepted *in the beloved*. And that basis remains secure even when we fail!

AN OLD TESTAMENT ILLUSTRATION

When the Israelites were in Egypt, God instructed them to sprinkle blood on the doorpost of their houses. The angel of Jehovah was to pass by the homes that night and kill all the firstborn in Egypt. The only exception would be those homes where blood had been applied. The blood would be for a "sign" upon the houses, and, when the angel saw the blood, he would bypass that particular home.

Let's use our imagination. What if one family decided to hang a list of its achievements on the door of the house? After all, wouldn't God be pleased with their kindness, prayerfulness, and generosity? The answer is obvious. They would have been victims of the plague. God said, "When I see the *blood* I will pass over you" (Exodus 12:13, emphasis added).

Another family, in their desire to be accepted by God, may have tacked another list of accomplishments to their door. These works were done in genuine devotion to Jehovah and included faithful prayer and separation from sin and sinners. Would that have met God's requirements? Again, no! Only *blood* could please God.

Similarly, Christians have prayed, read the Scriptures, and increased their giving in order to overcome their guilt completely. Their conscience (activated by Satan) tells them that they are failures and that God is not pleased with them. They try to make these accusations by appealing to some of their accomplishments. They hang all of their spiritual victories on the door of their lives, hoping that God will accept them. Satan is delighted! He knows they are hopelessly entangled in one certain failure after another. If they continue, they will end in despair.

Do you want to please God? Do you want His complete acceptance despite your personal failures? You can have that assurance by depending *solely* on Christ's sacrifice.

The purpose of reading the Scriptures and praying is so that our concept of God's salvation will be enlarged and so that we will understand more fully God's gracious (free) provision for all sin. In other words, all those necessary matters we have heard about—devotions, witnessing, prayer—have no *intrinsic* value in God's sight. Only in the beloved Son is God well pleased. And our lives on earth please God only to the extent that our prayers, Bible study, and Christian fellowship increase our appreciation (and application) of God's grace. Then we will voluntarily give ourselves to God in appreciation for what God has given us (Romans 12:1-2; Ephesians 2:8-10).

The implications of this are staggering. Every Christian is equally accepted by God; we all have equal access to fellowship with God.

## How Righteous Are We?

How righteous do you have to be in order to get to heaven? The answer is simple: as righteous as God. Of course we all come short of that. But God's standards don't change.

Fortunately, God has a plan to make us that righteous. It involves forgiving our sins but also much more. A Christian is one who is forgiven *and* has the righteousness of Christ credited to him. God accepts us like He accepts Christ.

Now, since any of us could die at any moment, God has already accepted us *forever* in Christ! That is, *legally*, all of our sins have already been forgiven; Christ's righteousness is ours.

Think of this: God sees believers as absolutely perfect. God sees us in Christ. And *nothing* you can do can change God's complete acceptance of you! Many Christians don't believe this. We are so accustomed to accepting people because of what they are and rejecting them for what they are not, that we believe God must operate like that, too. But if we take God at His word, we must believe that *nothing* we do can stop God from accepting us.

If we are permanently accepted by God, why is it necessary to confess our sins? Our sins block our fellowship, though not our acceptance, with God. To confess means to "agree with God" about our sin. It does not mean to beg, plead, or live in misery until we convince God we mean business. We simply agree that we have sinned and *freely* accept God's forgiveness. When we do this, God does not compromise His justice. "He is faithful and righteous to forgive us our sins and to cleanse us from all unrighteousness" (1 John 1:9).

The parable of the prodigal son illustrates this point. The wayward son had all of the legal rights of sonship; he had the father's continual acceptance, but he did not enjoy these privileges until he returned to his father and admitted his sins. Similarly, as believers, our acceptance with God is always secure; we have all the rights of sonship, but we must confess our sins to experience the inheritance that is ours.

## THE DIFFERENCES BETWEEN CHRISTIANS

Earlier in this book, we showed that the differences between unsaved people were only slight. If we judge Christians by their sins and private failures, the differences between them are not great either; all of us commit sins in our hearts. Why then are some Christians living joyfully and victoriously whereas others live in defeat?

The reason cannot be that some people are more "worthy" in the sight of God than others. Sometimes when we are in special need we ask for the prayers of outstanding Christians. But they do not have special access to God. Blood is blood, whether applied to your doorpost or mine. Christ's sacrifice is no better for one Christian than another! God accepts us on the same basis as the "greats" of the past.

Neither is it because some Christians are not prone to failure; all of us are. In fact, I've concluded that no Christian is an unqualified success. We all experience varying degrees of failure! The difference is in what we do with our mistakes and sins.

Some Christians understand clearly the basis of their acceptance and others don't. Some are not discouraged over failures, because they know that all sins have already been cared for in Christ. Others become preoccupied with their failures and try to find some righteousness *within themselves* to make them worthy to have fellowship with God. *That* is a key difference.

Are you discouraged? Defeated? All of us have been! Micah (a prophet of God, no less) also felt the sting of defeat. But he knew that it need not be permanent. "Do not rejoice over me, O my enemy. Though I fall I will rise; Though I dwell in darkness, the Lord is a light for me" (Micah 7:8). Here is a comment from a book of wisdom, "For a righteous man fails seven times, and rises again. But the wicked stumble in time of calamity" (Proverbs 24:16). Your defeats have been paid for. Say "Thank You" to God and live in fellowship with the Almighty.

### Forgiving Ourselves

God is not angry with you! He is not displeased with you, if you depend solely on the death and life of Christ for your acceptance.

But one difficulty remains. God is pleased with Christ's sacrifice. He has forgiven you, but *have you forgiven yourself?*

Many Christians are handcuffed by regret. This goes all the way from the widow who says, "If only I had persuaded my husband to go to the doctor earlier, he would not have died," to the person who believes that he has committed the unpardonable sin. By nature, we know that sin has to be paid for; consequently, some people nurse their regrets and cling to their grief. The reason? They believe that such an attitude is necessary to punish themselves. Unconsciously *they* want to pay for their sins.

For example, I know a widow who went to the grave of her husband every morning for fourteen years. Before his death, she had urged him to attend a special event with her. En route, an accident occurred, and later he died. God forgave her mistake (it was not a sin), but she never forgave herself. She felt that if she were ever happy again, it would mean both disrespect for her husband and an indication that she was not truly repentant.

If Christ has paid the penalty for our sins and failures, why should we try to add our continual regret to His work? Christ came to free us from the bondage of our sin toward God and from our slavery to past failures.

A well-known Christian was driving faster in the rain than was safe. As a result, he was in an accident, and his companion was killed. Regret? Of course! Deep anguish and remorse. Yet, that night, he relates that he saw more clearly than ever before. "The purpose of the cross was to repair the irreparable."

It is the deep, difficult heartaches that the cross was meant to cover. Christ's sacrifice is as good for big sins as it is for small ones. From God's perspective, there is no reason we must be defeated. We are always accepted in God's book, and if our fellowship is broken, it can be restored immediately.

John Newton had committed every sin imaginable. Yet later he understood the reason he could be totally righteous before God. He wrote,

> Amazing Grace, how sweet the sound
> That saved a wretch like me;
> I once was lost, but now am found,
> Was blind but now I see.

That grace is available for you and me. It is an insult to Christ if we believe His sacrifice was not enough for us!

# 6

## Do We Get by Scot-Free?

"I'm pregnant. My parents don't know it yet, neither does my boyfriend. I've got to tell somebody. Somebody has to tell me what to do." The speaker was a sixteen-year-old girl brought up in an evangelical church. She was a Christian—a nice Sunday school kid—the last one you'd expect to see in this condition.

So what do you do? Tell her it's her own fault and that she is getting what she deserves? Hardly. It *is* her own fault; she might be getting what she deserves; but it's too late to sermonize. The girl needs help.

What about God? Should you tell her that she should ask forgiveness, or would that be making it too easy for someone who should "get what she deserves"? Perhaps God should be brought into the picture only after she has suffered enough, after she has faced embarrassment at the hands of her family and friends?

Of course, this girl needs more than forgiveness. She needs acceptance, understanding, and wisdom. There will be embarrassment, humiliation, and (in certain related cases) church discipline. But so far as her relationship to God is concerned, so far as her *guilt* is concerned, do you encourage her to ask God's forgiveness, or should she come to God after she has gotten other matters straightened out?

It is odd that we should sometimes be tempted to begrudge someone the grace of God at the moment they need it the most. Often we self-righteously believe it unfair that those who sin so grossly should be forgiven so freely.

But forgiveness is already available for every sin that we will ever commit. There is no reason to delay her acceptance of God's grace. Right now, while she is sitting on a chair in your living room, she can be forgiven. Legally (in God's books), her sins that are scarlet can be cleansed like the freshly driven snow. After all, Christ did not come to call the righteous but *sinners* to repentance.

Too simple? Perhaps someone objects, "But if we tell people (especially young people) that forgiveness is readily available, they will live in deliberate sin, knowing they can always count on instant forgiveness." Such a response is wrong but encouraging! When someone says that God's unlimited forgiveness gives license to sin, it shows that they are beginning to understand the incredible generosity of God's grace!

When Paul argued that through Christ we can be forgiven for all our trespasses he stated, "But where sin increased, grace abounded all the more" (Romans 5:20). He knew that if the people understood him correctly—if he made his point clear—his readers would object by in effect saying, "Let us continue in sin that grace might increase!" (Romans 6:1). In other words, once we have grasped the unlimited favor God gives to us, the human (perhaps a better word is *carnal*) reaction is to assume that such teaching will encourage people to sin. Paul's answer is direct: "God forbid. How shall we, that are dead to sin, live any longer therein?" (Romans 6:2, KJV).

Yes, forgiveness is always available to those who repent. God is merciful beyond all human explanation. We can never sin too many times or too much for God to pardon us. We often think that God is like we are. We can forgive the same person a few times, but after that, we have had enough. But God doesn't impose limits on forgiveness. The blood of Christ is never inadequate. It can cover all sins.

Does God's grace encourage sin? Possibly there have been those who have deliberately sinned, flippantly presuming on God's goodness to forgive them. (I think if we were honest, all of us would admit that we have been guilty of that at some time.) But if we do not understand or fully appreciate God's grace, there is a much greater danger: the certainty of discouragement. Because we have been unwilling to explain grace in its fullest sense, many Christians simply do not come to God anymore. They are weary of sin and falsely assume God is weary of them, too.

Only those who understand God's unlimited forgiveness have the wisdom to confess their sins after personal failure. In my counseling, I've learned that most spiritual defeats result from ignorance. Many believers are in the dark as to how good God is and how completely Christ satisfied His requirements for all sin.

Easy believism? Yes! Thank God that the only requirement for forgiveness is to believe in Him whom He hath sent! To add to that any work or to insist that we must plead and beg for forgiveness is to mix faith and works and insult the Christ who died to save us.

Yes, forgiveness is always free. But that doesn't mean that confession is always easy. Sometimes it is hard. Incredibly hard. It is painful (sometimes literally) to admit our sins and entrust ourselves to God's care.

Think of those who sit in a church pew, convicted of covetousness, pride, and hypocrisy. Forgiveness is free, but admitting to those sins, making restitution, humbling ourselves, these matters are incredibly difficult—so difficult that many Christians would rather be carnal than thoroughly purged. As a result, they prefer simply to confess their sins generally. They want just enough pardon to remain on speaking terms with God, but the core of their lives remains untouched.

Here is the paradox: although forgiveness is free, few people want to receive it. By nature we don't want to admit our sins. If we do, we feel more comfortable in confessing our sins to God than in asking forgiveness of our friends (if we have wronged them). By nature, we don't mind religion, but we resist humility. A broken and contrite heart is not easy to come by.

This is why we often hear that the price of revival (discipleship) is incredibly high. It's not that God's grace costs us anything; it's just that we have to make so many changes when we accept grace in its fullest sense!

Can an unmarried, sixteen-year-old girl who is pregnant receive God's forgiveness freely? Yes. However, whether she will want that forgiveness, whether she will want to face the implications of admitting her sin to God and casting herself upon God's mercy is quite another matter. Remember, confession means that we face our sins head-on. Most of us prefer to dodge our sins, work them out ourselves, or, if possible, ignore them. Jeremiah says the heart is deceitful above all things. Little wonder we are experts at deceiving others and ourselves.

This unmarried girl can be forgiven, but the requirement is that she agree with God that *she* has sinned. As long as it's the boyfriend's fault, the parents' fault, or the church's fault, she cannot have fellowship with God.

There is also another lesson in this story: forgiveness wipes out guilt before God and restores us to fellowship. But forgiveness cannot eliminate the consequences of sin. Some sins have especially serious effects that can never be erased in this life. Let's consider this in more detail.

## The Social Consequences

All sins have consequences. Even the sins of the mind are not as harmless as we often suppose. True, there are sometimes no visible effects of sinful thoughts. Although all sins are conceived in the mind, they need not give birth to actions. But even so, evil thoughts weaken our moral and spiritual resistance to temptation. If we lust we will not necessarily commit the act of adultery, but the lust prepares the way for the overt act. Furthermore, there are some sins—great sins—that often exist solely in the mind. Pride and covetousness are examples.

Although we might not always (or ever) see the result of our thoughts, God judges us by them just the same. "As [a man] thinketh in his heart, so is he" (Proverbs 23:7, KJV). Christ severely rebuked the Pharisees who cleaned the outside of the cup but inside were full of robbery and self-indulgence (Matthew 23:25). He told them that they should clean their hearts first and then be concerned about outward conduct.

Yet, it is our actions that have the most far-reaching consequences. The pregnant sixteen year old could be forgiven, but the child would be born. The murderer who receives forgiveness is clothed in Christ's righteousness but must still serve his prison sentence. The carnal Christian who receives forgiveness for specific sins (and makes personal adjustments) can walk with God, but there is no way to restore the lost time.

Possibly, the most familiar biblical illustration of sin's consequences is David's story. In a moment of passion he committed adultery with Bathsheba. His story is unique because he was not an uncommitted, flippant man whose life was characterized by wickedness. He was chosen to be king precisely because he was "a man after God's own heart." David's experience reminds us that *none* of us is beyond the possibility of gross sin. Greater men than we have thrown away their purity in a moment of sensual passion. The one who believes he stands (i.e., the one who believes he or she could never do such a thing) is the most likely to fall.

David's experience also illustrates how difficult it is to ask for forgiveness. Undoubtedly, his conscience troubled him, but he did not want to face the painful consequences of confession. His guilt was so pronounced that it even affected his physical condition: "When I kept silent about my sin, my body wasted away through my groaning all day long. For day and night Thy hand was heavy upon me; my vitality was drained away as with the fever heat of summer" (Psalms 32:3-4). Yet, for all that, David did not repent of his sin.

Even when Nathan the prophet told the parable to illustrate David's sin, the king did not get the message. Finally, the prophet confronted David directly. Then David repented.

Did God forgive him? Yes. Even in the Old Testament era the repentant were forgiven. But the consequences were disastrous; God predicted that there would be fighting within David's family; his wives would be raped in broad daylight, and Bathsheba's son would die. In the end, David also lost his sons Absalom and Ammon.

Stiff consequences? Yes. But some sins—particularly sexual ones—have bitter repercussions. In Scripture, sexual immorality is especially singled out as one sin that is most harmful (1 Corinthians 6:17-20). Those who give their body to another in an illicit relationship (whether it is public knowledge or not) bear special emotional and moral scars.

Sometimes Christians, in order to dramatize God's complete forgiveness, say, "The bird with the broken wing will fly just as high again," implying that any sinner can be restored to his original usefulness if he truly repents.

I disagree. The story of David, plus a host of similar illustrations in contemporary life, prove that the bird with the broken wing often does *not* fly as high as he did before. Sometimes he never flies again! There are some consequences for specific sins that we will carry to our grave.

However, as emphasized earlier in this book, all is never lost. God does make the best of our consequences; He does use our self-inflicted problems for ultimate good. To return once more to the story of David, it was after he finally did confess his sins that he had the assurance of God's guidance again. The same psalm that speaks of how painful confession is also tells how satisfying God's leading is. God reminds David, "I will instruct you and teach you in the way which you should go; I will counsel you with My eye upon you. . . . Be glad in the Lord and rejoice you righteous ones, and shout for joy all you who are upright in heart" (Psalms 32:8, 11). When God forgives, He gives us the ability to rejoice, even in the middle of tragedies that are our own fault. The greatest sinner can yet give praise to God. The consequences might remain; the guilt does not.

## GOD'S DISCIPLINE

God does not punish Christians for sin. God disciplines His children, but He doesn't punish them. The distinction is this: punishment carries the idea of satisfying justice for a crime. But Christ satisfied the Father's justice. Therefore, God now disciplines us, that is, He brings problems and struggles into our lives so that we will not stray from the main road. He is not angry with us but disciplines us so that we can mature spiritually.

Of course God doesn't scold us or make us stand in the corner. But He does use the circumstances of life to keep us in line. In fact, He scourges (whips) every son that belongs to Him (Hebrews 12:6).

Those to whom the book of Hebrews was written were tempted to become discouraged because of persecution. They hadn't yet had to die for their faith, but they were on the verge of buckling under pressure.

These problems did not come to them because they were unlucky. Their circumstances were God's way of developing their faith and weaning them from the attractions of the world. God was disciplining them for their own good so that they might be partakers of His holiness (Hebrews 12:10). God disciplines *all* of his children (Hebrews 12:8), and if someone is not corrected by Him, he is an illegitimate child.

The upshot of this is that we should learn everything we can from the difficulties of life without complaining about the way our Father treats us.

Should we interpret all of our problems as the result of specific sins? The obvious answer is no. Those whose lives are filled with tragedy are not necessarily more sinful than those who are free from such difficulties. But in each instance we can be certain of one fact: God intends to teach us faith and conform us to Christ. As a result, He will not screen us from anything that will help us reach these goals.

Of course we do sometimes encounter difficulties as a direct result of specific sins. We've already emphasized that sins—especially *some* sins—have damaging consequences. But in many instances we may not know whether our tragedies are the direct result of specific sins. Often calamities hit us without any apparent connection between our actions and a given sin.

The point is this: *It isn't necessary to know why God sent us the misfortune in order to profit from it.* Just because we can't think of any specific reason for the trial doesn't mean that God had no reason for allowing it.

We can be sure that God's primary concern for us is always that we forsake our sins and develop the rich qualities of faith and joy *within* our circumstances. The writer of Hebrews observed that discipline is usually not welcomed, "yet to those who have been trained by it, afterwards it yields the peaceful fruit of righteousness" (12:11).

All of our difficulties—whether the result of our own sin or not—are custom-designed by God to teach us how to apply His grace. Even Paul had to learn that God's grace was sufficient for his thorn in the flesh.

Paul said he had *learned* to be content in every circumstance of life (Philippians 4:11). The implication is that contentment is not a quality that comes naturally. If Paul had to learn from poverty, shipwrecks, hunger, and imprisonment, perhaps we need a few roadblocks in our lives to learn the same lesson.

Tragically, many Christians who complain about life are not learning the lessons God wants to teach them. They are like a child who simply resents his parents' spankings and refuses to profit from them. Yet, the irony is that God often simply applies more pressure when we are too stubborn to get the message!

When some ships are brought into the harbor, they must be steered through the deepest section of the harbor or else be broken on the rocks. Similarly, some Christians have been spared personal shipwreck (even though they might not know it) when they have come through the deepest waters of misfortune.

Remember, God always disciplines in love. God cannot be angry with us, neither can He ever punish us since Christ received punishment for us. All of the ammunition of God's justice was exhausted for *our good*, that is, to lead us to more meaningful relationships with God.

Confession removes all guilt but not necessarily all consequences. God uses these circumstances (and the dilemmas of life in general) to develop rich qualities (the fruit of the Spirit) within us. Therefore, we can experience a joyful relationship with God, even when facing problems that are our own fault.

# 7

# A Foundation for Self-Acceptance

Mary looked as if she'd never had a problem in her life. She was friendly, attractive, and cheerful. But beneath that facade were feelings too deep for words—feelings of resentment, bitterness, and intolerable depression. In fact, she had contemplated suicide.

That she was a dedicated Christian made her problem more puzzling. Why did Christ not give her the fulfillment she craved? Why was she beset with uncontrollable resentment? She had spent countless hours in prayer asking God for deliverance, but to no avail. Although Christ came to set His people free, this woman was in bondage.

Mary's background provided the clue to her problem. Her father died when she was a child, and, as a result, she was entrusted to the care of a harsh stepfather who vented his bitterness on this unwanted child. When Mary (then three or four years old) would come to her stepfather for affection, she was brushed aside. One remark he made will always ring in her ears: "I'd like to throw you out! You should be pushed into a ditch."

Understandably, Mary grew up feeling guilty for simply being alive. She felt responsible for her stepfather's misery and developed deep feelings of inferiority. She knew that she would always be a failure. Furthermore, she believed she *deserved* to be one.

In later years, when friends showed concern for her, she resented it. *How could anyone ever love me?* she thought. She believed no person in his right mind would love someone as worthless as she. She even married a man whom she believed did not love her. *No sane, decent, respectable man would love me,* she unconsciously assumed. Thus, she settled for something less than love (at least from her perspective) when she promised to "love, honor, and obey."

Twenty years and four children later, she began verbalizing her true feelings. At first I believed she was looking for sympathy, fishing for compliments. But I was mistaken. This beautiful and intelligent woman believed she was the scum of the earth; she believed with all her heart, mind, and soul that she was and always would be a colossal failure, a gigantic zero.

Mary's self-image could not be changed merely by telling her that her opinion of herself was mistaken. Those who reject themselves cannot be convinced to accept themselves by pointing out their personal worth or accentuating their positive qualities. The point is they *feel* inferior, they *feel* worthless, they *feel* rejected. No amount of persuasion can convince them otherwise.

Consequently, beautiful people may actually believe they are ugly; talented people may believe they are inferior; and people who are loved may reject the love they so desperately crave.

Even those who have grown up in fine homes—Christian homes—often find difficulty with self-acceptance. A person who flunks college, fails on a business venture, or is fired from a job may find that it takes years for him to accept his failure. He may never regain the self-confidence he once had. But God has not left us without hope.

Fortunately, it is possible to accept ourselves even after we have failed. Even if we were rejected by our parents, friends, or marriage partner we can accept ourselves—failure and all. But we can only do this by facing our limitations and considering our lot in life from God's perspective.

When I speak of accepting our failures I don't mean that we should accept habitual sin as a way of life. Rather, I am suggesting that God wants us to put past failures behind us and not use them as an excuse for morbid introspection, pessimism, or depression. Self-acceptance means that we are at peace with ourselves, with others, and with God.

People reject themselves for many reasons: physical appearance, lack of ability and intelligence, or because of the failures of the past. Others, like Mary, have warped views of themselves because of their family background. Thank God this can be changed! The Scriptures provide the information necessary to be at peace with ourselves and be free from the bondage of self-rejection.

### ACCEPTING OUR LIMITATIONS

Our opinion of ourselves is formed largely by the attitude of others toward us. If, as children, we are ridiculed for our physical appearance or our lack of ability, we may develop deep-seated inferiority and the belief that we are doomed to be a failure.

Children are often unintentionally cruel in pointing out one another's physical idiosyncrasies. If a child is too fat, too skinny, too tall, or too short, he can become so self-conscious that he loses his self-respect and self-esteem. Sometimes the emotional scars are so deep that the person may never develop self-confidence again.

In fact, most people who reject themselves do so because they dislike their physical appearance. They look in the mirror and wonder where God was when they were put together. As a result they feel self-conscious, worthless, and inferior. They may unconsciously or consciously hate God because of the way He made them.

What do the Scriptures teach regarding our physical appearance? First, God fashioned us in our mother's womb (Psalms 139:13-16). Therefore, our appearance was determined by Him. In fact, God even takes responsibility for physical handicaps. To Moses he said, "Who has made man's mouth? Or who makes him dumb or deaf, or seeing or blind? Is it not I, the Lord?" (Exodus 4:11). God made us the way we are for a special reason. We must accept the fact that He knew what He was doing when we were assembled. We will never accept our physical features unless we thank God that He made us as He did.

Of course there may be some things about ourselves that we can change; our weight, for instance. If we are overweight we should diet, and all of us should take care of ourselves physically and work to improve our abilities. But God takes responsibility for the basic "raw material" we have to work with.

The first step? Thank God for the way He made you. *You* are special, distinct, and unique. You were not made from a common mold. Thank Him that you are special.

Second, we must see that God created us less than ideal (i.e., with our physical or functional handicaps) to teach us that the inward is more important than the outward. Rich qualities of character make a truly beautiful person. A Korean minister who had been the pastor of a large congregation of lepers made this observation: "Despite their leprosy, they were beautiful people *inside*."

Inside! Isn't that what God said to Samuel when he was trying to find a king for Israel? Samuel thought that one of the tall, impressive sons of Jesse would qualify. But God had other ideas. He explained to Samuel, "Do not look at his appearance or at the height of his stature, because I have rejected him; for God sees not as man sees, for man looks at the outward appearance, but the Lord looks at the heart" (1 Samuel 16:7). It's the *inside* that counts.

Peter taught the same truth in the New Testament. Since women (and men) are often conscious—perhaps too conscious—of their appearance, Peter taught that the emphasis should not be on the outward adorning: "But let it be the hidden person of the heart, with the imperishable quality of a gentle and quiet spirit, which is precious in the sight of God" (1 Peter 3:4). Our outward imperfections are a reminder of

God's priorities. He is concerned with character, not the deception of outward beauty.

On the surface it would seem that those who are especially good-looking have an advantage over the rest of us, and, to some extent, this is true. We are taught to worship the god of beauty early in life. Attractive children, teenagers, and adults are usually the most popular and the most accepted. Yet, inherent in such advantages are many dangers. Those who are physically attractive find it much more difficult to accept the onslaught of old age, and, even more important, they face greater temptations. The attractive are often lured into promiscuity and frequently sense they are loved for how they look rather than for what they are.

If we are dissatisfied with our appearance, God is trying to teach us to find our security *in Him*. He knows that if we were attractive we might find our satisfaction in the fleeting pleasure of popularity rather than the solid rock of inward godliness.

Others resent God because of their lack of intelligence or lack of ability. They spend their lives wishing they were like someone else; their conversation is filled with self-pity and self-derogatory comments. Perhaps they believe that such an attitude displays humility. They never seem to grow weary of informing others of their shortcomings.

Such an attitude is not humility; neither is it realism; it is sin. And there will be no victory over such an ungrateful attitude until it is confessed and forsaken.

God has given us our abilities. If we are gifted, we cannot take credit for it; if we lack abilities, that is no reason to complain. To the Corinthians, who prided themselves in their spiritual gifts, Paul wrote, "For who regards you as superior? And what do you have that you did not receive? But if you did receive it, why do you boast as if you had not received it?" (1 Corinthians 4:7). One of our temptations is to overestimate the importance of our abilities. Often we build up such an unrealistic self-image that we cannot—or, perhaps, will not—face our limitations. Or we may go to the other extreme and underestimate our gifts.

The solution? Take Paul's advice: "I say to every man among you not to think more highly of himself than he ought to think; but to think so as to have sound judgment, as God has allotted to each a measure of faith" (Romans 12:3). We must evaluate our abilities realistically, accept our limitations, and thank God for *whatever* He has given us.

History is filled with innumerable instances of people who refused to be stopped by handicaps, misfortune, and lack of ability. They understood that a lack of personal ability did not cramp God's power; indeed, His strength is made perfect in weakness. They were able to praise God for what He had given them, and, in the process, they accepted themselves for what they were.

Self-acceptance is basically a spiritual issue. What it boils down to is this: are we able to thank the Creator for the way He made us? If not, we are casting doubt on His wisdom; if we can thank Him, we display our belief that He knows what is best for us. And *that* will help us accept ourselves—limitations, failures, and all.

But even more than this, we must come to appreciate our value from God's perspective. Understanding His acceptance of us gives us the key to understanding ourselves.

## THEOLOGICAL CONSIDERATION

Theologians have often erred by not distinguishing between proper self-love (i.e., self-acceptance) and selfishness. It is true that we should not love ourselves in a self-centered way, but it is equally true that we must not hate ourselves. We must accept ourselves, for if we are not at peace with ourselves, we cannot be at peace with others or with God. The Scriptures teach that we should love our neighbor *as* we do ourselves. We cannot love our neighbor unless we, in a proper sense, love ourselves.

Sometimes we are told, "We are nothing in God's sight. We are worms before Him." In one sense this is true; namely, that we are rebellious sinners who cannot do one iota to please God on our own. But in another more profound sense, such a statement is patently false. Would Christ have died for us if we were worthless? Would He (pardon the thought) have died for worms?

The scriptural viewpoint is that all people are exceedingly valuable in God's sight, so valuable that God gave the best He had to redeem us. His investment in us is so great He could not possibly abandon us.

An illustration might help. Let us imagine a husband who invests his life's savings to buy a diamond for his wife. Would he be careless with it? Or would he treasure and protect it with painstaking care? The answer is obvious: since the diamond was purchased at a high cost, it will be protected, polished, and admired. Its value lies in its cost.

We were not bought with money but with the precious blood of Christ. If the value of an item depends on the price paid for it, the worth of each believer (and unbeliever, too, since Christ died for the whole world) is beyond calculation. Since God's investment in us is so great He is not about to abandon us. He is interested in protecting His valuables.

A poet can take a worthless sheet of paper, write a poem on it, and make it worth thousands of dollars. An artist can take a canvas, paint a picture, and the masterpiece becomes more valuable than gold. God takes sinners, redeems them with the sacrifice of His Son, and gives them the Holy Spirit as a pledge of His ownership. Then He elevates them to become joint heirs with Christ, His Son. Yet, some of these believers insist that they are worthless property!

To return to Mary, she began to make progress when she grasped the significance of God's investment in her as an individual. She realized that God is not an unwise speculator. He doesn't make foolish investments. In rejecting herself, Mary was, in effect, telling God that He is an unwise investor. He paid a high price for worthless property. If we feel worthless or hate ourselves, we insult Him.

In a sense, God's honor is at stake in us. David wrote that the Lord leads us in paths of righteousness, not merely for our own good, but for *His name's sake* (Psalms 23:3). Since we are His, He has the responsibility of protecting His investment. His reputation is at stake.

To repeat, regardless of how worthless we might feel, God thinks differently. Anyone—and particularly believers —can say, "I am valuable to God." To say less than that is to cast doubt on God's reputation. He knew what He was doing when He bought us at a high cost.

### Accepting in the Beloved

If you were a first-century slave who ran away from your owner, what would you expect as punishment when you returned? A flogging? Death?

That's what the slave Onesimus might have expected. But fortunately the apostle Paul intervened on his behalf. This incident illustrates what God has done for us.

Onesimus would probably have been glad simply to be forgiven. He'd have been glad if the past were forgotten and if he could begin again. Forgiveness brings great relief.

Many people believe that a Christian is simply a sinner whose sins are forgiven. They are grateful that God gives them a fresh start, and, as far as they are concerned, that is all they need. Yet, after repeatedly confessing the same sin, they become discouraged. Then they begin to wonder whether God's patience is wearing thin; perhaps He is not accepting them anymore.

Forgiveness is a precious gift! But forgiveness alone does not give us the security we need to live the Christian life. The forgiveness of specific sins does not guarantee our continual acceptance before God.

When Paul wrote a letter to Philemon on behalf of Onesimus, he requested more than forgiveness. He asked Philemon to accept Onesimus as he would accept the apostle himself. He wrote, "If then you regard me a partner, accept him *as you would me*" (Philemon 17, italics added). Onesimus was not to be merely a forgiven slave; he was to be received and treated *as if* he were the apostle Paul.

Let me say it once more. If your defeats and failures cause you to turn away from God, you don't understand God's grace. Christ died so that we would have the basis of acceptance before God that has *nothing* to do with our fluctuating experiences. Our acceptance depends on the sacrifice of Christ on the cross.

In God's sight there are only two classes of people, those who are in Christ and those who are outside of Him. And all those who are in Christ are accepted equally; there are no grades of perfection with God.

Of course, in actual experience Christians differ: some are carnal, others are godly, and the majority are somewhere in between. But there is no difference so far as *acceptance* is concerned.

We can't question Christ's acceptability to the Father. God the Father said that Christ is His beloved Son in whom He is well pleased. Yet we are just as pleasing to God as Christ! Christ, as it were, says to God the Father, "Receive these believers *as* You receive Me."

This illustrates the mind-boggling New Testament teaching that believers are not merely forgiven; they are not merely sinners minus their sins, but they are accepted before God as Christ is accepted! They are accepted in the Beloved (Ephesians 1:6).

Again, our acceptance before God is based squarely on Christ's acceptance before the Father. There can be no such thing as degrees of acceptance with God. He accepts perfection only for the reason that Christ alone is acceptable to the Father. The good news is that when we receive Christ as Savior, we are accepted *in Him*. Our acceptance before God is as certain as Christ's!

Perhaps you have flown in an airplane. Did the stewardess ask you whether you had a good day before you were permitted to board? Were you rejected if you were depressed?

Of course not. As far as the airline is concerned, you could be depressed, elated, or apathetic. Only one thing qualifies you for the flight: the right ticket. And that ticket has nothing to do with your feelings!

Imagine a man standing in the terminal with a ticket in his hand, refusing to enter the plane because he feels unworthy to fly! Such an attitude would prove that he doesn't understand the basis for his admittance to the plane. He would probably end up a nervous wreck and never get off the ground. He doesn't understand that his worthiness or unworthiness is not the issue; the *ticket* is what counts.

Think of the implications. If God (whose standards are far higher than ours) has completely forgiven and accepted us, why can we not accept ourselves? Why can we not believe His verdict in the matter and accept ourselves as He accepts us? If we have received the ticket, which Christ paid for on the cross, we have no need to feel unacceptable.

Perhaps now we can understand why those who reject themselves (and, as a result, experience deep depression) do not find help through prayer. Tim LaHaye, who has had vast experience in counseling, has observed that a high percentage of depressed people frequently pray. But their prayers remain unanswered because (1) they use the occasion to repeat their failures, indulge in self-pity, and remind God of their worthlessness; and (2) their prayer is, of necessity, one of unbelief. They spend most of their time praying that God will accept them, and they refuse to believe His word, namely, the fact that *He already has!*

We need not look within ourselves to find some reason that God should accept us. Neither should we believe that God rejects us because we are unworthy. True, we *are* unworthy, but our acceptance is unrelated to our unworthiness. We are received in Christ; His righteousness is attributed to us.

This is the heart of the doctrine of justification by faith. God declares us righteous. We are credited with all the perfection of Christ!

Have you accepted yourself, failures, limitations, physical handicaps, and all? If your faith is in Christ, *God has accept-*

*ed you* just as you are. To reject yourself is to reject God's grace.

Accepting ourselves does not mean that we condone sin or that we simply learn to adjust to continual spiritual failures. As explained above, God accepts a Christian who persistently lives in sin, but God is not honored by the life of such a Christian.

Here is the point. Our acceptance before God gives us the security to turn repeatedly to God for strength and forgiveness. *Our acceptance in heaven gives us the basis to live here on earth.* God's legal declaration—that we are credited with the righteousness of Christ—makes it possible for us to be free from guilt, free from the emotional scars of the past.

Mary illustrates the point. When she began to thank God for His acceptance of her through Christ, when she realized how valuable she was to God, her attitude toward herself began to change. At last she was free to live without self-condemnation, free to return to God for spiritual power, free to evaluate honestly her abilities and appearance. Although her stepfather did not accept her, she found comfort in David's words: "For my father and mother have forsaken me, but the Lord will take me up" (Psalms 27:10).

# 8

# The Detour Can Lead Back to the Main Road

The woman sat quietly, carefully pondering her next sentence. Then she leaned forward in her chair, as if to give special emphasis to each word. "God can't bless us. We can't be happy. *We should never have been married.*"

Her story? She was reared in a Christian home. As she grew older, she deeply resented her parents' restrictions, especially because they disapproved of the boys she dated. The arguments that erupted only drove a deeper wedge between their beliefs and hers. She determined to do as she pleased. And she did.

By the time she announced her wedding, she was already three months pregnant.

Deep within, she was bitter. She knew her parents had been right in what they had told her, but she was too proud to admit it. She swore her marriage would work.

It didn't.

Her husband was not the carefree and thoughtful man she had believed he was. She felt trapped because she *had* to marry him. He felt the same way about her.

She spent hours dreaming of what she *might* have done, whom she *might* have married, if she had not become attached to this—this thing. It was pride, the determination not to admit they were wrong, that held their marriage together.

Years later, she finally asked God to forgive her sins. Slowly she was able to work through her bitterness, depend on God's mercy, and accept herself for what she was. So far, her husband was unchanged.

And now she found herself wondering about God's will for her life. She wished that God could bless her and her husband. But could she honestly expect God's help in their marriage after her deliberate disobedience?

Maybe she was supposed to have been a missionary. There was little use trying to speculate. The fact remained that she was married to a man whom God never intended for her. How could she be happy now that she was *permanently* ("till death do us part") out of God's will?

What happens when Christians marry the wrong partner, refuse to accept God's call to be a missionary, or bypass countless opportunities because of unbelief? Can they ever again prove that "good and acceptable and perfect will of God"?

Sometimes we get the impression that the will of God is like an egg, a heavenly Humpty-Dumpty. Presumably, God expects us to do a balancing act as we walk an invisible tightrope. One mistake—or, at the most, two—and no one, not even God, can put Humpty-Dumpty together again.

Of course it is true that one sin (or even an error in judgment) can be costly. One immoral relationship, one selfish choice, or one bypassed opportunity can have devastating consequences. But we must remember that God is never finished with anyone who repents. Anyone can be forgiven; anyone can yet do the will of God.

Let me explain.

## God's Ideal Will

Does God have an ideal plan for everyone's life? To answer this, let us begin one step further back: Does God have an ideal plan for the world? Presumably, an ideal world was the Garden of Eden; His ideal people were Adam and Eve.

Sin ruined this perfect setup. Disobedience brought evil and death to the human race. Sin even affected the planet, and all of nature was cursed.

Did the Fall of man cause an emergency in heaven? Was God in despair, thinking that mankind could never have fellowship with Him again?

No! God did not have to hurriedly depend on a make-shift backup plan. He was not caught off guard. Christ's coming was not a last-minute decision made in the wake of a disaster. Redemption was planned long before sin entered the world (Titus 1:2).

God, who knows and controls all things, had already planned to take a ruined world and incorporate it into His program. Since Adam sinned, God has been working *in, with,* and *in spite of* sinful conditions.

The ideal world was ruined; but God instituted another "ideal" plan, that is, the plan of redemption. God chose to use evil to accomplish His ultimate purpose. Evil is not an enemy that took God by surprise. God has not chosen to destroy evil by one sovereign act. Rather, He has chosen to let it exist and redeem us from it. Where sin abounds, grace *does* much more abound!

To talk about the "ideal" life is quite futile. Since we were all born as children of wrath, we have all experienced sins and failures. The only ideal life will be in heaven, and if you are reading this, you're not there!

Of course, within the context of our sinful human condition, God undoubtedly has a plan for everyone's life. It includes such matters as our vocation, marriage partner (or lack of one), and even minute details of everyday life. The very hairs of our head are numbered. But all such plans are made by taking our sinful condition into account. For God, there are no contingencies; He knows the end from the beginning.

What if we should err on one point or another? What if we disobey God and sin greatly? Or marry the "wrong" one?

God will not be caught off guard. He will not be forced to activate emergency equipment. *He is as prepared to help us in our sin as He was to help Adam in his.*

God is a specialist in the sin disease. His Son died to remedy our situation. And if we repent and seek Him, *He will make the best arrangement possible within the context of our failure.*

As a result, we never reach the place where God is no longer willing to direct us. True, we might damage God's plan and pay the consequences. But if we repent, God will make the best of every situation. He is well prepared to work in and through conditions that are less than ideal.

To understand how this works in practice, let's consider four examples.

Example one: I know a man who believed that God wanted him to be a missionary in Europe. He refused to go. Later he yielded himself to God, and now he is an effective witness to others on this continent. He ends each day with the satisfaction of having been guided by God.

God is never short on ideas. He never says, "You blew it! I can't work you in." He does not run a union that can handle only a prescribed quota of workers. We are not permanently unemployed in the kingdom of heaven because we've shown up late for work. Neither are we on a waiting list, knowing that someone else must retire before we are hired. If we are willing to do anything (even things we thought we were not trained for), our God can use us.

Example two: A woman who came to me for counsel has a struggling marriage. As a Christian, she had married a non-Christian. She has paid dearly for that decision.

But now she has finally submitted herself totally to God. As a result, God is blessing her. The rough edges of her character are being smoothed by the struggles of her marriage. Her self-made predicament is teaching her the rich qualities of love, joy, peace, and patience.

Sometimes the going is tough, but God isn't through with her. She has already led her children to Christ.

Example three: Remember Jonah? God said, "Go to Nineveh." Jonah said, "No, I'm going to Tarshish." He ended up in the stomach of a fish. Was he in God's will? In one sense he was not, for he should have been going to Nineveh. But because of his disobedience, God prepared the fish for Jonah. The fish (and its appetite) was arranged under God's directive will. Jonah was disobedient, but God had other plans for His servant. The plan included a scary ride to Nineveh.

Remember, God is concerned that we stay in His will. He went to the trouble of preparing a fish, a storm, and even loaded the sailors' dice so that Jonah would get back on course. If God did this for a prophet who deliberately disobeyed, think of what He will do for those who fully commit their ways to Him.

Example four: Jephthah was an illegitimate child, "the son of a harlot" (Judges 11:1). After he grew up, he was forced out of his home because of his discredited birth. Later he was asked to return to his relatives and fight the Ammonites.

Does God have a purpose for a man who is the unintended product of an illicit sexual relationship? Can God use someone who, strictly speaking, should never have been born? Yes. "Now the Spirit of the Lord came upon Jephthah. . . . So Jephthah crossed over to the sons of Ammon to fight against them; and the Lord gave them into his hand" (Judges 11:29, 32).

Many people have had the crushing experience of being rejected by their parents. Often they develop such a low self-image that they are convinced that no one—including God —could possibly love them. Perhaps they are humiliated by the circumstances of their conception or their debased surroundings.

Here is good news: God can incorporate *any* repentant sinner into His program! When our father and mother forsake us, He will take us up (Psalms 27:10). There is no such thing as a situation beyond God's control.

### KNOWING GOD'S WILL

God does not want us to be ignorant of His will. Too often we think of the will of God as mystical or private information that can be known only by those who are "called" into vocational Christian work. Yet, the Scriptures say to us all, "Do not be foolish, but understand what the will of the Lord is" (Ephesians 5:17). God does not play hide-and-seek; He wants us to know His will.

Unfortunately, many Christians are confused at this point. They think of the will of God almost solely in geographical terms: Where shall we live? Or as a vocational decision: What should my occupation be? But all of these decisions are secondary; they fall into place after the most important aspects of God's will have been done.

It sounds trite, but the will of God is spelled out clearly for us in Scripture. God has desires that apply to all Christians. He does not have one will for missionaries and another for bricklayers. True, God may lead them into different vocations, but His primary will for all of us is the same.

What does God want *you* to do? A group of people asked Jesus, "What shall we do, that we may work the works of God?" (John 6:28). That is a sensible question. Christ answered, "This is the work of God, that you believe in Him whom He has sent" (v. 29). God's first purpose for our lives is that we transfer our trust from ourselves to Christ, that we believe in Him. What does God want *you* to do? First, He wants you personally to trust Christ as your Savior.

Second, God wants you to live in moral purity. "For this is the will of God, your sanctification; that is, that you abstain from sexual immorality. . . . For God has not called us for the purpose of impurity, but in sanctification" (1 Thessalonians 4:3, 7). God wants us to be free from sensuality, both in our actions and in our thoughts. Many Christians have secret moral sins that have captivated their minds. Some have already given up in the struggle. God wills that we learn to apply Christ's victory to ourselves. *That* is His will for you and me.

What else? "In everything give thanks; for this is God's will for you in Christ Jesus" (1 Thessalonians 5:18). An attitude of thankfulness shows our faith in God's providence.

Sometimes Christians say, "I want to glorify God in my life." But what does that mean? How do you glorify God? Who is qualified to glorify the Almighty? Here is the answer: "Whoso offereth praise glorifieth me" (Psalms 50:23, KJV).

It is also God's will that we do our routine duties with enthusiasm and joy. Listen to what Paul wrote to slaves who were often mistreated and expected to do the most humiliating chores. He urged them to be obedient, and then added that they should serve "in the sincerity of your heart, as to Christ; not by way of eye service, as men-pleasers, but as slaves of Christ, doing the will of God from the heart" (Ephesians 6:5-6).

What is God's will for a homemaker who dislikes washing dishes and clothes and who lives with an ungrateful husband? It is to do her work with joy, just as if she were doing these things for Christ.

What is God's will for a man who dislikes both his employer and his job? It is to work as though Christ is the one who hands him the paycheck at the end of the week. *That* is the will of God.

There are numerous other commands in Scripture relating to our basic attitudes (Romans 12). But all of these commands, including those referred to above, state specifically what God's will is for us. Yet, remarkably, these commands can be applied to *all* Christians, even those whose lives have a history of failures and sins. Since God is primarily concerned about our attitudes and responses, *anyone* can do the will of God. Even if we have made unwise choices, bypassed opportunities, or sinned miserably, it is not too late to begin to do what God wants us to do!

## God's Specific Direction

But what about other choices that involve God's will, those which are not mentioned in the Bible? Obviously, Scripture cannot tell us whether we should become missionaries to another country or whether we should go to college. Each of us makes a host of such decisions daily. How do we determine God's will in these matters?

The formula is quite simple. If we are obedient in the plan God has revealed, He is obligated to guide us in decisions that are unrevealed. If we houseclean our attitudes, values, and desires, if we seek first the kingdom of God and His righteousness, these other matters will be added unto us.

God has an indefinite number of ways to block us if we are going the wrong way and to create opportunities if we are going the right way. For example, He guides us by the advice of others and the desires He puts within us.

What about Brian and his wife described in chapter 1? They failed as missionaries. Is God finished with them? No. God can use their failure to teach them lessons on faith and acceptance. They can still do the will of God! By accepting their failure and giving God their future, they can be both blessed and a blessing to others.

What about the woman who married an unbeliever? If she accepts God's forgiveness and seeks His will, she will experience God's guidance. In fact, I've known many Christians in similar circumstances who have done just that. If we are obedient to God's Word, He is faithful to guide us in the mundane experiences of life.

But the hard part is this: we have to confess and forsake our sins. After David sinned with Bathsheba, his fellowship with God was repaired only when he admitted his guilt— with all of its implications. He realized that "the sacrifices of God are a broken spirit; a broken and a contrite heart, O God, Thou wilt not despise" (Psalms 51:17).

One day some ink was accidently spilled onto a beautiful and expensive handkerchief. The mess was observed by an artist who decided to make the best of the situation. So he drew a picture on the cloth and used the blotch of ink as part of the scenery. God is well-equipped to do that for us, if we are prepared to let Him. The cost? A broken and a contrite heart.

It is never too late to do God's will. Failures of the past sometimes curtail our ministry, but they need not poison our attitude. The past cannot be changed, but our response to it can be. If we acknowledge God in all our ways, He will yet direct our paths!

# 9

## There Is a Price

The tragedy made headlines for ten days. Radio and television stations kept replaying the story. As people exchanged greetings in stores and on the street, this event surfaced as the number-one topic of conversation. A murder is always news, but this one made the community stagger in disbelief.

The story? A mother was murdered by her own fifteen-year-old son. The young rebel had killed the one who had borne and nurtured him. The ordeal was even more shocking because the people involved were Christians. The father had studied for the ministry and was a lay preacher. Now he suffered the humiliation of standing beside the casket of his wife, who was the victim of their own flesh and blood.

The man became disillusioned with God and bitter with other believers. He felt justified in his attitude for one good reason: fellow believers, who should have stood with him through this painful experience, rejected him. "Any man with a family like that should never hold office in a church again," they reasoned.

Eight years later, the brokenhearted man suffered a second crushing blow: one of his other sons committed suicide. "For ten years I lived one-half inch from hell," he said. "No one will ever know the darkness I experienced." Like water spilled on the ground, the past could not be reclaimed. There was only the future, and that looked as black as the darkness of the past.

When I met this father at a conference, I could scarcely believe my eyes and ears. Beside me was a radiant man whose strength was quite literally found in the "joy of the Lord" (Nehemiah 8:10). As might be expected, he spoke of the past with hesitation; to share the sensitive details of personal tragedy cannot be done easily or flippantly. But there was love in his voice, radiance on his face, and optimism as he spoke about the future. In fact, he was scheduled to share in different churches how God had transformed a person who was a bitter, defeated failure into a victorious, Spirit-filled disciple. One person who knew him well said, "The apostle of bitterness is now the apostle of love."

How does God take a Christian who lives one-half inch from hell and make him live one-half inch from heaven? It's not easy. There is a price to be paid. The divine Surgeon must be permitted to use His scalpel to cut, cleanse, and break so healing can take place. In fact, such spiritual surgery is more painful than physical surgery. God does not use an anesthetic; He does not do His work while we are asleep. God can take any brokenhearted believer and make him or her a radiant, loving person. But when He performs such heart operations His children are wide awake.

He often begins by prying us loose from our misguided notions of what yieldness to God means. Shorn of our superficiality, we are finally forced to accept the drastic treatment we really need.

Let's consider some of the shallow notions of what commitment to God involves. Then we will be more ready to see how God changed an apostle of bitterness into an apostle of love.

### CLEARING THE GROUND

Perhaps the most widely held misconception within the evangelical community is the belief that yieldness to the will of God involves little more than standing in a dedication service to sing "I Surrender All." Countless defeated Christians have responded to such appeals without any measurable results. Yet such believers have conned themselves into believing that they are yielded to God because they responded to a challenge to follow Christ. Perhaps they are; perhaps not.

There are several basic weaknesses in many so-called dedication services. Often we are challenged to do something heroic for God, for example, become a missionary, give more money, or witness to our neighbors. We are told (and in a qualified sense this is true) that God wants strong, courageous Christians who can weather the difficulties of life and emerge unscathed. Young people are challenged to do more for God (one youth leader says God wants "gutsy" Christians). Consequently, those who respond to a "challenge" determine that they will witness for Christ, reject the attraction of the world, and be dedicated Christians.

The difficulty with such an approach is this: if often appeals only to natural, human inclinations. The challenge to be different, to witness, or become a missionary can be accepted without the slightest understanding of the power of the Holy Spirit or what commitment to Christ really means. Consider: hundreds of young people leave well-paying jobs and go to other countries with the Peace Corps. Every cult in the world has committed followers who are willing to accept a life of poverty and, if necessary, die for its cause. Even political activists who espouse no religion are often willing to work sacrificially for their stated goals. If we ask people to dedicate themselves to the Christian cause, we often are simply employing the same motivations used by sects all over the world. And this, I believe, is why most so-called dedication services have little or no effect on the Christian community. It is not a lack of sincerity but a lack of understanding that is at stake. Perhaps this is why one Christian, after dedicating himself to God countless times, borrowed a line from *Alice in Wonderland* to describe his spiritual experience: "I have to run real fast just to stay in the same place!"

Of course, God does want us to be willing to be missionaries, to witness, and to be courageous. But as we shall see, these qualities are the by-product of a more radical transformation God wants to do in our hearts.

Our misunderstanding of true commitment might explain why thousands of half-hearted Christians are under the comfortable illusion that they are dedicated to God. They have all the right credentials to prove it: they go to church, give a percentage of their income to missionaries, and for the most part stay out of trouble. They might be dedicated to the cause of Christ and yet be controlled by purely human motivation. As Charles Spurgeon once said, "Some Christians are healed before they are wounded; they are clothed before they have seen their nakedness." Consequently, they may be oblivious to their true spiritual condition.

How do we make progress in surrendering fully to the will of God? Let's consider that now.

### BEGIN WITH SIN

Firmly entrenched within every human being lies a most deceptive presupposition, namely, that circumstances and other people are responsible for our responses to life. "If only my son had not murdered my wife . . . if only the people within the church had accepted me . . . if only . . ." So reasoned the man referred to earlier, who spent a decade one-half inch from hell. But when God began to close in on him, he came to an inescapable conclusion: bitterness is always sin, regardless of how many cruel circumstances crush us or other people fail us. There was no way for him to be delivered from the nightmare of the past without calling his bitterness *sin*.

This man could have stood in a hundred dedication services, prayed an equal number of prayers for God's help, and still be the victim of uncontrollable emotional trauma. The unvarnished fact is this: God does not accept excuses for sin.

Whenever we can pinpoint sin in our lives, we are on the way to true spiritual progress—after all, there is an excellent remedy for sin! But it is not enough simply to confess our sins (although confession is all that is necessary for forgiveness) if we want to be delivered from sin's power. We must go a step further and accept the fact that God also has a remedy for the sin nature within us. Confessing our sins is often like sawing branches off a tree; but if we do not want the tree to grow, it is more effective to strike at its roots. That is why God, the divine Surgeon, is not concerned only that we confess our sins; He goes directly for our hearts.

We cannot appreciate this until we see how helpless we are to change our inner motivations and emotions. We cannot overcome bitterness by making a New Year's resolution. "This year I will not be bitter." God has to show us how destitute we are apart from Him. Sometimes He does this by our study of the Scriptures, but often the lessons of Scripture must be reinforced by the ugly tragedies of life. The man who lost his wife at the hand of his son made a revealing statement: "For ten years I was strong and defeated; now I am weak and victorious." Did you get that? To be strong in ourselves is defeat; to be helpless in ourselves makes us candidates for God's power.

I've known "successful" Christians who have not learned that lesson—Christians who have gone as missionaries, witnessed to others, and yet have lived defeated albeit dedicated lives. The call of the Peace Corps, cults, and political revolutionaries is to the strong, the courageous, and the shrewd. The call of God is to the weak, the helpless, and the broken. In Christianity the strong are defeated, the weak are victorious. As Paul said, "When I am weak, then [not two weeks later] I am strong" (2 Corinthians 12:10). To respond to a heroic challenge is relatively easy, but to accept the words of Christ, "Apart from me you can do nothing" (John 15:5), is difficult. I doubt whether any one of us knows how spiritually hopeless we are apart from Him. No wonder we need the Holy Spirit to show us how bad off we really are.

Perhaps now we can understand why so many people who pray "Lord help me" never receive the help they expect. They want the Lord to take their fleshly (that is, carnal) abilities and add to them His power, making them strong enough to cope with the difficulties of life. But our selfish motivation is so abhorrent to God that He will not do that. He is not in the business of helping the humanly strong become stronger; rather He takes the weak and makes them strong *in Himself.*

This is why failure can be a stepping-stone if we respond to it in the right way. Anything that helps us see ourselves as the rebellious sinners we really are is a help. When the mask of self-righteousness has been torn from us and we stand stripped of all of our accustomed defenses, we are candidates for God's generous grace. When God takes us apart piece by piece, we identify with the pain Paul felt when he cried, "In me (that is, in my flesh,) dwelleth no good thing" (Romans 7:18, KJV). If it takes a hundred failures to learn that, it is worth it. Because apart from that experience, we never make any spiritual progress. On God's scorecard this truth is a square one.

What next? Once we have confessed our sin and admitted our helplessness, we must accept as true that statement of Paul, "Knowing this, that our old man is crucified with him, that the body of sin might be destroyed, that henceforth we should not serve sin" (Romans 6:6, KJV). This is God's remedy for the self-life (that is, the part of me that wants to be in control instead of God).

Here is what we must do: we must realize that Christ won a legal victory over our selfish nature when He died on the cross. I cannot crucify my old nature, but Christ can and did. Now the victory He won can be applied to me by a deliberate act of faith, that is, by accepting His victory as mine.

This does not mean that we will not have our sin nature anymore; it is not a matter of saying, "I've arrived!" No, it is the beginning of being free from slavery to myself and to humanly uncontrollable desires. Without this act of faith in Christ's victory, we will always be controlled by the forces of sin. A life of victory and fulfillment will always be a mirage in the middle of an endless desert.

How could a man who was the victim of such tragedy be delivered from bitterness and depression? "I got on my knees," he recalls. "I confessed my sin, which I had justified for so long—then I accepted the fact that Christ had already won the victory for me."

With eyes still hot with tears he went to those whom he had resented to ask their forgiveness. He was finally a free man.

Does it happen overnight? Sometimes. This man was changed so suddenly because he was so desperate. But for most of us it takes time. The Bible says we are to "grow in grace." Our faith becomes stronger as we study the Scriptures and mature spiritually.

Christ has pried all of our excuses from us; His victory is great enough for any failure—it is good for broken hearts of all shapes and sizes. As the once bitter man put it, "For years I underestimated what Christ can do!"

Have you?

## A New Commitment

Once we have come this far, we are ready to commit ourselves—our past, present, and future—to God. The word *commit* means to deliver into another's charge. It involves transferring the responsibility for your life to another Person.

When South Vietnam fell to the rule of the Viet Cong, hundreds of people wanted to flee from the armies that ravaged the countryside. Thousands fled to airfields and seaports hoping to escape the coming disaster. When some families saw that they could not leave, many mothers gave their babies to men aboard a ship. They did this hoping that their children would be better off being with strangers than suffering starvation, war, and death. That was surely the most pathetic sight I have ever seen on television. Think of it. Mothers committed their children to people they did not know. They parted, knowing full well they would never see those children again.

This tragic story illustrates two facts about commitment: (1) the mothers trusted the judgment of those (in this case, strangers) to whom they gave their children; they believed others would do what was best for the children; and (2) there was no possibility of having their children back—the act was final. Quite apart from how they would feel about it in the future, the transfer of authority had been made.

What does it mean to commit ourselves to God? For one thing, it is an act of faith. It is the belief that God is well qualified to take care of what we give to Him. Fortunately, we do not have to commit our lives to Someone whom we do not know or to a Being who does not know what is best. Paul had every reason in the world to believe that God was able to keep that which he had committed to him (2 Timothy 1:12). If God does not know what is best for us, who would? Certainly not ourselves, since our knowledge is so fragmentary and distorted. Can you be sure you will be alive for another five years? Can you guarantee five minutes? Only God, who knows the future and understands the implications of eternity, is a trustworthy guide.

Also, our commitment is not based on feelings. To return to the sad plight of the Vietnamese mothers: regardless of how they felt later, the outcome could not be changed. Feelings had nothing to do with the commitment once it was made.

Many people give themselves to God, only to feel that their burdens are back on their own shoulders once again. They repeatedly give themselves to God and are engulfed in the slough of despair. But commitment to God is based on the One to whom the commitment is made—not on the feelings of the one who makes the commitment. Speaking of this, Henry Teichrob wrote:

> A shareholder does not lose his place in the corporation because he feels tired or ill or even unhappy. His benefits in the corporation rest on the fact that he is a shareholder. His "commitment" to the corporation provides the benefits as a shareholder. The fact of the matter rather than the feelings, determines the outcome.[1]

1. Henry Teichrob, "The Committed Way," *Brigade Leader* (Fall 1973): 19.

Our commitment to God is not taken back just because we feel that the burden is back upon our own shoulders. Once we have given a matter to God, that commitment is not nullified by the fluctuations of our emotions or the bitter struggles of personal experience.

### LIVE FROM THE INSIDE OUT

What does it mean to be filled with the Holy Spirit? Does it mean that we smile all the time? Should we expect that all who walk in the Spirit should look alike, act alike? No.

To walk in the Spirit is to have Christlike responses to the experiences of life. The fruit of the Spirit essentially involves our attitudes toward the many and varied situations we all face. To be controlled by the Spirit means that we are not controlled by what happens on the outside but by what is happening on the inside.

Recall once more that man who experienced a decade of failure. He says, "I've learned that no man can make me hate him!" What he means is obvious—the most bitter experiences of life need not make us bitter; the most obnoxious individuals need not make us resentful. The power of God within enables us to accept the circumstances without.

And how do we walk in the Spirit? Like committing ourselves to God, it is an act of faith. It is not a matter of the way we feel or whether we have had an indescribable experience. "The just shall *live* by his faith" (Habakkuk 2:4, KJV).

We do not have to beg the Holy Spirit to control us—He delights in doing so. The reason He indwells those of us who are Christians is that His fruit, the fruit of the Spirit, might blossom in our lives. The only obstacle that blocks the ministry of the Holy Spirit within us is sin. Paul urged us not to grieve the Holy Spirit, and in the same context gives a list of sins that rob us of spiritual power—anger, bitterness, and gossip, to name a few (Ephesians 4:28-32). If our lives are free of known sin, we can begin each day by committing ourselves to God and anticipating the guidance of the Holy Spirit. We need never think that we have to overcome the Spirit's reluctance; He has been freely given to us in order that He might control us.

We must choose to depend on the Holy Spirit for power, just as we depend on Christ's death for forgiveness. We all know that the basis of our forgiveness is Jesus Christ's death on the cross; similarly, the basis of the gift of the Holy Spirit is Christ's ascension (John 7:39; Acts 2:33). Just as we receive forgiveness by faith, and we prove our faith by thanking God for Christ's death, so we accept the ministry of the Holy Spirit by faith and thank God for Christ's glorification. Forgiveness and the work of the Holy Spirit are both accepted by saying thank-you to God.

Let me illustrate it this way. If you bought a two-volume book and carelessly left one volume at the store, what would you do when you got home? You would return to the store and get the other volume. Since you paid for both, you need not be content with just one. Similarly, salvation has two aspects—one is forgiveness and the other is the ministry of the Holy Spirit. Both have been provided, paid for. We experience them by faith in saying thank-you to God for what He has *already* done.

Remember this: the Holy Spirit is more willing to control us than we are willing to let Him. He will empower any believer who is willing to remove the obstacles to spiritual growth and begin each day with faith in the Spirit's presence and ministry.

Failure helps us learn these lessons. The key question is whether we are prepared to pay the price that God demands to turn our failure into success. That price is admitting our failure, repenting of the sin that causes it, and applying the cross to our sinful nature. Only then can we live a committed life and walk in the Spirit once again.

What God did for a bitter, defeated man, He can do for us all. Why not let Him, just now?

# 10

## But I'm So Messed Up

A divorce shatters all family relationships. The wife feels hurt and cheated; the husband is often bitter against his ex-wife. Children are treated like pawns on a chessboard.

No one knew this better than a certain woman reared in a remote village. She had married well, she thought. As a new bride, she dreamed about the security and happiness her marriage would bring. Perhaps her expectations were unrealistic; perhaps she was too preoccupied with her own ambitions to recognize the first signs of tensions in her marriage.

After a few initial arguments, she and her husband hoped they could reconcile their differences. But the tensions between them mushroomed. Eventually they agreed that they could not live together any longer. The decision was agonizing but, from all appearances, necessary. They were divorced. Only those who have lived through the trauma of divorce can understand this woman's anguish.

True, divorces are common. But their increasing number does not lessen the hurt. This woman was so deeply grieved that she felt she could never share her life with someone else again.

But time heals all wounds, or at least lessens the pain of the initial blow. After she had pulled herself together emotionally, she eventually met a man who seemed to have all of the qualities her first husband lacked. Rather than face the future with loneliness and insecurity, the woman accepted the man's proposal. *This* marriage would be a success.

Despite this optimism, her second marriage showed signs of strain. At first the irritations were manageable. The woman dared not let herself think that this marriage would end like the first. Yet, the foundations of their relationship began to crumble. Patching up their differences was like trying to support a teetering building with wallpaper. Something fundamental was wrong; the resources needed to make this marriage work were lacking. Before long, the end was in sight. The result, a second divorce.

Some women would have buried their frustrations in their career. They would have relocated in another city, gone back to school, or learned a skill. But this woman could not. Her family believed not only that a woman's place was at home but that the woman was to be obedient to the whim of her husband. Furthermore, in her locality, no jobs were available to women. All she knew—all she could know—was the household chores, the drudgery of the routine.

It is not surprising that the decision to marry again was made easily. But now, the woman was bitter, angry at God, and disgruntled with men. This time she married without even calculating the risk. If her marriage didn't work, another divorce would rescue her from the bonds of her meaningless vows. She was crushed by guilt and filled with resentment.

She was married for only a short time. Predictably, she experienced a third divorce.

Then a fourth.

Then a fifth.

Any further marriage vows would have been a mockery. Since chastity was no longer an option, she decided not to bother with the formality of another wedding. When she met the sixth man, they decided to live under common law.

And then? Then she met Jesus Christ.*

*John 4:1-30.

Her confrontation with Christ was quite accidental, so far as she was concerned. It began as just an ordinary day for this woman, another day to ponder her meaningless existence. At noon she left her home to trudge a quarter of a mile to get a bucket of water at the town well. In the background was Mount Gerizim; to her right was Mount Ebal.

From a distance she saw a man sitting at the well. As she came closer, she recognized that He was a Jew.

"Give Me a drink," the man said.

The woman was startled. She knew the hostility of Jews towards the Samaritans, who were a mixed race. How could this man stoop to drink from *her* vessel?

"How is it that You, being a Jew, ask me for a drink since I am a Samaritan woman?" she asked.

Ignoring her question, the man directed her thoughts to another topic: "If you knew the gift of God, and who it is who says to you, 'Give Me a drink,' you would have asked Him, and He would have given you living water."

Living water? The man did not even have a bucket! How could He draw water from this deep well? How could He promise *living* water? Was He as great as Jacob who had dug the well? Hardly.

But the woman was wrong. This man *was* greater than Jacob. Or, at least, He claimed to be. "Everyone who drinks of this water shall thirst again, but whoever drinks of the water that I shall give him shall never thirst; but the water that I shall give him shall become in him a well of water springing up to eternal life." The words flowed from His lips.

The woman listened incredulously. But the man spoke with such assurance that she was willing to test His promise. "Sir, give me this water, so I will not be thirsty, nor come all the way here to draw."

What a relief, if she would not have to carry water from the well each day! But Christ did not offer her water like that in Jacob's well. He did not come to eliminate physical and temporal needs. He came to supply the deeper need of spiritual thirst.

In order for the woman to grasp His offer, He said, "Go call your husband, and come here."

With embarrassment, the woman replied, "I have no husband."

Christ, nodding in agreement, added, "You have well said, 'I have no husband'; for you have had five husbands, and the one whom you now have is not your husband; this you have said truly."

How did He know this? She'd never seen Him before. The woman suspected that He might be another Jewish prophet. So she said, "Our fathers worshiped in this mountain, and you people say that in Jerusalem is the place where men ought to worship."

Christ's reply was startling. He did not tell her she must go to Jerusalem to worship, as the Jewish leaders insisted. Rather, He said, "Woman, believe Me, an hour is coming when neither in this mountain, nor in Jerusalem, shall you worship the Father. . . . But an hour is coming, and now is, when the true worshipers shall worship the Father in spirit and truth; for such people the Father seeks to be His worshipers. God is spirit, and those who worship Him must worship in spirit and truth."

God was not pleased with either the worship at Gerizim or Jerusalem. He looked for real worshipers, those whose hearts wanted fellowship with Him.

Standing before Christ was a woman who had had five unsuccessful marriages and was presently living in adultery with a sixth man. Morally, her life was beyond repair. Was there any hope for her? Christ offered her forgiveness. And he suggested that she was one whom the Father was seeking to be a worshiper.

## God Is Seeking Worshipers

It is odd that we should so often forget why God made us. We busy ourselves with earning money and cram our spare moments with pleasure. We talk glibly about "serving the Lord" and being busy for Him. But often we forget that such matters are secondary; they are the by-product of true worship. And if we haven't learned to be worshipers, it doesn't really matter how well we do anything else.

What does the Father seek? Missionaries? Pastors? Generous laymen? Christ taught that the Father seeks worshipers. *Worshipers* satisfy His desires. *Worshipers* please Him. Are *you* a worshiper?

Consider the familiar verse: "But if we walk in the light as He Himself is in the light, we have fellowship with one another, and the blood of Jesus His Son cleanses us from all sin" (1 John 1:7). This does not merely mean that if we walk in the light we have fellowship with other Christians: it means that if we walk in the light we have fellowship with God, and He has fellowship with us. We and God have fellowship one with another.

We not only have the privilege of having fellowship with God, but *God desires to have fellowship with us!* He seeks our fellowship. He seeks our worship.

How selfish we are! We often go to church to see what is in it *for us*; we read the Bible so *we* will receive a blessing; we pray so that God will fulfill *our* wishes; we look to God to supply *our* needs. Everything (our church, devotions, and service) is judged by how it profits us!

Isn't it time we reversed our priorities? Isn't it more important that God be satisfied than that we are? If God seeks worshipers, should we not learn (if we don't yet know) how to worship Him in spirit and truth? Is this not more important than teaching Sunday school, witnessing, or tithing?

Often Christians ask, If God already knows our needs, why should we have to ask Him for anything? Consider George Macdonald's reply:

> What if he knows prayer to be the thing we need first and most? What if the main object in God's idea of prayer be the supplying of our great, our endless need—the need of Himself? . . . Hunger may drive the runaway child home, and he may or may not be fed at once, but he needs his

mother more than his dinner. Communion with God is the
one need of the soul beyond all other need: prayer is the
beginning of that communion.[1]

In other words, the reason we must ask God for things
He already intends to give us is that He wants to teach us dependence, especially our need for Himself.

God is looking for worshipers. And if the religious elite
are too proud or too busy to learn to worship Him, He seeks
the worship of those whose lives are trapped in moral ruin.
Perhaps they, like the woman of Samaria, can more readily
appreciate God's forgiveness; perhaps they are better candidates for two-way fellowship with the Creator! The Father
seeks such to worship Him.

### THE ELEMENTS OF WORSHIP

Christ's statement gives us the clue to what worship involves. First, it is not confined to geographical location. The
Jews worshiped at Jerusalem; the Samaritans worshiped on
Mount Gerizim. Yet, Christ said the time had come when
people would worship God neither at Jerusalem nor at Gerizim. Worship does not happen because of correct geography.

How often Christians assume they have worshiped God
simply because they have been in church. We are told that
the church building is "God's house" (an inaccurate designa-
tion borrowed from the Old Testament Temple) and conclude that worship *must* take place there. Not necessarily.
God was not pleased with the worship at Jerusalem (the Holy
City). Neither is He impressed with beautiful cathedrals.

Are you ready for this? It is possible to attend church
regularly, participate in the service, and not worship God at
all. Worship isn't listening to a sermon, appreciating the harmony of the choir, and joining in singing hymns. It isn't even
prayer; for prayer can be the selfish expression of an unbroken heart.

1. C. S. Lewis, *George Macdonald: An Anthology* (New York: Macmillan, 1948),
pp. 51-52.

Worship goes deeper. Since God is Spirit, we fellowship with Him with our spirit; that is, the immortal and invisible part of us meets with God, who is immortal and invisible.

Prayer may be worship; singing may be worship; reading the Scriptures may be worship—but not necessarily.

Second, we must worship in truth, without hypocrisy or any form of dishonesty. The people in Isaiah's day were not condemned because they sang the wrong songs; neither did God judge them because they prayed unorthodox prayers. They even brought the prescribed sacrifices. Were they worshiping God? Here is Christ's answer, quoting Isaiah: "Rightly did Isaiah prophesy of you hypocrites, as it is written, 'This people honors Me with their lips, but their heart is far away from Me. But in vain do they worship Me, teaching as doctrines the precepts of men' " (Mark 7:6-7). The content of their prayers did honor God. They did bring the prescribed sacrifices. But their hearts (their spirits) were far from God.

What goes though your mind when you attend church? Do you wonder how your clothes compare with those of the person next to you? Are you self-conscious, anxious to make an impression on those you meet? Do you anticipate the end of the meeting so that you can greet your friends? Do you find it difficult to concentrate on what's going on because you are day-dreaming about business or pleasure? If so, *you have not met God.* You have honored Him with your lips, but your heart is far from Him!

The greatest commandment is not "Thou shalt not commit adultery," neither is it "Thou shalt not bear false witness," nor even "Thou shalt not steal." These are needful, but the greatest commandment—the most important—is, "You shall love the Lord your God with all your heart, and with all your soul, and with all your mind" (Matthew 22:37). If our greatest desire—our real ambition—is not to love God, we are not pleasing to Him. Period.

Finally, Christ taught that the Father *seeks* worshipers. That seems odd! Would not all people—especially Christians —want to worship the Father? Would it not be more appropriate for us—the creatures—to want to meet the Creator? That might be more appropriate, but that is not the way it is! The Father, the almighty God, does the seeking. And my guess is that there are relatively few who respond.

The reason? Many of us are not thirsty for God because we have quenched our thirst at other fountains! Consider God's word to Jeremiah: "For my people have committed two evils: they have forsaken Me, the fountains of living waters, to hew for themselves cisterns, broken cisterns, that can hold no water" (Jeremiah 2:13). They forsook the fountain of living water and drank from man-made cisterns.

Thirst must be quenched! If our desires are not met by God, we will quickly find something else to alleviate our thirst. And when we become satisfied with stagnant water holes, the more difficult it is to seek the fresh stream.

To change the figure of speech slightly, if we are not nourished by the bread from heaven, we will satiate ourselves with crumbs from the world. And once we have become addicted to the world's nourishment, our appetite for God is spoiled. Many of us are so satisfied with ourselves that God's request for worship appears to be an intrusion. We don't like to interrupt our schedules to seek Him.

For example, we have become addicted to affluence. A professor in a leading evangelical seminary remarked that the greatest difficulty with the men who came to study was that they had been reared in middle or upper middle-class homes. As a result, they had never learned to trust God for anything tangible. They were reared in homes where there was always enough money for food and clothes.

Few of us have ever had to pray in sincerity, "Give us this day our daily bread." We have never needed God quite that desperately. And if we have never had to trust God for earthly things, we find it more difficult to trust Him for heavenly things.

We've also absorbed the world's love of pleasure. Paul predicted that in the last days people would love pleasure more than they love God (2 Timothy 3:4). That day is here. Consider this: Are we as willing to go into debt for the work of God as we are for a vacation to Hawaii? Are the pleasures at God's right hand as appealing as a promotion or unexpected salary increase?

Repeatedly, God warned the Israelites that bumper crops and productive gardens would turn them away from Him (Deuteronomy 6:1-12). Their history as well as ours has confirmed one fact: *it is almost impossible to develop true worshipers in affluent surroundings.* Recall Christ's words about how hard it is for the rich to enter the kingdom of heaven. Who needs God when there are no pressing emergencies? Why should we take the time and effort to know Him when we are doing so well by the strength of our own hands?

We are puzzled as to why the saints of the past had such a passion to seek God, when we sense no such need ourselves. Martin Luther prayed as much as three hours on days that were especially busy; Hudson Taylor and John Wesley did the same. Such devotion can't be understood by those who pay their respects to God on Sunday and find no special need for Him during the week.

It was in exile as slaves in a foreign land that the sons of Korah sang, "As the deer pants for the water brooks, so my soul pants for Thee, O God" (Psalms 42:1). Seldom have we been that thirsty!

Although God seeks worshipers, we continue to use Him for selfish ends. He is prayed to in emergencies, and His Son is used to forgive our sins. But we are satisfied with that much. We want a religion that is convenient, one that demands a minimum of our time and effort.

But those who have drunk deeply of the living water discover that the world's fountains are but muddy water holes in comparison. Malcolm Muggeridge, a distinguished English journalist, in his book *Jesus Rediscovered* wrote,

> I may, I suppose, regard myself [as] or pass for being, a relatively successful man. People occasionally stare at me in the streets—that's fame. I can fairly easily earn enough to qualify for admission to the higher slopes of the Internal Revenue—that's success. Furnished with money and a lit-

tle fame even the elderly, if they care to, may partake of trendy diversions—that's pleasure. It might happen once in a while that something I said or wrote was sufficiently heeded for me to persuade myself that it represented a serious impact on our time—that's fulfillment. Yet, I say to you—and I beg you to believe me—multiply these tiny triumphs by a million, add them all together, and they are nothing—less than nothing, a positive impediment—measured against one draught of that living water Christ offers to the spiritually thirsty, irrespective of who or what they are.[2]

Did you understand what Muggeridge was saying? He is famous, wealthy, and influential; yet, these triumphs, if multiplied by a million, are still nothing in comparison to "one draught of that living water Christ offers to the spiritually thirsty."

Remember Beth, described in chapter 1? She probably will never serve God in public; she likely will never have a successful marriage; even her good name may be lost forever. Success (as we often think of it) is no longer a possibility for her. Is there anything she can do to please the Father? Yes!

The invitation Christ gave to the woman of Samaria includes Beth, and it includes you and me. Worship is possible even for those who are victims of an unhappy marriage or crushing emotional experiences. It's a possibility for us all. *Those who truly worship, truly serve.* The Father seeks such to worship Him.

2. Malcolm Muggeridge, *Jesus Rediscovered* (New York: Doubleday, 1969), p. 61.

# 11

# A Formula for Accomplishment

I was gifted with a vivid imagination. Reared in a rural area, I had ample time to think about the future. Sometimes I imagined I was a businessman, sometimes an airplane pilot, sometimes an evangelist. One persistent characteristic of my daydreams was this: regardless of the vocation I chose, I was always a smashing success!

Of course, I realized that these escapades of my imagination could never come to be—at least, not all of them could! But I cherished the hope that those dreams would become reality. For the most part they haven't.

This discrepancy between the ideal (what we imagine ourselves to be) and the real self (what we actually are) causes conflicts. The middle-aged are especially prone to experience deep disillusionment. For many years they have visualized themselves as a success, but now their dreams may be far from fulfilled. As one man put it, "I'm forty-five. I thought I would have it made by now, but what has happened? I am where I started, if anything, a bit further back." He passed his prime without the achievement he wanted.

Even greater disappointment comes to many people in their sixties. They have saved money faithfully for their retirement and have made starry-eyed plans about what they will do with their leisure time. Now that they have reached the "paradise" of retirement, they are either too lonely or too sick to enjoy it. It's like patiently following a rainbow only to discover that there is no pot of gold at the end!

Looking back, I realize that I am not nor shall I ever be the person I visualized in my youth. I've had to accept my limitations and realistically evaluate my gifts.

I'm not complaining. I've had the opportunity to attend several schools, teach in Bible school, pastor a church, and do some writing. But my daydreams were unrealistic. Most of them will never come to be.

Perhaps this is the way it should be. For God has been trying to teach me that we don't have to do everything we had planned to do; we don't have to reach all of our goals in order to qualify for "success" in His eyes.

In fact, it is often when we are striving to reach our goals (even valid ones) that God breaks into our lives and reorganizes our priorities. Soon we learn that His notion of success differs from ours.

Let me explain. I was busy accomplishing my goals, earning graduate degrees, preaching, teaching, and writing. I was so busy that I scarcely had time to ask God to rubber-stamp my plans! Of course, theoretically I wanted to do these things only for Him. But a rather insignificant incident changed the direction of my life.

A Christian man in California had a sign on his desk that read, "You may not be accomplishing as much as you think you are." That observation began cleaning the cobwebs out of my mind. Here I was, doing more than most other Christians (or so I thought). But I couldn't shake the suspicion that that sign spoke the truth about me. Inwardly, I knew that my activities were not as significant as I thought them to be. God could do without me. He didn't need me to accomplish His work in the world. True, I was busy. But I began to suspect that I wasn't doing much for God.

Then another incident happened. I was hospitalized for a week for what I had mistakenly taken to be heart attack. I began to reflect over my life. If I died today would I have any regrets? What would I do differently if I knew I would die within one year? Or ten?

I was forced to re-evaluate my priorities. What did God want me to do on earth? What was He seeking? Educated Christians? "Successful" pastors? Popular writers? No. At least, these are not number one on His list. He was seeking worshipers! He was looking for men and women who knew Him. "The people who know their God will display strength and take action" (Daniel 11:32). In fact, the Scriptures teach, "The eyes of the Lord move to and fro throughout the earth that He may strongly support those whose heart is completely His" (2 Chronicles 16:9).

Obviously, the activities we do *for* God are secondary. Above all else, God is looking for people who long for communication with Him. That's why Paul said that he counted everything but dung (KJV) that he might know Christ (Philippians 3:8-10). J. I. Packer observed that when Paul says these words, he not only means that he considers his past accomplishments as worthless but also that he does not live with them constantly in his mind. Packer asks, "What normal person spends his time nostalgically dreaming of manure?"[1] Paul's single passion was to know Christ. He didn't want anything—even his prized achievements—to detract him from this goal.

Now, since I wasn't accomplishing as much as I thought I was, since my ministry was something less than spectacular, I decided to try an experiment. It was this: rather than have my activities rotate around myself and my ministry, I would sincerely attempt (not just verbally, as I had done countless times before) to make my life rotate around God. In other words, He would be brought from the fringes into the very center of my life.

Remember Copernicus? He was the astronomer who rejected the theory that the planets rotate around the earth. He found it difficult to explain planetary motion according to this scheme. So he proposed a new theory, namely, that the sun is the center of the universe. With this theory, he found

1. J. I. Packer, *Knowing God* (Downers Grove, Ill.: InterVarsity, 1973), p. 21.

that the motion of heavenly bodies could be more easily explained.

I knew I needed my own "Copernican revolution." Until now, my world was at the core of my life. God was worked in only when needed. Now I decided that He would be on center stage, and my world—schedules, sermons, and exams—would rotate around Him. This, of course, necessitated some adjustments.

### Working on the Specifics

The first practical problem was *time.* Although in theory I had always put God first, no one would have guessed it by looking at my schedule. The spare moments I used for Him were wedged between other deadlines. Now some adjustment was necessary. I began by blocking out forty-five minutes of each day for one purpose: to know and worship God. I decided it wouldn't even matter whether God would answer my prayers. In fact, my requests were cut to a minimum. These forty-five minutes were not for me, they were for *Him.*

How do we begin to honor the Almighty? I took my cue from Psalms 50:23: "Whoso offereth praise glorifieth me" (KJV). In the New Testament, it is put this way: "In everything give thanks; for this is God's will for you in Christ Jesus" (1 Thessalonians 5:18). Throughout the Bible there are scores of direct references to praising God. Worship (which is our response to God's revelation) always produces praise.

So after a brief time of confession, I would begin to thank God for His attributes. Then I'd recount all the blessings that He gives us in Christ (there are at least thirty). I thanked Him for excellent health, my family, my schedule, and my irritations. In short, I thanked Him for everything except sin.

The more I studied the Scriptures, the more I realized that this was a dimension of worship I had been neglecting. David said, "Bless the Lord, O my soul" (Psalms 103:1). This does not mean that mortal man can bless the immortal God. Our thanksgiving (which is a response to God's blessing) is often referred to in the Old Testament by the same word as the blessing itself. To bless the Lord means to praise Him for His blessings! The rest of Psalms 103 is a magnificent illustration of how God is honored; it is by recounting His attributes and goodness to His people. Anyone who wants to can glorify God! "Whoso offereth praise glorifieth me."

Second, I knew that God was pleased with His Word. "I will bow down toward Thy holy temple, and give thanks to Thy name for Thy lovingkindness and Thy truth; for Thou hast magnified Thy word according to all Thy name" (Psalms 138:2). God's promises are backed by the honor of His name.

In fact, there are at least two (perhaps more) promises of success in the Scriptures. In each case the formula is the same. To Joshua, God said that if he would meditate in the book of the law day and night and be careful to do all that is written in it, "Then you will make your way prosperous, and then you will have success" (Joshua 1:8). The same promise is given in Psalms 1 to those who meditate in the law of God day and night: "He will be like a tree firmly planted by streams of water, which yields its fruit in its season, and its leaf does not wither, and in whatever he does, he prospers" (v. 3).

I realized I would have to readjust my thinking habits to meditate continually (or, at least, more often) in the Scriptures.

So I determined to think (in an unhurried way) about several verses each day. I was surprised at how often I had read the Bible without "seeing" (and it *does* take observation) how much of it applied to me. Previously, I had memorized whole chapters of the Bible, but often I had never thought of the significance of what I quoted. Now, with my mind sufficiently free of stray thoughts, God was teaching me truths I had not experienced before. I began to learn a startling truth —namely, that I didn't know as much as I thought I did! Progress was slow (and still is), but gradually I found that concentration on the Word was possible—and meaningful.

Along with my praise and Bible study, I would often read a devotional book or spend time in evaluating my life.

But I tried to keep the focus primarily on God's honor, rather than merely presenting Him with a list of needs, although I sometimes did that, too.

I had determined to try this experiment and continue it whether it "got results" or not. That is, I was not looking for spiritual power, great answers to prayer, or spectacular blessings. For a change I hoped to honor God without asking, "What's in it for me?"

Perhaps you have guessed what happened. I kept my appointments, prepared sermons, and did some writing—and everything became easier. Did not Christ say that if we seek first the kingdom of God and His righteousness that many other things would be added unto us? I realized what I had always known theoretically: that time spent with God is not wasted. A man who is chopping a tree is not wasting time when he sharpens his ax! The woodcutter who is too busy to sharpen his ax loses in the long run.

Isaiah put it vividly: "Yet those who wait for the Lord will gain new strength; they will mount up with wings like eagles, they will run and not get tired, they will walk and not become weary" (Isaiah 40:31).

## A Return to Basics

My new approach to Christian living taught me several lessons. I was a bit surprised to discover that God had been, in many ways, a stranger to me. Maybe that's why it is so difficult for some of us to trust God in a crisis: we are forced to commit ourselves to Someone we don't know very well. Of course, we cannot know God fully, and we certainly cannot understand all His ways. But learning about Him in the Scriptures and then talking to Him directly develops the trust relationship, and without faith it is impossible to please Him (Hebrews 11:6).

A poem by Nancy Spiegelberg vividly describes the experience of those who determine to know God better:

Lord
    I crawled
    across the barrenness
        to You
        with my empty cup
uncertain
    in asking
        any small drop
        of refreshment.
if only
        I had known You
        better
I'd have come
running
with a bucket.[2]

Isn't that true of us all? If we knew God better, we could trust Him for more. If we understood that we were created for fellowship with Him, we'd spend more time fulfilling that purpose. I've began to learn that fellowship with God leads to faith; it develops trust.

Although we become Christians instantaneously by faith in Christ, knowing God and developing faith is a gradual process. The simple fact is that some Christians know God better than others. There are no shortcuts to spiritual maturity. It takes time to be holy.

I also realized that the best motivation for spiritual maturity is not the prospect of freedom from sin but the prospect of knowing the living God. Of course all forms of sin must be condemned. But people will face up to their sins only when their appetite for God is aroused.

Teenagers don't leave their bicycles until they want a car; beggars don't leave their crumbs until they are offered a ham sandwich. Similarly, sin is unattractive only when seen next to genuine two-way fellowship with the Creator.

2. Nancy Spiegelberg, in *Decision*, November 1974. © 1974 by the Billy Graham Evangelistic Association. Used by permission.

All of us know "average" Christians who are glad they accepted Christ's forgiveness, but they mistakenly believe that this is all that Christianity is. They believe that a Christian is simply a sinner minus his (or her) sins. They've never experienced anything beyond that. Consequently, church is boring, reading the Bible is a chore, and praying is a waste of time. (None of the above is as exciting as football, for instance.)

The answer? It's not merely to condemn carnality but to develop a thirst for something better. Until we've known by experience that the pleasures at God's right hand are better than the pleasures of the world, we won't change our lifestyles.

Another thing happened to me. I found myself less concerned about my reputation as one who is "successful." God's approval became more important than that of my friends. Of course, I am still conscious of other people's opinions and, for that matter, conscious of my reputation. But I can rejoice more easily when others are more "successful" than I. I've begun to play the game for the Coach rather than the unpredictable applause of the fans.

Remember the story of the disciples who were elated with their success? They came to Christ and announced, "Lord, even the demons are subject to us in Your name." Christ replied, "Nevertheless do not rejoice in this, that the spirits are subject to you, but rejoice that your names are recorded in heaven" (Luke 10:17, 20). God has had to slap me across the face for rejoicing in the wrong things! Slowly I'm learning that my joy must be in God and not in what He allows me to accomplish.

Finally, whenever I missed my appointment with God, I noticed it immediately. "O taste and see that the Lord is good; how blessed is the man who takes refuge in Him!" (Psalms 34:8). My appetite for God was increasing. And just like skipping meals, skipping my appointment with God created hunger. As Christ said to the lukewarm Laodicean church, to those who would let Him in, "I will come in to him, and will dine with him, and he with Me" (Revelation

3:20). Two-way fellowship with the Lord of the universe! That's enough to whet even the most carnal taste buds. Is it any wonder that meeting God is more satisfying than being introduced to the famous people of this world?

When a Christian dies, we often say, "He went to be with the Lord." I know what we mean. But unfortunately that expression might betray a shallow understanding of our relationship with God *now*. Paul said that we *are* in Christ —crucified, buried, risen, and seated with Him in heaven (Ephesians 2:6). That means we are as close to God as Christ is; we are already "with the Lord." Death brings only a different kind of relationship. But our proximity to God will never be closer than it is now, and He is available for fellowship. Are you?

If you are like me, you will never reach all of your goals. Your "real" self will never match your "ideal" self. Face that fact. Don't live in a dreamworld, thinking of what you *could* have done or even *should* have done. Success, as we usually think of it, is simply not an option for everyone. But fellowship with God is! And if the chief end of man is to know God and enjoy Him forever, *that* goal is possible for you. Try it. You can't go wrong.

After all, you may not be accomplishing as much as you think you are!

# 12

## When Is It Too Late to Begin?

"The best years of my life are over. I've made my share of mistakes. I'd give anything to relive it, but it's gone forever. Should I bother beginning *now*?" The man who said these words had buried his wife a few weeks earlier. Theirs had not been a happy marriage. He and his wife squabbled about the relatives and about their children. Throughout the years, his wife had depended more on her mother than on him. He in turn was not strong enough to be the leader in his household.

The sins of the past affected the next generation. The children had suffered. The hurts and insults of the past could not be changed. It was too late to talk to this man about what he *should* have done. As Shakespeare observed, "What has been done cannot be undone."

But what about the future? Is there still an opportunity to live a meaningful life, a chance to work in God's vineyard? Any possibility for rewards at the judgment seat?

If we were asked to set up a reward system for believers, we would probably work out a detailed merit scale. Those who sacrificed many years serving God would receive a large reward; those who served for a short time would receive a small reward. Naturally, we would try to be fair to all.

Surprisingly, Christ taught that God doesn't give rewards that way. He told a parable that on the surface is puzzling. In fact, it seems that God is unfair.

In Palestine, the grapes ripen toward the end of September, and after that, the rains begin to fall. If the harvest is not gathered in quickly, it is ruined. Any worker is welcome, even if he can only do an hour's work.

Christ taught that the kingdom of heaven is like a landowner who went out early in the morning to hire workers. Those who began at nine o'clock agreed to work for one denarius. Other workers came at twelve noon and some as late as five o'clock.

Here is the surprise: when they lined up at the end of the day to receive their wages, *everyone* received the same—one denarius. As might be expected, the first group grumbled, "These last men have worked only one hour, and you have made them equal to us who have born the burden and the scorching heat of the day" (Matthew 20:12). Imagine paying employees equally without even checking their time cards!

Perhaps the most obvious lesson from this parable is that seniority in the kingdom of heaven does not imply superiority. We will not be judged by how long we serve but by *how* we serve. For example, some Christians die in their youth. If rewards were based on the number of years of service, they would never have a chance to be rewarded like the veteran workers.

God is generous! These men did not all do the same work, but they did receive the same pay. Think of how good God is. He gives us the physical, mental, and spiritual ability to work in his kingdom, and then He rewards us for doing it!

The landowner (who represents Christ in the parable) says to the complainers, "Is it not lawful for me to do what I wish with what is my own? Or is your eye envious because I am generous?" (Matthew 20:15). We might resent seeing our friends receive wages for something they didn't do. We might become especially irritated if we did more and received less. But God delights in giving, and if we are envious of others, it shows that we have missed a basic lesson in living the Christian life. More of that later.

A second observation is that quantity is not as important as quality. Remember Paul's words in 1 Corinthians 3? Some Christians spend their lives accumulating wood, hay, and stubble, all of which will be burned in the day of judgment. Others have gold, silver, and precious stones that will endure the test. A few gems held in the hand are worth more than a gigantic pile of rubble!

You see, it is possible to work for Christ just as a non-Christian works for his company. We can serve with selfish motivation or for personal fulfillment. All such work, though done in God's name, will not receive God's approval. The distinction is whether we have served out of gratitude to God and dependence on Him or whether we worked with purely human motivation.

One mistake made by those who came to the vineyard at nine o'clock in the morning was this: they worked for what *they* could get out of it! They didn't lift a finger until they "agreed" (probably some haggling went on) with the landlord for a denarius a day. They wanted to know what was expected of them and what they could expect in return.

This group of workers were like students who want to know how many classes they can cut so that they can be sure to use their quota! They were like Christians who want to know whether to tithe on their net or gross income so they don't have to give more than expected!

Notice also their critical attitude. They grumbled because they were envious at what others received. Self-righteously, they reminded the landlord, "[We] have borne the burden and the scorching heat of the day" (Matthew 20:12). They looked with pride on their own accomplishments; they forgot that no man (in God's kingdom) is accepted because of his sacrificial achievements.

God doesn't "pay" us because we have worked for Him. We are given rewards (which we don't deserve) because He is generous! We see this principle clearly in salvation, but we don't always see it in the Christian life. We all admit that we will be in heaven solely because of God's grace. But we forget that any reward we get will be because of God's grace, too.

It's not a matter of saying, "Lord I've served you for thirty years, I will expect thirty crowns!" No. God has the right to give us whatever *He* wishes, and if He gives *nothing*, that would be fair, too. Remember, God owes us nothing. *Whatever* we get is because of God's goodness.

A third observation is already obvious: the first group of workers didn't realize that serving the keeper of the vineyard (Christ) carries its own reward. The second and third groups of workers did not agree to work for a certain amount. They left that up to the landowner, believing that he would do whatever was right. They were just glad for the chance to work in his vineyard.

Working for Christ, out of sheer appreciation for what He has done, is in itself the highest privilege. The one who comes to the vineyard late is to be pitied because he didn't have the thrill of spending his entire life serving the Lord. But even for him, there will be reward—a *generous* reward —at the end of the day.

Too late to begin? Never. God is still hiring workmen, even those who are of retirement age! Remember, no one has to be unemployed in God's vineyard.

## WHERE TO BEGIN?

Perhaps you are one who has come to work in the kingdom at five o'clock. True, the hour is late. How much better if you had worked in the Father's vineyard all the day. Whether you are a Christian who had spent your life in the "far country" of selfishness or are an unbeliever who has never known the Keeper of the vineyard, realize this: *it is better to show up for work in the kingdom of heaven at sunset than not to show up at all!*

If in the end you should receive a reward, it will be because of God's grace; but then those who receive rewards for working all day will receive their reward on the same basis.

Where should you begin? We've become so accustomed to judging ourselves by our performance (and this is not all wrong) that we forget that in God's books, what we *are* is more important than what we *do.*

God's will is that we be conformed to the image of Christ (Romans 8:29). In practical terms, that means that God wants to develop the same character traits in us as exist in Christ. We are to react to the situation of life as Christ did.

Of course, this does not mean that we simply roll up our sleeves and determine to live differently. The radical purity of heart that God demands—the rich qualities of love, joy, peace, and patience—are not the product of practice. Rather, they are supernatural characteristics that are developed by dependence on the Holy Spirit (Galatians 5:22-23).

It is a deadly error to suppose that the Christian life can be lived by sheer willpower, abstaining from a given list of sins or fitting into an expected mold. Once we have understood the deep change God wants to bring about, we will see that His demands are so great that only He can supply what He demands! In short, living an acceptable Christian life requires constant fellowship *with* and dependence *on* the living God.

That is why those who have failed miserably are often the first to see God's formula for success. Those who believe they are doing well, often the ones who are faithful in their "work" for the Lord, are the last to appreciate their need for the Holy Spirit's constant power. Most autobiographies of "successful" godly men and women confirm this truth: those who (figuratively) went to the highest mountains also experienced the deepest valleys. In fact, you can't have a mountain without valleys! It is the broken and the contrite heart that God does not despise.

What next? God always wants us to be involved with people. Paul was getting anxious to die and be with Christ, which was far better, but then he realized that it was better still that he live a while longer. Why? Because he could be a blessing to others and encourage them in the faith (Philippians 1:23-26). Our responsibility is to show love to all people in *specific* actions of kindness. Those who offer someone a cup of cold water in the name of the Lord will not lose their reward.

Perhaps you are an invalid in bed. Why not phone a friend and tell him that you will pray for him constantly? Or why not write some letters of encouragement to missionaries or lonely friends? "Truly I say to you, to the extent that you did it to one of these brothers of Mine, even the least of them, you did it to Me" (Matthew 25:40).

Recently, during a trip to Washington, D.C., my wife and I visited the Tomb of the Unknown Soldier at Arlington National Cemetery. After World War I, the American government had the bodies of four unknown soldiers brought to Washington, D.C. Then Sergeant Edward Younger arbitrarily selected one of these four to be buried where the Tomb of the Unknown Soldier would be built. On the tomb are inscribed these words: "Here rests in honored glory an American soldier known but to God."

As I stood there, I realized that all of us will die as unknowns. We may be remembered by our friends, but succeeding generations will forget us. Even today, of the 180,000 graves in Arlington, tourists visit only a few, such as John F. Kennedy's, his brother Robert's, and the Tomb of the Unknown Soldier.

As the years pass, the names of many heroes are obliterated from the minds of men. Yes, we die as unknowns. And when that happens, many things we thought important will be irrelevant. All that will remain is what will not be burned up at the Bema, the judgment seat of Christ, those things that have the dimension of the supernatural. The rich qualities of faith, love, and joy that Christ gave us are all that will survive.

What should we be doing today? We should be discovering the power of a personal God in an age that rejects the supernatural. Then others who see us will not pity us because we are Christians. They will discover that our lives defy human explanation.

God is at work completing His plan before His Son returns to the earth to wrap up history. He wants us to rise above the pessimism, despair, and cynicism of our age. He wants us to display the presence of the supernatural, to rejoice always, pray without ceasing, and in everything give thanks.

It's never too late to begin!

# 13

## Shedding the Grasshopper Complex

A man who was losing his memory went to his doctor for advice. He received this diagnosis: "We cannot help your memory without impairing your eyesight. The choice is yours. Would you rather be able to see or to remember?" The man thoughtfully replied, "I would rather have my eyesight than my memory. I'd rather see where I am going than remember where I have been!"

This story (which is probably apocryphal) reminds us of something we need to hear: at this present moment, our future is more important than our past. We have no claim on the past, but we do have a claim on the future. The past is closed; the future is yet open for new possibilities. But we cannot live meaningful lives in the future if we are tied to the failures or successes of the past. Paul was an example for us all: "But one thing I do: forgetting what lies behind and reaching forward to what lies ahead, I press on toward the goal for the prize of the upward call of God in Christ Jesus" (Philippians 3:13-14).

A basic prerequisite for progress in the Christian life is to learn from the past without being controlled by it. Many Christians are "hung up" on their past. They have tried and failed and are determined never to try again. Their past performance is their excuse for present impotence. If they could choose, they'd prefer their memory to their eyesight. They are blinded to the possibilities of the future because of the memories of the past. Paul reminds us that sometimes it is better to forget than to remember.

But let us assume that you have the assurance of God's forgiveness; suppose that you realize that God is willing to make the best of your past. You want to change the direction of your life. Now what? How should you face the future? How do you tackle your hang-ups? Here are some necessary steps.

First, *consciously include God in every aspect of your life.* Remember the story of the Israelites at Kadesh-barnea? Twelve men were sent to spy out the land of Canaan. They found the land to be productive, just as God had promised. But ten of the twelve spies were shaken with fear, the fear of failure. The Canaanites had walled cities; the Israelites were accustomed only to tents; furthermore, there were "giants" in the land, the sons of Anak.

The result? The majority report read, "We became like grasshoppers in our own sight, and so we were in their sight" (Numbers 13:33). The Israelites were small, the Canaanites were giants; the Israelites were open to attack, the Canaanites lived in fortified cities. Conclusion: failure is inevitable. *Grasshoppers don't win wars.*

Notice that when the spies saw *themselves* as grasshoppers ("We became like grasshoppers in our own sight"), it was then they assumed that the Canaanites thought of them as grasshoppers, too ("And so we were in their sight"). Of course this wasn't true! The Canaanites were scared of the Israelites because rumors of Jehovah's power had reached them (Joshua 2:9-11).

But when you see yourself as a grasshopper, nothing— not even obvious facts—makes the slightest difference. The "grasshopper complex" is the most crippling of all psychological attitudes.

Perhaps the greatest single sin of Christians in any century is the mistake made by the spies: *facing human problems with human resources*. Whether it is preparing a church budget, deciding to share our faith, or tackling our personal problems, the question often is, How much can *I* do? As a result, perpetual failure is inevitable. Instead of comparing our problems with God, we compare them to ourselves. Little wonder we soon feel like grasshoppers (or, at best, pygmies) among an army of giants.

Christ's disciples were guilty of the same sin of unbelief. When Christ suggested that the multitude be fed, Philip checked their resources and concluded, "Two hundred denarii worth of bread is not sufficient for them, for every one to receive a little" (John 6:7). The best Philip could do was to match human resources with human needs. The result: there was simply not enough food to go around.

The boy who gave his lunch to Christ saw the same problem, but apparently, he had enough insight to include Christ in his calculations. Maybe Christ could go beyond human resources; maybe He could do the supernatural; maybe He was relevant to pressing problems. The boy was right.

Why did the spies succumb to the "grasshopper complex" at Kadesh-barnea? First, it began with negative thinking: "We are not able to go up against the people, for they are too strong for us" (Numbers 13:31). The spies thought of more reasons why they couldn't do it than why they could. Second, they exaggerated the situation: "We are like grasshoppers." Unbelief always distorts the facts. A Christian who refuses to trust God for problems as they arise will magnify his difficulties. A pessimist is not only well aware of the negative side of every circumstance but also invents added reasons why failure should be expected.

Third, the next step of unbelief was their desire to return to Egypt (Numbers 14:2-3). People who haven't experienced God's power constantly hover between their faith in God and their desire to succumb to the world. As James reminds us, "A double-minded man [is] unstable in all his ways" (James 1:8). Fourth, they became ignorant of God's will. The next day they decided to conquer the land by themselves. What was the result of this foolish decision? Without God, they were beaten as easily as grasshoppers (Numbers 14:44-45).

All of these disastrous consequences followed because ten men looked at themselves and concluded that they could not cope with the situation. Perhaps they reasoned, "Sure, God is with us, but we have to be realistic!" Maybe they even thought that their attitude displayed humility: "Who are we to think that we can achieve such victory?" But God was angry with them. Why? Because they did not compare the cities and the giants with God; they only compared these obstacles with themselves.

Undoubtedly, God often puts us in situations that are too much for *us* so that we will learn that no situation is too much for *Him.* Goliath was stronger than David; the Midianites were stronger than Gideon; and the storm on Galilee was beyond the control of the disciples. But neither these problems nor ours are too difficult for God.

Do you consciously include God in *all* your plans? Do you face the future with optimism, knowing that nothing is too hard for the Lord? Or is your life characterized by *human* abilities, *human* responses, and *human* resources? Only those who learn to expose each new situation to the living God are delivered from the curse of the grasshopper complex.

Second, *choose a specific difficulty in your life and trust God to conquer it.* Many people who have either psychological or emotional problems do so because they have skeletons in their closet, skeletons that they have tried to hide from others and from God. The trauma of asking others to forgive them or the fear of repeated failure has filled them with pessimism and resentment. But those who are prepared to face themselves with their weaknesses and fears can be freed from such bondage.

Wes Pippert, a Washington-based reporter with United Press International, said that early in life he was afraid of most things. He made a rational decision to acknowledge the fear and proceed to do everything he was afraid of. The result was emancipation. He no longer was afraid, or he had consciously decided to disregard his fears.[1]

Think of what troubles you most at this moment. Your hot temper? Your inability to love others? Are you afraid that your children will go astray? Do you fear the future? Face those problems directly by giving them to God. "Casting all your anxiety upon Him, because He cares for you" (1 Peter 5:7).

The Scriptures teach that all of the spiritual battles that we face have already been conquered by Christ on the cross (Colossians 2:15). God is honored when we simply say "Thank You" for what Christ has already done. If the Israelites had taken God at His word, they would have realized that Canaan was already theirs (Joshua 1:3). It was simply a matter of acting in faith. Canaan could have been theirs if they had believed that God does not deceive His people.

Let me repeat. Choose the difficulty that troubles you the most. Trust God either to remove it, or, if it is not sin, trust God to give you the grace to accept it with joy. If you act on your own, you'll be as easily routed as the Israelites. But if God be for us, who can be against us?

Third, *don't become content with too little; ask God for new areas of ministry and experience.* Even if you think of yourself as a "victorious" Christian, choose to meet even greater challenges. It is heartbreaking to see many Christians who are either content with failure or content with using only a fraction of their potential. This book was written to help those who have failed, which includes all of us to a greater or lesser degree. Failure is not God's plan for us! Neither does He want us to live below par. The Israelites were more content to wander in the wilderness than they were to tackle walled cities. Such sinful contentment, which always leads to *dis*contentment, is the result of unbelief.

Remember Caleb? He was not easily satisfied. At the age of eighty-five, he might have been pardoned for wanting a

1. Wes Pippert, "Ambition, the Ethics of Success," *His* (February 1975): 31.

small home next to the seashore and a garden in the back-yard. After all, he had already participated in many victories; why not let someone else conquer the new territory?

Is he content with that? No, he wants to conquer the mountain God promised him. So he takes the city of Hebron with its Anakims and fortified walls (Joshua 14:12-15). Here was a man who believed that God specialized in victory, not defeat. He was not afflicted with the grasshopper complex.

True, we should be content with our surroundings and our lot in life (Philippians 4:11), but we should never be content with our experience of God's power. Like Paul, we should press on toward the goal for the prize of the high calling of God in Christ Jesus (Philippians 3:14).

Ask God for a mountain! Ask Him for the wisdom to see new challenges that can only be met with His help. Perhaps He wants you to tell your neighbor about Christ; maybe He wants you to have a ministry of encouragement; or He might want you to change the spiritual atmosphere of your home. *Trust God for something that only He can do!* You'll be amazed at the results. "For the eyes of the Lord move to and fro throughout the earth that He may strongly support those whose heart is completely His" (2 Chronicles 16:9). God calls us to live lives we cannot live, so that we must depend on Him for supernatural ability. We are called to do the impossible, namely, to live beyond our natural ability. Someone has said, "If you've never been called to the impossible, you haven't been called."

I've always liked the prayer of Jabez: "Oh that Thou wouldst bless me indeed, and enlarge my border, and that Thy hand might be with me, and that Thou wouldst keep me from harm, that it may not pain me!" (1 Chronicles 4:10). Here was a man who did not feel guilty about asking God to bless him and enlarge the influence of his life. And because he asked this for God's glory, Scripture assures us, "God granted him what he requested." Don't be satisfied until you have seen God conquer the unconquerable!

Fourth, *have a positive rather than negative approach to life.* Many Christians refuse to develop a positive attitude. The reason is simple: they *plan* to fail. Athletic coaches often notice that a player will develop what J. K. Summerhill called a "loser's limp." A player sometimes develops a limp in order to have an excuse for not doing better. Without the limp, he would have to bear the responsibility for incompetence, but with it, he believes that he can't be blamed for a poor performance.

Many Christians constantly complain, "You can see how badly I am handicapped by _____." They would be floundering in bewilderment if their handicap were suddenly removed! Their weakness, whether it be their personality, appearance, lack of ability, or difficult circumstances, has been their security; it provides the rationale for their failure. The truth is they do not want to exchange their pessimism for optimism. They choose to emphasize the negative rather than the positive so that they have a ready-made excuse for not making the grade. They assure us that they have already lost the race even before it has begun.

How can we overcome the "loser's limp"? It is by determining that each day will be a challenge to let God display His power. I've found that my best mental preparation for a positive attitude is to begin each day reminding myself of God's promises. Here are a few: "For nothing will be impossible with God" (Luke 1:37). "We know that God causes all things to work together for good to those who love God, to those who are called according to His purpose" (Romans 8:28). "I can do all things through Him who strengthens me" (Philippians 4:13). Of course, there are many more such promises. Reminding ourselves of them gives us the proper perspective on life.

After you have recited these promises, thank God for everything—your trials, blessings, and challenges. Thanksgiving is a sign of trust; if we believe that all things work together for good, we will be able to be thankful in the most depressing circumstances. Paul's advice is basic to our victory: "In everything give thanks; for this is God's will for you in Christ Jesus" (1 Thessalonians 5:18).

Even if you don't *feel* particularly thankful, thank God for your blessings in Christ (e.g., forgiveness, acceptance, and righteousness), and your attitude will change. I've found that the most difficult struggle is to begin to consciously thank God for all things; then when I think of all God's blessings, my second difficulty is to know when to quit.

Try this right now. List as many blessings as you can, and thank God for each one. In a few moments you will view your problems from a different perspective and face life more objectively. God wants us to be optimists, not pessimists; He wants winners, not losers.

Fifth, *learn to encourage other Christians.* Consider the following statements: "I am the subject of depression of spirit so fearful that I hope none of you ever get to such extremes of wretchedness as I go to . . . personally, I have often passed through this dark valley [of depression]."

"I was very melancholy, I may say, on Saturday evening. The old scenes reminded me of my ministry, and this accompanied with such regret for past failures."

Who spoke these words? Carnal Christians who were living with one foot in the world? A new convert who didn't understand the basis of God's acceptance? Hardly. The first statement was made by one of the world's greatest and most successful preachers—Charles Haddon Spurgeon. The second is recorded in the diary of Andrew Bonar, an outstanding saint and friend of Robert McCheyne.

The point is obvious: everyone—including the greatest saints—experiences regret, unbelief, and the reality of failure. Remember what we said earlier: even successful Christians experience varying degrees of failure. If we compare ourselves with Christ, there isn't much difference between us.

We are all cut from the same piece of cloth. No matter how successfully we may hide our problems, we are still much the same *inside.* Bible records and church history reveal to us that many of God's servants have at times handed God their resignation.

Paul wrote that God "comforts us in all our afflictions so that we may be able to comfort those who are in any affliction with the comfort with which we ourselves are comforted by God" (2 Corinthians 1:4). God expects us to use *our* failures and *His* comfort to be a help to others. Spurgeon could be a blessing to thousands of people because he knew and understood despair. On a less spectacular level, we can be an encouragement to others by sharing our failures and our victories with them. One of my great encouragements was to become friends with those who were personally acquainted with A. W. Tozer. This man, who knew God so intimately, had days when he was so discouraged he felt he could not continue as a minister. Imagine! A man who instructed thousands in the deep things of God often felt he was a miserable failure. He, too, was made of flesh and blood.

If Tozer felt he was a failure, maybe it's not so surprising that we feel that way too. He needed encouragement. So do we.

The most persistent problem in the church is discouragement, and if we do not freely commend people for what they are, they will simply say, "What's the use"—and quit.

A minister, who resigned from his church because of utter discouragement, was inundated with reports of blessing —at his farewell. The people did not want to see him leave; they testified of his effective ministry among them. If they had done that a year earlier, they could have rescued a man from the slough of despondency.

Do you want to make a lasting impact on someone's life? Find a lonely or discouraged Christian. Listen to his needs and tell your personal struggles to him. Your honesty may be as refreshing as a cool stream on the great Sahara. Pray together. Remember, your problems are destined to help us help others.

Let me repeat the fifth step: learn to affirm and encourage the lives of others. As a by-product of encouraging others, you will strengthen yourself. Mutual fellowship produces individual blessing.

Finally, let the words of Peter Marshall become your motto: "It is better to fail in a cause that will ultimately succeed than to succeed in a cause that will ultimately fail."

Better to love God and die unknown than to love the world and be a hero; better to be content with poverty than to die a slave to wealth; better to have taken some risks and lost them than to have done nothing and succeeded at it; better to have lost some battles than to have retreated from the war; better to have failed when serving God than to have succeeded when serving the devil. What a tragedy to climb the ladder of success, only to discover that the ladder was leaning against the wrong wall!

God specializes in the impossible. When we positively accept His grace, our failures can be turned into success. Only a big God can do such big miracles. Isn't it time we shed the grasshopper complex? After all, God specializes in success, not failure. "He raises the poor from the dust, and lifts the needy from the ash heap, to make them sit with princes, with the princes of His people" (Psalms 113:7-8).

Moody Press, a ministry of the Moody Bible Institute, is designed for education, evangelization, and edification. If we may assist you in knowing more about Christ and the Christian life, please write us without obligation: Moody Press, c/o MLM, Chicago, Illinois 60610.

"A friend handed me this book at about midnight, and come two or three in the morning, I was still reading. It's a wonderful and inspiring story that brightens your perspective, giving you a sense of security, clarity, and warmth."

—DONALD MILLER, AUTHOR, *BLUE LIKE JAZZ*

"Don Piper's ninety minutes in heaven changed his life and his perspective. Reading his book will give you the assurance that God is faithful to bring you through even the most horrific of circumstances. May his eyewitness account of the hope that lies before you change your perspective of this life as well!"

—MICHAEL CARTER, CBN CHIEF FINANCIAL OFFICER

"Captivating and well written, this book holds your attention and often holds your heart. Don tells his story, his experience that all Christians long to hear. His experience will lift your spirit and soften your pain."

—RON HILL, PASTOR, THE FELLOWSHIP OF SAN ANTONIO

# 90
## MINUTES IN
# HEAVEN

## A TRUE STORY
### *of* DEATH & LIFE

## DON PIPER
### WITH CECIL MURPHEY

Revell
Grand Rapids, Michigan

Published by Fleming H. Revell
a division of Baker Publishing Group
P.O. Box 6287, Grand Rapids, MI 49516-6287

Thirty-seventh printing

Printed in the United States of America

Library of Congress Cataloging-in-Publication Data
Piper, Don 1950–
    90 minutes in heaven : a true story of life & death / Don Piper with Cecil Murphey.
        p.      cm.
    Includes bibliographical references.
    ISBN 10: 0-8007-5949-4 (pbk.)
    ISBN 978-0-8007-5949-0 (pbk.)
    1. Heaven—Christianity. 2. Future life—Christianity. 3. Near-death experiences—Religious aspects—Christianity. 4. Death—Religious aspects—Christianity. I. Murphey, Cecil B.   II. Title.   III. Title: Ninety minutes in heaven.
    BT846.3.P56 2004
    231.7'3'092—dc22                                              2004006778

To the prayer warriors . . .
You prayed; I'm here!

# CONTENTS

# ACKNOWLEDGMENTS

I wrote this book in self-defense. In the years since 1989 I have seldom satisfied anyone with quick answers or brief encounters retelling my experiences. On radio, on TV, in newspapers, and from countless pulpits and other speaking engagements, I have generally left more unanswered questions than satisfactory responses. People consistently have wanted to know more . . . always more. I wrote three different manuscripts about this experience to satisfy inquiring minds. None of them satisfied me. That's when I prevailed upon one of America's distinguished authors to partner with me to write a book that would answer the most compelling issues concerning my death and life. Cecil Murphey, author of very successful biographies of such luminaries as Franklin Graham, Truett Cathey, B. J. Thomas, Dino Karsanakas, and Dr. Ben Carson, gave me the perspective I wanted to write the book I needed to write. You're holding it now.

Cec has become a devoted friend, confidant, and mentor. Indeed, one of the blessings of writing this book has been to know Cec Murphey. His passion for this project is felt on every page. Thank you, Cec! You are deeply appreciated. Likewise, the Knight Agency's Deidre Knight's belief in this project is much appreciated. And Dr. Vicki Crumpton of Baker Publishing Group is a person I have grown to admire. Her dedication to seeing this story in print is cherished.

I want to thank the staff of both Memorial Hermann Medical Center's Trauma Unit and St. Luke's Episcopal Hospital in Houston for their devotion to the healing arts. Special thanks to Dr. Thomas Greider, my orthopedic surgeon since that fateful night of January 18, 1989.

Precious people of God from many churches have allowed me to serve them. Not only were their prayers crucial to my survival but their presence has been a blessing to my ministry. Deep gratitude goes to South Park Baptist Church of Alvin, Texas, God's great prayer warriors. I would like to acknowledge the special contributions of First Baptist Church, Airline Baptist Church, and Barksdale Baptist Church, all of Bossier City, Louisiana. My father in the ministry, Dr. Damon V. Vaughn, former pastor of the first two of those churches is owed an immeasurable debt.

For standing faithfully with me in the days since my accident I express undying love for the First Baptist Church of Rosharon, Texas, along with Hunters' Glen and Murphy Road Baptist Church of Plano, Texas. Since 1996 I have called First Baptist Church of Pasadena, Texas, my place of service. Your support for this project has been sweet and unwavering. Thank you all for your patience, forbearance, prayers, and love.

To Anita Onerecker and her late husband, Dick, thank you for allowing God to use you so dramatically. To all my friends, brothers and sisters in Christ, who prayed so passionately, I thank you. Only God knows your sacrifices and kindnesses. Most of all, I thank my friends of many years, Cliff McArdle and David Gentiles, true gifts from God. Whether day or night, convenient or imposition, expedient or sacrificial, you have always been faithful. And thank you all for encouraging me to see this book to fruition.

Finally, I want to express profound gratitude to my wife's parents, Eldon and Ethel Pentecost, and my own parents, Ralph and Billie Piper, for their incalculable sacrifices and faithful support. To my three children, Nicole, Chris, and Joe, I say . . . God has given me children so much better than I could have ever deserved. I am highly blessed. How can I say thank you for all you have meant to me, even more so since that Wednesday so long ago? And to my wife of thirty years, Eva, no one should ever have had to do the things you've had to do for me. But you did them, faithfully, compassionately, and without hesitation. Of all my family and friends, only Eva comes closest to really knowing how painful this journey has been each day, for she has endured it with me. Eva, you are a gift from God.

Lord, you know I haven't always understood the whys of what has happened, but I've never stopped trusting you. I pray, Abba Father, that this humble effort to tell my story pleases you and blesses many. Amen.

DON PIPER
FEBRUARY 2004

*Don with sons Chris and Joe in 1982.*

# PROLOGUE

I died on January 18, 1989.

Paramedics reached the scene of the accident within minutes. They found no pulse and declared me dead. They covered me with a tarp so that onlookers wouldn't stare at me while they attended to the injuries of the others. I was completely unaware of the paramedics or anyone else around me.

Immediately after I died, I went straight to heaven.

While I was in heaven, a Baptist preacher came on the accident scene. Even though he knew I was dead, he rushed to my lifeless body and prayed for me. Despite the scoffing of the Emergency Medical Technicians (EMTs), he refused to stop praying.

At least ninety minutes after the EMTs pronounced me dead, God answered that man's prayers.

I returned to earth.

This is my story.

# THE ACCIDENT

That is why we can say with confidence,
"The Lord is my helper,
so I will not be afraid.
What can mere mortals do to me?"

The Baptist General Convention of Texas (BGCT) holds annual statewide conferences. In January 1989, they chose the north shore of Lake Livingston where the Union Baptist Association, composed of all Baptist churches in the greater Houston area, operates a large conference center called Trinity Pines. The conference focused on church growth, and I went because I was seriously considering starting a new church.

The conference started on Monday and was scheduled to end with lunch on Wednesday. On Tuesday night, I joined a BGCT executive and friend named J. V. Thomas for a long walk. J. V.

15

had become a walker after his heart attack, so we exercised together the last night of the conference.

Months earlier, I had begun thinking that it was time for me to start a new congregation. Before embarking on such a venture, I wanted as much information as I could get. I knew that J. V. had as much experience and knowledge about new church development as anyone in the BGCT. Because he had started many successful churches in the state, most of us recognized him as the expert. As we walked together that night, we talked about my starting a new church, when to do it, and where to plant it. I wanted to know the hardships as well as the pitfalls to avoid. He answered my seemingly endless questions and raised issues I hadn't thought about.

We walked and talked for about an hour. Despite the cold, rainy weather, we had a wonderful time together. J. V. remembers that time well.

So do I, but for a different reason: It would be the last time I would ever walk normally.

On Wednesday morning the weather worsened. A steady rain fell. Had the temperature been only a few degrees colder, we couldn't have traveled, because everything would have been frozen.

The morning meetings started on time. The final speaker did something Baptist preachers almost never do—he finished early. Instead of lunch, the staff at Trinity Pines served us brunch at about ten thirty. I had packed the night before, so everything was stowed in my red 1986 Ford Escort.

As soon as we finished brunch, I said good-bye to all my friends and got into my car to drive back to the church where

I was on staff, South Park Baptist Church in Alvin, a Houston bedroom community.

When I started the engine, I remembered that only three weeks earlier I had received a traffic ticket for not wearing a seat belt. I had been on my way to preach for a pastor friend who was going to have throat surgery. A Texas trooper had caught me. That ticket still lay on the passenger seat, reminding me to pay it as soon as I returned to Alvin. Until I received the ticket, I had not usually worn a seat belt, but after that I changed my ways.

When I looked at that ticket I thought, *I don't want to be stopped again.* So I carefully fastened my seat belt. That small act would be a crucial decision.

There were two ways to get back to Houston and on to Alvin. As soon as I reached the gates of Trinity Pines, I had to choose either to drive through Livingston and down Highway 59 or to head west to Huntsville and hit I-45, often called the Gulf Freeway. Each choice is probably about the same distance. Every other time to and from Trinity Pines I had driven Highway 59. That morning I decided to take the Gulf Freeway.

I was relieved that we had been able to leave early. It was only a few minutes after 11:00, so I could get back to the church by 2:00. The senior minister had led a group to the Holy Land and left me responsible for our midweek service at South Park Church. He had also asked me to preach for the next two Sundays. That night was a prayer meeting, which required little preparation, but I needed to work on my sermon for the following Sunday morning.

Before I left Alvin, I had written a draft for the first sermon titled "I Believe in a Great God." As I drove, I planned to glance over the sermon and evaluate what I had written so far.

Many times since then I've thought about my decision to take the Gulf Freeway. It's amazing how we pay no attention to simple decisions at the time they're made. Yet I would remind myself that even the smallest decisions often hold significant consequences. This was one of those choices.

I pulled out of Trinity Pines, turned right, and headed down Texas Highway 19. That would take me to Huntsville and intersect with I-45, leading to Houston. I didn't have to drive far before I reached Lake Livingston, a man-made lake, created by damming the Trinity River. What was once a riverbed is now a large, beautiful lake. Spanning Lake Livingston is a two-lane highway whose roadbed has been built up above the level of the lake. The road has no shoulders, making it extremely narrow. I would have to drive across a long expanse of water on that narrow road until I reached the other side. I had no premonitions about the trip, although I was aware of the road's lack of shoulders.

At the end of the highway across the lake is the original bridge over the Trinity River. Immediately after the bridge, the road rises sharply, climbing the bluff above the Trinity's riverbed. This sharp upturn makes visibility a problem for drivers in both directions.

This was my first time to see the bridge, and it looked curiously out of place. I have no idea of the span, but the bridge is quite long. It's an old bridge with a massive, rusty steel superstructure. Other than the immediate road ahead, I could see little, and I certainly didn't glimpse any other traffic. It was a dangerous bridge, and as I would learn later, several accidents had occurred on it. (Although no longer used, the bridge is still there. The state built another one beside it.)

I drove at about fifty miles an hour because it was, for me, uncharted territory. I braced my shoulders against the chill inside the car. The wind made the morning seem even colder than it was. The steady rain had turned into a cloudburst. I would be happy to finally reach Alvin again. About 11:45 A.M., just before I cleared the east end of the bridge, an eighteen-wheeler driven by an inmate, a trusty at the Texas Department of Corrections, weaved across the center line and hit my car head-on. The truck sandwiched my small car between the bridge railing and the driver's side of the truck. All those wheels went right on top of my car and smashed it.

I remember parts of the accident, but most of my information came from the accident report and people at the scene.

From the description I've received from witnesses, the truck then veered off to the other side of the narrow bridge and side-swiped two other cars. They were in front of the truck and had already passed me going in the opposite direction. The police record says that the truck was driving fast—at least sixty miles an hour—when it struck my car. The inexperienced driver finally brought the truck to a stop almost at the end of the bridge.

A young Vietnamese man was in one vehicle that was hit, and an elderly Caucasian man was in the other. Although shaken up, both drivers suffered only minor cuts and bruises. They refused help, so the paramedics transported neither man to the hospital.

Because of the truck's speed, the accident report states that the impact was about 110 miles an hour. That is, the truck struck me while going sixty miles an hour, and I was carefully cruising along at fifty. The inmate received a citation for failure to control his vehicle and speeding. Information later came out that the inmate wasn't licensed to drive the truck. At the prison, supervisors had asked for volunteers to drive their truck to pick up food items and bring them back. Because he was the only volunteer, they let him drive their supply truck. Two guards followed close behind him in another state-owned pickup.

After the accident, the truck driver didn't have a scratch on him. The prison truck received little damage. However, the heavy vehicle had crushed my Ford and pushed it from the narrow road. Only the bridge railing stopped my car from going into the lake.

According to those who were at the scene, the guards called for medical backup from the prison, and they arrived a few minutes later. Someone examined me, found no pulse, and declared that I had been killed instantly.

I have no recollection of the impact or anything that happened afterward.

In one powerful, overwhelming second, I died.

# 2
# MY TIME
# IN HEAVEN

He was afraid and said, "How awesome is this place! This is none
other than the house of God; this is the gate of heaven."

GENESIS 28:17

W hen I died, I didn't flow through a long, dark tunnel.
I had no sense of fading away or of coming back. I
never felt my body being transported into the light.
I heard no voices calling to me or anything else. Simultaneous
with my last recollection of seeing the bridge and the rain, a light
enveloped me, with a brilliance beyond earthly comprehension
or description. Only that.

In my next moment of awareness, I was standing in heaven.

Joy pulsated through me as I looked around, and at that moment I became aware of a large crowd of people. They stood

21

in front of a brilliant, ornate gate. I have no idea how far away they were; such things as distance didn't matter. As the crowd rushed toward me, I didn't see Jesus, but I did see people I had known. As they surged toward me, I knew instantly that all of them had died during my lifetime. Their presence seemed absolutely natural.

They rushed toward me, and every person was smiling, shouting, and praising God. Although no one said so, intuitively I knew they were my celestial welcoming committee. It was as if they had all gathered just outside heaven's gate, waiting for me.

The first person I recognized was Joe Kulbeth, my grandfather. He looked exactly as I remembered him, with his shock of white hair and what I called a big banana nose. He stopped momentarily and stood in front of me. A grin covered his face. I may have called his name, but I'm not sure.

"Donnie!" (That's what my grandfather always called me.) His eyes lit up, and he held out his arms as he took the last steps toward me. He embraced me, holding me tightly. He was once again the robust, strong grandfather I had remembered as a child.

I'd been with him when he suffered a heart attack at home and had ridden with him in the ambulance. I had been standing just outside the emergency room at the hospital when the doctor walked out and faced me. He shook his head and said softly, "We did everything we could."

My grandfather released me, and as I stared into his face, an ecstatic bliss overwhelmed me. I didn't think about his heart attack or his death, because I couldn't get past the joy of our reunion. How either of us reached heaven seemed irrelevant.

I have no idea why my grandfather was the first person I saw. Perhaps it had something to do with my being there when he died. He wasn't one of the great spiritual guides of my life, although he certainly influenced me positively in that way.

After being hugged by my grandfather, I don't remember who was second or third. The crowd surrounded me. Some hugged me and a few kissed my cheek, while others pumped my hand. Never had I felt more loved.

One person in that greeting committee was Mike Wood, my childhood friend. Mike was special because he invited me to Sunday school and was influential in my becoming a Christian. Mike was the most devoted young Christian I knew. He was also a popular kid and had lettered four years in football, basketball, and track and field, an amazing feat. He also became a hero to me, because he lived the Christian lifestyle he often talked about. After high school, Mike received a full scholarship to Louisiana State University. When he was nineteen, Mike was killed in a car wreck. It broke my heart when I heard about his death, and it took me a long time to get over it. His death was the biggest shock and most painful experience I'd had up to that time in my life.

When I attended his funeral, I wondered if I would ever stop crying. I couldn't understand why God had taken such a dedicated disciple. Through the years since then, I had never been able to forget the pain and sense of loss. Not that I thought of him all the time, but when I did, sadness came over me.

Now I saw Mike in heaven. As he slipped his arm around my shoulder, my pain and grief vanished. Never had I seen Mike smile so brightly. I still didn't know why, but the joyousness of the place wiped away any questions. Everything felt blissful. Perfect.

23

More and more people reached for me and called me by name. I felt overwhelmed by the number of people who had come to welcome me to heaven. There were so many of them, and I had never imagined anyone being as happy as they all were. Their faces radiated a serenity I had never seen on earth. All were full of life and expressed radiant joy.

Time had no meaning. However, for clarity, I'll relate this experience in terms that refer to time.

I saw my great-grandfather, heard his voice, and felt his embrace as he told me how excited he was that I had come to join them. I saw Barry Wilson, who had been my classmate in high school but later drowned in a lake. Barry hugged me, and his smile radiated a happiness I didn't know was possible. He and everyone that followed praised God and told me how excited they were to see me and to welcome me to heaven and to the fellowship they enjoyed.

Just then, I spotted two teachers who had loved me and often talked to me about Jesus Christ. As I walked among them, I became aware of the wide variety of ages—old and young and every age in-between. Many of them hadn't known each other on earth, but each had influenced my life in some way. Even though they hadn't met on earth, they seemed to know each other now.

As I try to explain this, my words seem weak and hardly adequate, because I have to use earthly terms to refer to unimaginable joy, excitement, warmth, and total happiness. Everyone continually embraced me, touched me, spoke to me, laughed, and praised God. This seemed to go on for a long time, but I didn't tire of it.

My father is one of eleven children. Some of his brothers and sisters had as many as thirteen children. When I was a kid, our family reunions were so huge we rented an entire city park in Monticello, Arkansas. We Pipers are affectionate, with a lot of hugging and kissing whenever we come together. None of those earthly family reunions, however, prepared me for the sublime gathering of saints I experienced at the gates of heaven.

Those who had gathered at Monticello were some of the same people waiting for me at the gates of heaven. Heaven was many things, but without a doubt, it was the greatest family reunion of all.

Everything I experienced was like a first-class buffet for the senses. I had never felt such powerful embraces or feasted my eyes on such beauty. Heaven's light and texture defy earthly eyes or explanation. Warm, radiant light engulfed me. As I looked around, I could hardly grasp the vivid, dazzling colors. Every hue and tone surpassed anything I had ever seen.

With all the heightened awareness of my senses, I felt as if I had never seen, heard, or felt anything so real before. I don't recall that I tasted anything, yet I knew that if I had, that too would have been more glorious than anything I had eaten or drunk on earth. The best way I can explain it is to say that I felt as if I were in another dimension. Never, even in my happiest moments, had I ever felt so fully alive. I stood speechless in front of the crowd of loved ones, still trying to take in everything. Over and over I heard how overjoyed they were to see me and how excited they were to have me among them. I'm not sure if they actually said the words or not, but I knew they had been waiting and expecting me, yet I also knew that in heaven there is no sense of time passing.

I gazed at all the faces again as I realized that they all had contributed to my becoming a Christian or had encouraged me in my growth as a believer. Each one had affected me positively. Each had spiritually impacted me in some way and helped make me a better disciple. I knew—again one of those things I knew without being aware of how I had absorbed that information—that because of their influence I was able to be present with them in heaven.

We didn't talk about what they had done for me. Our conversations centered on the joy of my being there and how happy they were to see me.

Still overwhelmed, I didn't know how to respond to their welcoming words. "I'm happy to be with you," I said, and even those words couldn't express the utter joy of being surrounded and embraced by all those people I loved.

I wasn't conscious of anything I'd left behind and felt no regrets about leaving family or possessions. It was as if God had removed anything negative or worrisome from my consciousness, and I could only rejoice at being together with these wonderful people.

They looked exactly as I once knew them—although they were more radiant and joyful than they'd ever been on earth.

My great-grandmother, Hattie Mann, was Native American. As a child I saw her only after she had developed osteoporosis. Her head and shoulders were bent forward, giving her a humped appearance. I especially remember her extremely wrinkled face. The other thing that stands out in my memory is that she had false teeth—which she didn't wear often. Yet when she smiled at me in heaven, her teeth sparkled. I knew they were her own, and when she smiled, it was the most beautiful smile I had ever seen.

Then I noticed something else—she wasn't slumped over. She stood strong and upright, and the wrinkles had been erased from her face. I have no idea what age she was, and I didn't even think about that. As I stared at her beaming face, I sensed that age has no meaning in heaven.

Age expresses time passing, and there is no time there. All of the people I encountered were the same age they had been the last time I had seen them—except that all the ravages of living on earth had vanished. Even though some of their features may not have been considered attractive on earth, in heaven every feature was perfect, beautiful, and wonderful to gaze at.

Even now, years later, I can sometimes close my eyes and see those perfect countenances and smiles that surprised me with the most human warmth and friendliness I've ever witnessed. Just being with them was a holy moment and remains a treasured hope.

When I first stood in heaven, they were still in front of me and came rushing toward me. They embraced me, and no matter which direction I looked, I saw someone I had loved and who had loved me. They surrounded me, moving around so that everyone had a chance to welcome me to heaven.

I felt loved—more loved than ever before in my life. They didn't say they loved me. I don't remember what words they spoke. When they gazed at me, I *knew* what the Bible means by perfect love. It emanated from every person who surrounded me.

I stared at them, and as I did I felt as if I absorbed their love for me. At some point, I looked around and the sight overwhelmed me. Everything was brilliantly intense. Coming out from the gate—a short distance ahead—was a brilliance that was brighter than the light that surrounded us, utterly luminous. As soon as I stopped gazing at the people's faces, I realized that everything around me glowed with a dazzling intensity. In trying to describe the scene, words are totally inadequate, because human words can't express the feelings of awe and wonder at what I beheld.

Everything I saw glowed with intense brightness. The best I can describe it is that we began to move toward that light. No one said it was time to do so, and yet we all started forward at the same time. As I stared ahead, everything seemed to grow taller—like a gentle hill that kept going upward and never stopped. I had expected to see some darkness behind the gate, but as far ahead as I could see, there was absolutely nothing but intense, radiant light.

By contrast, the powerful light I had encountered when I met my friends and loved ones paled into darkness as the radiance and iridescence in front of me increased. It was as if each step I took intensified the glowing luminosity. I didn't know how it could get more dazzling, but it did. It would be like cracking open the door of a dark room and walking into the brightness of a noonday sun. As the door swings open, the full rays of the sun burst forth, and we're momentarily blinded.

I wasn't blinded, but I was amazed that the luster and intensity continually increased. Strange as it seems, as brilliant as everything was, each time I stepped forward, the splendor increased. The farther I walked, the brighter the light. The light engulfed me, and I had the sense that I was being ushered into the presence of God. Although our earthly eyes must gradually adjust to light or darkness, my heavenly eyes saw with absolute ease. In heaven, each of our senses is immeasurably heightened to take it all in. And what a sensory celebration!

A holy awe came over me as I stepped forward. I had no idea what lay ahead, but I sensed that with each step I took, it would grow more wondrous.

Then I heard the music.

# HEAVENLY MUSIC

## 3

Then I looked again, and I heard the singing of thousands and millions of angels around the throne and the living beings and the elders.

REVELATION 5:11

As a young boy I spent a lot of time out in the country and woods. When walking through waist-high dried grass, I often surprised a covey of birds and flushed them out of their nests on the ground. A whooshing sound accompanied their wings as they flew away.

My most vivid memory of heaven is what I heard. I can only describe it as a holy swoosh of wings.

But I'd have to magnify that thousands of times to explain the effect of the sound in heaven.

It was the most beautiful and pleasant sound I've ever heard, and it didn't stop. It was like a song that goes on forever. I felt awestruck, wanting only to listen. I didn't just hear music. It seemed as if I were part of the music—and it played in and through my body. I stood still, and yet I felt embraced by the sounds.

As aware as I became of the joyous sounds and melodies that filled the air, I wasn't distracted. I felt as if the heavenly concert permeated every part of my being, and at the same time I focused on everything else around me.

I never saw anything that produced the sound. I had the sense that whatever made the heavenly music was just above me, but I didn't look up. I'm not sure why. Perhaps it was because I was so enamored with the people around me, or maybe it was because my senses were so engaged that I feasted on everything at the same time. I asked no questions and never wondered about anything. Everything was perfect. I sensed that I knew everything and had no questions to ask.

Myriads of sounds so filled my mind and heart that it's difficult to explain them. The most amazing one, however, was the angels' wings. I didn't see them, but the sound was a beautiful, holy melody with a cadence that seemed never to stop. The swishing resounded as if it was a form of never-ending praise. As I listened I simply *knew* what it was.

A second sound remains, even today, the single, most vivid memory I have of my entire heavenly experience. I call it music, but it differed from anything I had ever heard or ever expect to hear on the earth. The melodies of praise filled the atmosphere. The nonstop intensity and endless variety overwhelmed me.

The praise was unending, but the most remarkable thing to me was that hundreds of songs were being sung at the same time—all of them worshiping God. As I approached the large, magnificent gate, I heard them from every direction and realized that each voice praised God. I write *voice,* but it was more than that. Some sounded instrumental, but I wasn't sure—and I wasn't concerned. Praise was everywhere, and all of it was musical, yet comprised of melodies and tones I'd never experienced before.

"Hallelujah!" "Praise!" "Glory to God!" "Praise to the King!" Such words rang out in the midst of all the music. I don't know if angels were singing them or if they came from humans. I felt so awestruck and caught up in the heavenly mood that I didn't look around. My heart filled with the deepest joy I've ever experienced. I wasn't a participant in the worship, yet I felt as if my heart rang out with the same kind of joy and exuberance.

If we played three CDs of praise at the same time, we'd have a cacophony of noise that would drive us crazy. This was totally different. Every sound blended, and each voice or instrument enhanced the others.

As strange as it may seem, I could clearly distinguish each song. It sounded as if each hymn of praise was meant for me to hear as I moved inside the gates.

Many of the old hymns and choruses I had sung at various times in my life were part of the music—along with hundreds of songs I had never heard before. Hymns of praise, modern-sounding choruses, and ancient chants filled my ears and brought not only a deep peace but the greatest feeling of joy I've ever experienced.

As I stood before the gate, I didn't think of it, but later I realized that I didn't hear such songs as "The Old Rugged Cross" or "The Nail-Scarred Hand." None of the hymns that filled the air were about Jesus' sacrifice or death. I heard no sad songs and instinctively knew that there are no sad songs in heaven. Why would there be? All were praises about Christ's reign as King of Kings and our joyful worship for all he has done for us and how wonderful he is.

31

The celestial tunes surpassed any I had ever heard. I couldn't calculate the number of songs—perhaps thousands—offered up simultaneously, and yet there was no chaos, because I had the capacity to hear each one and discern the lyrics and melody.

I marveled at the glorious music. Though not possessed of a great singing voice in life, I knew that if I sang, my voice would be in perfect pitch and would sound as melodious and harmonious as the thousands of other voices and instruments that filled my ears.

Even now, back on earth, sometimes I still hear faint echoes of that music. When I'm especially tired and lie in bed with my eyes closed, occasionally I drift off to sleep with the sounds of heaven filling my heart and mind. No matter how difficult a day I've had, peace immediately fills every part of my being. I still have flashbacks, although they're different from what we normally refer to as flashbacks. Mine are more flashbacks of the sounds than the sights.

As I've pondered the meaning of the memory of the music, it seems curious. I would have expected the most memorable experience to be something I had seen or the physical embrace of a loved one. Yet above everything else, I cherish those sounds, and at times I think, *I can't wait to hear them again—in person.* It's what I look forward to. I want to see everybody, but I know I'll be with them forever. I want to experience everything heaven offers, but most of all, I want to hear those never-ending songs again.

Obviously, I can't really know how God feels, but I find joy and comfort in thinking that he must be pleased and blessed by the continuous sounds of praise.

In those minutes—and they held no sense of time for me—others touched me, and their warm embraces were absolutely real. I saw colors I would never have believed existed. I've never, ever felt more alive than I did then.

I was home; I was where I belonged. I wanted to be there more than I had ever wanted to be anywhere on earth. Time had slipped away, and I was simply present in heaven. All worries, anxieties, and concerns vanished. I had no needs, and I felt perfect.

I get frustrated describing what heaven was like, because I can't begin to put into words what it looked like, sounded like, and felt like. It was perfect, and I knew I had no needs and never would again. I didn't even think of earth or those left behind.

I did not see God. Although I knew God was there, I never saw any kind of image or luminous glow to indicate his divine presence. I've heard people talk about going inside and coming back out the gate. That didn't happen to me.

I saw only a bright iridescence. I peered through the gate, yearning to see what lay beyond. It wasn't an anxious yearning, but a peaceful openness to experience all the grace and joy of heaven.

The only way I've made sense out of that part of the experience is to think that if I had actually seen God, I would never have wanted to return. My feeling has been that once we're actually in God's presence, we will never return to earth again, because it will be empty and meaningless by comparison.

For me, just to reach the gates was amazing. It was a foretaste of joy divine. My words are too feeble to describe what took place.

As a pastor, I've stood at the foot of many caskets and done many funerals and said, "To be absent from the body is to be present with the Lord to those who love him and know him."

I believed those words before. I believe them even more now.

After a time (I'm resorting to human terms again), we started moving together right up to the gate. No one said it, but I simply knew God had sent all those people to escort me inside the portals of heaven.

Looming just over the heads of my reception committee stood an awesome gate interrupting a wall that faded out of sight in both directions. It struck me that the actual entrance was small in comparison to the massive gate itself. I stared, but I couldn't see the end of the walls in either direction. As I gazed upward, I couldn't see the top either.

One thing did surprise me: On earth, whenever I thought of heaven, I anticipated that one day I'd see a gate made of pearls, because the Bible refers to the gates of pearl. The gate wasn't made of pearls, but was pearlescent—perhaps *iridescent* may be more descriptive. To me, it looked as if someone had spread pearl icing on a cake. The gate glowed and shimmered.

I paused and stared at the glorious hues and shimmering shades. The luminescence dazzled me, and I would have been content to stay at that spot. Yet I stepped forward as if being escorted into God's presence.

I paused just outside the gate, and I could see inside. It was like a city with paved streets. To my amazement, they had been constructed of literal gold. If you imagine a street paved with gold bricks, that's as close as I can come to describing what lay inside the gate.

Everything I saw was bright—the brightest colors my eyes had ever beheld—so powerful that no earthly human could take in this brilliance.

In the midst of that powerful scene, I continued to step closer to the gate and assumed that I would go inside. My friends and relatives were all in front of me, calling, urging, and inviting me to follow.

Then the scene changed. I can explain it only by saying that instead of their being in front of me, they were beside me. I felt that they wanted to walk beside me as I passed through the iridescent gate.

Sometimes people have asked me, "How did you move? Did you walk? Did you float?" I don't know. I just moved along with that welcoming crowd. As we came closer to the gate, the music increased and became even more vivid. It would be like walking up to a glorious event after hearing the faint sounds and seeing everything from a distance. The closer we got, the more intense, alive, and vivid everything became. Just as I reached the gate, my senses were even more heightened, and I felt deliriously happy.

I paused—I'm not sure why—just outside the gate. I was thrilled at the prospect and wanted to go inside. I knew everything would be even more thrilling than what I had experienced so far. At that very moment I was about to realize the yearning of every human heart. I was in heaven and ready to go in through the pearlescent gate.

During that momentary pause, something else changed. Instead of just hearing the music and the thousands of voices praising God, I had become part of the choir. I was one with them, and they had absorbed me into their midst. I had arrived at a place I had wanted to visit for a long time; I lingered to gaze before I continued forward.

Then, just as suddenly as I had arrived at the gates of heaven, I left them.

# 4

# FROM HEAVEN TO EARTH

Even when I walk
   through the dark valley of death,
I will not be afraid,
   for you are close beside me.
Your rod and your staff
   protect and comfort me.

PSALM 23:4

The EMTs pronounced me dead as soon as they arrived at the scene. They stated that I died instantly. According to the report, the collision occurred at 11:45 A.M. The EMTs became so busy working with the others involved, that it was about 1:15 P.M. before they were ready to move me. They checked for a pulse once again.

I was still dead.

*Above: Don's Ford Escort after the accident. The roof was removed to extract Don and was laid back on top after the car arrived at the wrecking yard. Below: The accident scene.*

The state law said they had to pronounce me dead officially before they could remove my body from the scene of the accident. Unless they declared me dead, an ambulance would have to transport my body to a hospital. That county didn't have a coroner, but I learned later that a justice of the peace could declare me dead, and then they could remove my body.

Ambulances had come from the prison, the county, and Huntsville. Except for one, all of them left without taking back any patients. The last one was preparing to leave. From information I've pieced together, someone had arranged for an unmarked vehicle to take my body to a mortuary.

They had called for the Jaws of Life[1] to get me out of the smashed car. Because I was dead, there seemed to be no need for speed. Their concern focused on clearing the bridge for traffic to flow again.

When the truck came in at an angle and went right over the top of me, the truck smashed the car's ceiling, and the dashboard came down across my legs, crushing my right leg. My left leg was shattered in two places between the car seat and the dashboard. My left arm went over the top of my head, was dislocated, and swung backward over the seat. It was still attached—barely.

That left arm had been lying on the driver's side door, because I had been driving with my right hand. As I would learn later, the major bones were now missing, so my lower left arm was just a piece of flesh that held the hand to the rest of the arm. It was the same with the left leg. There was some tissue just above my knee that still fed blood to the calf and foot below. Four and a half inches of femur were missing and never found. The doctors have no medical explanation why I didn't lose all the blood in my body.

Glass and blood had sprayed everywhere. I had all kinds of small holes in my face from embedded glass. The steering wheel had pounded into my chest. Blood seeped out of my eyes, ears, and nose.

Just from seeing the results of the crash, the EMTs knew I had to have sustained massive head injuries and that my insides were completely rearranged. When he first felt no pulse, one of the EMTs covered me with a waterproof tarp that also blocked off the top of the car. They made no attempt to move me or try to get me out immediately—they couldn't have anyway, because it would have been impossible for them to drag or lift me out of the vehicle without the Jaws of Life.

One thing that sped help to the scene was that the two prison guards in the pickup truck immediately called for emergency assistance from the prison. Otherwise, we would have been too far away for any emergency vehicle to get to us quickly.

They examined the drivers of the other two cars; both of them were uninjured and refused medical attention. The prisoner who drove the truck sustained no injuries. As soon as the EMTs determined he was all right, they transported him back to the prison. Police halted all traffic on the bridge and waited for the ambulance to arrive. While they waited, traffic backed up for miles in both directions, especially the direction I had come from. It was only a narrow two-lane bridge, not wide enough for a car to turn around. Even if the waiting traffic could have turned around, they would have had to drive an extra forty or fifty miles around the lake to reach another road leading to their destination.

From the backed-up traffic, Dick and Anita Onerecker walked at least half a mile to the scene of the accident. Dick and Anita had started a church in Klein, which is north of Houston. Both had spoken at the conference I'd just attended. I'm not positive we actually met at Trinity Pines, although we may have. For years I had heard of Dick Onerecker, but that conference was the first time I had ever seen him.

On Wednesday morning, the Onereckers left Trinity Pines a few minutes before I did. By Houston standards, that January morning was extremely cold. As they sped along, Anita said, "I'm really chilled. Could we stop for coffee? I think that would warm me up."

Dick spotted a bait shop right on Lake Livingston, so they pulled over. Apparently, while they were buying coffee, I drove past them.

Many times afterward, Dick would bury his face in his hands and say, "You know that could easily have been us. It should have been us, but because we stopped and you drove past us, you got hit."

Before the Onereckers reached the bridge, the accident had occurred and traffic had started to back up. People got out of their cars and milled around, asking questions and sharing their limited information.

After Dick and Anita got out of their car, they asked fellow drivers, "What's going on up there?"

The word had passed down that there had been a serious auto accident. "A truck crashed into a car" was about all anyone knew.

Dick and Anita stood around a few minutes, but nothing happened, and more cars lined up behind them. Sometime between 12:30 and 12:45, they decided to walk to the accident site. When they saw a police officer, Dick said, "I'm a minister. Is there anybody here I can help? Is there anyone I can pray for?"

The police officer shook his head. "The people in those two cars," he said and pointed, "are shaken up a little bit but they're fine. Talk to them if you'd like."

"What about the other vehicle? The one with the tarp over it?"

"The man in the red car is deceased."

While Dick talked to the officer, Anita went over to the other vehicles. She gave her barely touched coffee to the old man.

Dick would later tell it this way: "God spoke to me and said, 'You need to pray for the man in the red car.'" Dick was an outstanding Baptist preacher. Praying for a dead man certainly ran counter to his theology. *I can't do that,* he thought. *How can I go over there and pray? The man is dead.*

The rain had become a light drizzle, but Dick was oblivious to his surroundings. Dick stared at the officer, knowing that what he would say wouldn't make sense. Yet God spoke to him so clearly that he had no doubt about what he was to do. God had told him to pray for a dead man. As bizarre as that seemed to him, Dick also had no doubt that the Holy Spirit was prompting him to act.

"I'd like to pray for the man in the red car," Dick finally said to the officer.

"Like I said, he's dead."

"I know this sounds strange, but I want to pray for him anyway."

The officer stared at him a long time before he finally said, "Well, you know, if that's what you want to do, go ahead, but I've got to tell you it's an awful sight. He's dead, and it's really a mess under the tarp. Blood and glass are everywhere, and the body's all mangled."

Dick, then in his forties, said, "I was a medic in Vietnam, so the idea of blood doesn't bother me."

42

"I have to warn you—" The man stopped, shrugged, and said, "Do what you want, but I'll tell you that you haven't seen anybody this bad."

"Thanks," Dick said and walked to the tarp-covered car.

From the pictures of that smashed-down car, it's almost impossible to believe, but somehow Dick actually crawled into the trunk of my Ford. It had been a hatchback, but that part of the car had been severed. I was still covered by the tarp, which he didn't remove, so it was extremely dark inside the car. Dick crept in behind me, leaned over the backseat, and put his hand on my right shoulder.

He began praying for me. As he said later, "I felt compelled to pray. I didn't know who the man was or whether he was a believer. I knew only that God told me I had to pray for him."

As Dick prayed, he became quite emotional and broke down and cried several times. Then he sang. Dick had an excellent voice and often sang publicly. He paused several times to sing a hymn and then went back to prayer.

Not only did Dick believe God had called him to pray for me but he prayed quite specifically that I would be delivered from unseen injuries, meaning brain and internal injuries.

This sounds strange, because Dick knew I was dead. Not only had the police officer told him but he also had checked for a pulse. He had no idea why he prayed as he did, except God told him to. He didn't pray for the injuries he could see, only for the healing of internal damage. He said he prayed the most passionate, fervent, emotional prayer of his life. As I would later learn, Dick was a highly emotional man anyway.

Then he began to sing again. "O what peace we often forfeit, O what needless pain we bear, all because we do not carry everything to God in prayer!"[2] The only thing I personally know for certain about the entire event is that as he sang the blessed old hymn "What a Friend We Have in Jesus," I began to sing with him.

In that first moment of consciousness, I was aware of two things. First, I was singing—a different kind of singing than the tones of heaven—I heard my own voice and then became aware of someone else singing.

The second thing I was aware of was that someone clutched my hand. It was a strong, powerful touch and the first physical sensation I experienced with my return to earthly life.

More than a year would lapse before I understood the significance of that hand clasping mine.

# 5
# EARTH TO HOSPITAL

But they were looking for a better place, a heavenly homeland.
That is why God is not ashamed to be called their God, for he
has prepared a heavenly city for them.

HEBREWS 11:16

I'm not certain what the world record is for exiting a wrecked
car, but Dick Onerecker must have surely broken it that
Wednesday afternoon. When a dead man began to sing
with him, Dick scrambled out of that smashed car and raced
over to the nearest EMT.

"The man's alive! He's not dead! He's alive!"

Who would have believed him? A preacher had started to
pray for a man who had been dead for an hour and a half. Then
he dashed across the road shouting, "That man has come back
to life!"

The EMT stared.

"He's alive! The dead man started singing with me."

The words didn't make sense as Dick thought of them later, but he could only keep yelling, "He's singing! He's alive!"

"Oh really?" a paramedic asked.

"I'm serious, this man's alive."

"We're medical professionals. We know a dead guy when we see him. That guy is *dead*."

"I'm telling you, that man just sang with me. He's alive."

"The justice of the peace is on his way here." He explained that although they knew I was dead, they couldn't move my body until someone in authority actually declared me dead. "But I can tell you this much: He is dead." The man turned away from Dick and refused to go over to my car.

Several ambulances had already arrived and departed.

Dick walked up in front of the remaining ambulance and said to the driver, "That man is alive. Go look at him."

The EMT began to act as if he handled feebleminded people all the time. "Please, we know our business. That man is—"

"Listen to me! I'm going to lie down on this bridge, and if you don't come over here, you're going to have to run over me."

"He's dead."

"Then humor me. Just feel his pulse," Dick pleaded.

"Okay, we'll check on him for you," the man said, mumbling under his breath. He walked over to the car, raised the tarp, reached inside, and found my right arm. He felt my pulse.

Everyone leaped into action. They began trying to figure out how to get me out. They could have taken me out on one side, but it would have been without my left leg. There was no clearance from the dashboard between my left leg and the seat, so they would have had to amputate. My leg was barely hanging on to my body anyway. I'm not sure they could have gotten my right leg out either. The point is that even though they could have gotten me out without the equipment, they would have left some of me in the car. They decided to wait on the proper equipment. They got on the phone and ordered the Jaws of Life to hurry from Huntsville, which was at least thirty miles away. I'm sure they did whatever they could for me, but I remember nothing. I remained vaguely conscious of people moving around me, touching me, and talking. I heard voices, but I couldn't make sense of anything they said. Dick refused to leave me. He got back inside the car, where he was able to kneel behind me, and he continued to pray until the Jaws of Life arrived. Only after they lifted me into the ambulance did he leave my side. When the EMTs lifted me out of the car, I remember that it involved a number of men—at least six or seven. As they moved me, I heard them talking about my leg. One of them said something about being careful so that my left leg didn't come off.

My system was in shock, so I felt no pain—not then, anyway. That came later.

They laid me on a gurney and started to roll me toward the ambulance. A light mist sprayed my face, and I saw nothing except the superstructure of the bridge above me. I was unable to move my head. I heard people walking around and glass crunching under their feet. They kept their voices low, so I had trouble following what they were saying.

I remember thinking, *Something terrible has happened here, and I think it's happened to me.* Even when I knew they were moving me into the ambulance, I felt weightless.

I don't remember anything about the ambulance ride, but later I learned that we went to two hospitals, both of which were little more than rural clinics.

"There's nothing we can do for him," I heard one doctor say as he examined me. "He's not going to make it. You may have gotten him out of the car alive, but it won't do any good. He's past hope."

They put me back inside the ambulance and drove away. I vaguely remember when they pulled up at the Huntsville Hospital, a fairly large regional medical center. It was about 2:30 P.M.

By then the authorities had notified my wife, Eva. She teaches school, and someone had called the school to tell her about the accident. Someone else called the schools where our three children attended. Church members picked up our children and took them to their homes to keep them until they heard from Eva.

No one knew then that I had died hours earlier. For the first hours after I returned to earth, they had no idea how extensive my injuries were. Even though they knew nothing specific, church people began to pray for my recovery. They called others to join with them.

Eva found out I had died from Dick Onerecker almost two weeks after the accident on one of Dick's visits to see me in the hospital. It was only then that she understood just how bad it had been. Also, by that time our insurance agent, Ann Dillman, a member of South Park, had brought pictures of the wreckage after it had been moved from the bridge. Eva says it was quite some time before she really understood how bad it was. She says she probably didn't pay attention to the bad news on purpose because she was trying to focus on immediate matters at hand.

Our children, other family members, and friends then began to piece together just how horrendous the accident was and how close I came to not surviving it.

⁓⚬⚬⁓

One of the EMTs said, "We're here now. You're going to be all right."

I was aware of being wheeled into the hospital. I stared uncomprehendingly at a large number of people who pulled back to make space and watched the gurney roll past them. Faces stared down at me, and our eyes met for a split second as the gurney kept moving.

They took me into a room where a doctor was waiting for me. It's strange, but the only thing I recall about the doctor who examined me was that he was bald. He spent quite a while checking me over. "Mr. Piper, we're going to do everything we can to save you," he must have said three times. "You're hurt bad, seriously hurt, but we'll do all we can." Despite his words, I later learned that he didn't expect me to survive. But he did everything he could to give me hope and urge me to fight to stay alive. Several people moved around me. They were obviously trying to save my life, but I still felt no pain. It was like living in some kind of twilight state where I could feel nothing and remained only vaguely aware of what went on around me.

"We have your wife on the phone," someone said. They patched her through on the telephone to the emergency room. A nurse laid the phone beside my ear, and I remember talking to Eva, but I can't recall one word either of us said.

Eva remembers the entire conversation. According to her, the only thing I said was, "I'm so sorry this happened."

"It's okay, Don. It's not your fault."

Over and over I kept saying, "I'm so sorry. I just wanted to come home. Please bring me home." In some kind of childlike way, I suppose I felt that if I couldn't be in my heavenly home, I wanted to be back in my earthly one.

I was alert enough to know that they wanted to transport me on a Life Flight helicopter to Hermann Hospital Trauma Center in Houston. But they decided that the weather was too bad and the cloud ceiling too low, so their helicopter couldn't take off.

My condition was deteriorating rapidly, and they didn't know if I was going to survive the afternoon. Despite that, the medical team made a significant decision: They decided to put me back inside an ambulance for the eighty-mile trip to Houston. They didn't have the facilities to take care of me. Hermann Hospital was the only place for me if I was to have any chance to survive.

They brought around a new ambulance. It's amazing that as injured as I was—and they still thought I could "expire" at any second—I became aware of little things such as the fresh odors of a new vehicle, especially the fresh paint.

"You're our first patient," the attendant said as we drove away.

"What?"

"You're the first person to ever ride in this ambulance," he said. "We're going to take you to Houston. We'll get you there as fast as we can."

"How fast do I go?" the driver asked the attendant who sat next to me.

"As fast as you can."

"How fast is that?" the driver asked again.

"Put the pedal to the metal! We've got to get there—*now!*"

Before we started the trip, I still had felt no pain. I was in and out of consciousness. I felt weightless, as if my mind had no connection with my body. However, about ten minutes down the road, a slight throbbing began. At first, I became aware of a tiny pain in my left arm. Then my left leg throbbed. My head started to ache. Within minutes I hurt in so many places, I couldn't localize any of it. My entire body groaned in agony and screamed for relief. The full force of the trauma invaded my body. It felt as if every part of my body had been wounded, punched, or beaten. I couldn't think of a single spot that didn't scream out in pain. I think I cried out but I'm not sure. Every beat of my heart felt like sledgehammers pounding every inch of my body.

"You've got to do something! Please!" I finally pleaded. That much I remember. "Medicine—just something to—"

"I've given you all I can."

"You've given me all you can?" His words didn't make sense. If they'd given me medication, why was I feeling so much pain? "Please—"

"I can't let you go unconscious," the attendant said. "You have to remain awake."

"Please—just something to—"

I couldn't understand why I had to remain awake. If they'd just knock me out, the pain would go away. "Please," I begged again.

"I'm sorry. I really am, but I can't give you anything else. You've already had enough to throw most people into a coma. You're a fairly big guy, but I just can't let you go unconscious."

I'm sure I whimpered, moaned, or even screamed several times during the rest of the torturous ride. The vehicle rocked back and forth, in and out of traffic, and the entire time the siren blared. It was the most painful, nightmarish trip of my life.

Even now I can close my eyes and feel the ambulance vibrating and bumping on the shoulder of the road as it took the curves.

One of the EMTs said something about rush-hour traffic just getting heavy, so I assumed it must be around 5:00. Momentarily, I wondered how it could be so late in the day.

The drive seemed interminable, although I think I passed out several times from the pain. We finally arrived at the emergency room in Houston at Hermann Hospital.

It was 6:20 P.M. Six and a half hours had passed from the time of the accident.

By the time I reached the hospital in Houston, thousands of people were praying. They spread the word so that members in hundreds of churches also prayed for my recovery. For the next few days, word spread about my injuries, and more people prayed. Over the years, I've met many of those who asked God to spare my life. Perhaps some of you reading this book prayed for my survival and recovery. I can only add that the prayers were effective: I lived, and I'm still alive.

As the EMTs lifted my gurney out of the ambulance, I spotted Eva's face. Next to her stood a deacon from our church. I felt as if they were looking at some lost puppy, given my pathetic appearance. They were amazed, gawking, but saying nothing.

Eva stared at me. Until that moment, I had been only vaguely aware of what was going on with my body. The pain had not abated, but I still had not reasoned out that I had been in an accident. It didn't occur to me that I was dying.

As I stared into her face, I recognized the anguish in her eyes. She probably said something to try to comfort me, I don't know. What stays with me is that I sensed her pain and that she feared I wouldn't live.

That's when I knew I must have been in really bad shape—and I was. My chest had already turned purple, and medics had bandaged almost every part of my body. Tiny pieces of glass were embedded in my face, chest, and head. I was aware that tiny shards had fallen out of my skin and rested on the gurney next to my head.

No one had to tell me that I looked hideous. Anyone who knew me wouldn't have recognized me. I wondered how Eva had known who I was.

My pain was off the scale. Once inside the trauma center, a nurse gave me a shot of morphine—and then followed up with several more shots. Nothing helped. Nothing dulled the pain.

Shortly after my arrival at Hermann, they sent me to surgery, where I remained for eleven hours. Under anesthesia, I finally felt no pain.

Our dear friend Cliff McArdle valiantly stayed with Eva throughout the night. Cliff, my best friend David Gentiles, and I had been ministry friends since our graduation from seminary and remain close to this day.

By the time I was conscious again, it was Thursday morning. When I opened my eyes, somehow I knew that I had become the first patient in a newly opened ICU pod. One nurse was cleaning my wounds while another was putting me into traction. I could feel that she was putting rods between my ankle and my arm. I heard myself scream.

"We've done an MRI on you," the doctor said. Until then I wasn't aware that he was also in the room. "You're very seriously injured, but the good news is that you have no head or thoracic injuries."

At the time, I didn't care where my injuries were. The throbbing pains were racing through my body. I hurt more than I thought was humanly possible.

I just wanted relief.

When Dick Onerecker came to see me two weeks after the accident, I had just been moved from the ICU to a hospital room. He told me about God telling him to pray for me and that he had done that for several minutes.

"The best news is that I don't have any brain damage or any internal injuries," I said.

Dick chuckled. "Of course you don't. That's what God told me to pray for, and God answered."

"You believed that? You believed that God would answer that prayer?"

"Yes, I did," he said. "I knew with all the other injuries you had incurred that God was going to answer my prayer."

It took a few seconds for me to absorb what he'd said. From the force and intensity of the impact, I would have had internal injuries. Even the doctor had commented—in amazement—that I had neither head nor thoracic injuries.

"I'll tell you this," I said. "I know I had internal injuries, but somewhere between that bridge and this hospital I don't anymore."

Tears ran down Dick's face, and he said, "I know. I wish I could pray like that all the time."

# 6
# THE RECOVERY BEGINS

And we can be confident that he will listen to us whenever we ask him for anything in line with his will. And if we know he is listening when we make our requests, we can be sure that he will give us what we ask for.

1 JOHN 5:14–15

Pain became my constant companion. For a long time I would not know what it was like not to hurt all over my body.

Despite that, within a few days of the accident, I began to realize how many miracles had occurred. I refer to them as miracles—although some may call them fortunate circumstances—because I believe there are no accidents or surprises with God.

First, I wore my seat belt. I shamefully admit that I had not "bothered" to wear one until I got ticketed. That morning, I had consciously belted myself in.

Second, the accident happened on the bridge. What if it had happened on the open highway across the lake when I was headed toward the bridge? My car would have plunged down at least thirty feet into the lake, and I would have drowned.

Third, I had no head injuries. Anyone who saw me or read the medical report said it was impossible that I suffered no brain damage. (Eva still jokes that on occasion she's not so sure I didn't.) Just as bewildering to all the medical people was that the accident affected none of my internal organs. That fact defied all medical explanation.

Fourth, orthopedic surgeon Dr. Tom Greider, who was on duty at Hermann Hospital that day, saved my leg. Dr. Greider "just happened to be" one of the few experts in the United States who deals with such bizarre trauma. He chose to use a fairly new, experimental procedure, the Ilizarov frame. He performed the surgery one week after my accident. The implanted Ilizarov not only saved my leg, but also allowed them to lengthen the bone in my left leg after I had lost four inches of my femur in the accident. The femur is the largest bone in the human body and quite difficult to break.

When Dr. Greider examined me, he faced a choice. He could use the Ilizarov frame or amputate. Even if he chose to use the Ilizarov frame, there was no guarantee that I would not lose the leg. In fact, at that stage, he wasn't even certain I would pull through the ordeal. A less-skilled and less-committed doctor might have amputated, assuming it wouldn't make much difference because I would die anyway.

Fifth, people prayed for me. I have thousands of cards, letters, and prayer-grams, many from people I don't know in places I've never been who prayed for me because they heard of the accident. I've since had people tell me that this experience changed their prayer lives and their belief in the power of prayer.

On the night I entered Hermann Trauma Center, I was in surgery for eleven hours. During that operation, I had the broken bone in my right leg set. My left forearm had to be stabilized because two inches of each bone were missing. My left leg was put into traction because four and a half inches of femur were missing. During the operation, an air tube was mistakenly inserted into my stomach. This caused my stomach to inflate and my lungs to deflate. It would be several days before they discovered that this was the cause of the swelling in my stomach. Further complicating my breathing, I was unable to be elevated, and I developed pneumonia. I nearly died a second time.

Because of many bruises and the severity of my obvious wounds, my doctors hardly knew where to start. Other less serious problems became obvious weeks later. Several years passed before they discovered a fractured pelvis that they had missed initially.

I lay on my bed with needles everywhere, unable to move, dependent on the life-support apparatus. I could barely see over the top of my oxygen mask. During most of those days in the ICU, I was in and out of consciousness. Sometimes I'd wake up and see people standing in front of my bed and would wonder, *Am I really here or am I just imagining this?*

Monitors surrounded me, and a pulse oximeter on my finger tracked my oxygen level. Because I wasn't getting enough oxygen, the alarm went off often, bringing nurses racing into my room.

The ICU in Hermann is near the helipad; helicopters took off and landed at all hours of the day. When I was awake, I felt as if I were in a Vietnam movie. There were no clocks in the room, so I had no concept of time.

Other people lay in beds near me, often separated by nothing more than a curtain. More than once I awakened and saw orderlies carrying out a stretcher with a sheet over the body. As a pastor, I knew that many people don't leave the ICU alive.

*Am I next?* I'd ask myself.

Although I asked the question, the pain prevented my caring. I just wanted not to hurt, and dying would be a quick answer.

I had experienced heaven, returned to earth, and then suffered through the closest thing to hell on earth I ever want to face. It would be a long time before my condition or my attitude changed.

Nightmarish sounds filled the days and the nights. Moans, groans, yells, and screams frequently disrupted my rest and jerked me to consciousness. A nurse would come to my bed and ask, "Can I help you?"

"What are you talking about?" I'd ask. Sometimes I'd just stare at her, unable to understand why she was asking.

"You sounded like you're in great pain."

*I am,* I'd think, and then I'd ask, "How would you know that?"

"You cried out."

That's when I realized that sometimes the screams I heard came from me. Those groans or yells erupted when I did something as simple as trying to move my hand or my leg. Living in the ICU was horrible. They were doing the best they could, but the pain never let up.

"God, is this what I came back for?" I cried out many times. "You brought me back to earth for this?"

My condition continued to deteriorate. I had to lie flat on my back because of the missing bone in my left leg. (They never found the bone. Apparently, it was ejected from the car into the lake when my leg was crushed between the car seat and dashboard.) Because of having to lie flat, my lungs filled with fluid.

Still not realizing my lungs were collapsed, nurses and respiratory therapists tried to force me to breathe into a large plastic breathing device called a spirometer to improve my lung capacity.

On my sixth day, I was so near death that the hospital called my family to come to see me. I had developed double pneumonia, and they didn't think I would make it through the night.

I had survived the injuries; now I was dying of pneumonia. My doctor talked to Eva.

"We're going to have to do something," he told her. "We're either going to have to remove the leg or do something else drastic."

"How drastic?"

"If we don't do something, your husband won't be alive in the morning."

That's when the miracle of prayer really began to work. Hundreds of people had been praying for me since they learned of the accident, and I knew that. Yet, at that point, nothing had seemed to make any difference.

Eva called my best friend, David Gentiles, a pastor in San Antonio. "Please, come and see Don. He needs you," she said.

Without any hesitation, my friend canceled everything and jumped into his car. He drove nearly two hundred miles to see me. The nursing staff allowed him into my room in ICU for only five minutes.

Those minutes changed my life.

I never made this decision consciously, but as I lay there with little hope of recovery—no one had suggested I'd ever be normal again—I didn't want to live. Not only did I face the ordeal of never-lessening pain but I had been to heaven. I wanted to return to that glorious place of perfection. "Take me back, God," I prayed, "please take me back."

Memories filled my mind, and I yearned to stand at that gate once again. "Please, God."

God's answer to that prayer was "no."

When David entered my room, I was disoriented from the pain and the medication. I was so out of it that first I had to establish in my mind that he was real. *Am I hallucinating this?* I asked myself.

Just then, David took my fingers, and I felt his touch. Yes, he was real.

He clasped my fingers because that was all he could hold. I had so many IVs that my veins had collapsed; I had a trunk line that went into my chest and directly to my heart. I used to think of my many IVs as soldiers lined up. I even had IVs in the veins in the tops of my feet. I could look down and see them and realize they'd put needles in my feet because there was no place left on my body.

"You're going to make it," David said. "You have to make it. You've made it this far."

"I don't have to make it. I'm not sure . . . I . . . I don't know if I want to make it."

"You have to. If not for yourself, then hold on for us."

"I'm out of gas," I said. "I've done all I can. I've given it all I can. I don't have anything else to give." I paused and took several breaths, because even to say two sentences sapped an immense amount of energy.

"You have to make it. We won't let you go."

"If I make it, it'll be because all of you want it. I don't want it. I'm tired. I've fought all I can and I'm ready to die."

"Well, then you won't have to do a thing. We'll do it for you."

Uncomprehending, I stared at the intensity on his face.

"We won't let you die. You understand that, Don? We won't let you give up."

"Just let me go—"

"No. You're going to live. Do you hear that? You're going to live. We won't let you die."

"If I live," I finally said, "it'll be because you want me to."

"We're going to pray," he said. Of course, I knew people had been praying already, but he added, "We're going to pray all night. I'm going to call everybody I know who can pray. I want you to know that those of us who care for you are going to stay up all night in prayer for you."

"Okay."

"We're going to do this for you, Don. You don't have to do anything."

I really didn't care whether they prayed or not. I hurt too badly; I didn't want to live.

"We're taking over from here. You don't have to do a thing— not a thing—to survive. All you have to do is just lie there and let it happen. We're going to pray you through this."

He spoke quietly to me for what was probably a minute or two. I don't think I said anything more. The pain intensified—if that was possible—and I couldn't focus on anything else he said.

"We're going to take care of this." David kissed me on the forehead and left.

An all-night prayer vigil ensued. That vigil marked a turning point in my treatment and another series of miracles.

The pneumonia was gone the next day. They prayed it away. And the medical staff discovered the error with the breathing tube.

On that seventh day, in another long surgery, Dr. Greider installed the Ilizarov device so that I could sit up and receive

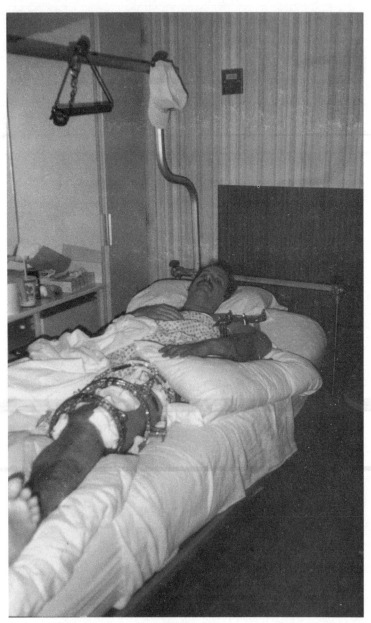

*Don wearing the Ilizarov bone growth device.*

breathing treatments. They also deflated my stomach, which allowed my lungs to inflate.

Normally, hospitals require six months of counseling before they will authorize the use of the Ilizarov frame. In my case, the medical staff could give Eva no guarantee that the experimental procedure would work. They also told her that using the Ilizarov frame would cause me considerable physical pain as well as extraordinary emotional and psychological distress. Worse, they warned that even after going through all of that, I might still lose my leg.

"This is extremely painful and takes months—maybe years— to recover," the surgeon said to Eva. Again he reminded her of the worst that could happen—that I might still lose the leg. "However, if we don't go this route, we have no choice but to amputate."

He quietly explained that if they amputated they would fit me with a prosthesis, and I'd have to learn to walk with it.

Eva had no illusions about the extent of my injury or how long I would have to endure excruciating pain. She debated the pros and cons for several minutes and prayed silently for guidance. "I'll sign the consent form," she finally said.

The next morning, when I awakened after another twelve hours of surgery, I stared at what looked like a huge bulge under the covers where my left leg had been. When I uncovered myself, what I saw took my breath away. On my left leg was a massive stainless steel halo from my hip to just below my knee. A nurse came in and started moving around, doing things around my leg, but I wasn't sure what she did.

I became aware of Eva sitting next to my bed. "What is that?" I asked. "What's she doing?"

"We need to talk about it," she said. "It's what I agreed to yesterday. It's a bone-growth device. We call it a fixator. It's the only chance for the doctors to save your left leg," she said. "I believe it's worth the risk."

I'm not sure I even responded. What was there to say? She had made the best decision she could and had been forced to make it alone.

Just then, I spotted wires leading from the device. "Are those wires going through my leg?"

"Yes."

I shook my head uncomprehendingly. "They're going *through* my leg?"

"It's a new technique. They're trying to save your leg."

I didn't know enough to comment. I nodded and tried to relax.

"I believe it will work," she said.

I hoped she was right. Little did I know that nearly a year later I would still be staring at it.

# DECISIONS AND CHALLENGES

7

Can anyone ever separate us from Christ's love? Does it mean he no longer loves us if we have trouble or calamity, or are persecuted, or are hungry or cold or in danger or threatened with death? (Even the Scriptures say, "For your sake we are being killed every day; we are being slaughtered like sheep.")

ROMANS 8:35–36

One of the most difficult things for me—aside from my own physical pain—was to see the reaction of my family members and close friends. My parents live in Louisiana, about 250 miles from Houston, but they arrived the day after my first surgery. My mother is a strong woman, and I always thought she could handle anything. But she walked into the ICU, stared at me, and then crumpled in a faint. Dad had to grab her and carry her out.

Her collapse made me aware of how pitiful I looked.

Most of those first days remain a blur to me. I wasn't sure if people really visited me or if I only hallucinated—and from what Eva and the nurses told me, I sometimes was delirious.

The hospital allowed visitors to come in each day, a few at a time. Even when they said nothing, their sad, pitying eyes made it clear to me how they felt. I write *clear to me* because I know how I perceived them. In retrospect, I may have been mistaken. I suspect I was so positive I would die—and I wanted to—that I saw in their eyes what I was feeling about myself.

Accurate or not, I felt as if they were staring at a mangled body and not a living person, that despite the assuring and comforting words they spoke, they expected me to die at any moment. I wondered if they had come to pay their last respects before I closed my eyes forever.

Though my pneumonia was gone, we still had to treat its aftermath. Nurses came in every four hours for respiratory therapy treatments. They beat on my chest and forced me to breathe through a plastic mouthpiece an awful-smelling, terrible-tasting stuff that was supposed to coat my lungs. This treatment would prevent the pneumonia from recurring and help restore my lungs. I'd wake up and see people coming in, and I'd think, *Oh no, here we go. They're going to make me breathe that stuff and pound on me and try to get the phlegm dislodged.* As painful as they were, the treatments worked. Dr. Houchins, the head of the Hermann trauma team, came in several times a day. What Dr. Houchins may have lacked in bedside manner, he made up in sheer bulldog determination not to lose any of his patients.

He demanded that I breathe. "Don't quit now. Don't quit. Keep trying." It wasn't just the words he spoke, but—as sick as I was—I felt as if he fought right alongside me. "Don't give up. Keep trying."

Often I didn't have the energy to breathe and just stopped trying.

I saw the pained expression on his face and then watched his features contort into an angry intensity. "Did you hear what I said? Do it! Now! Breathe and cough! Do it."

I shook my head. I just didn't have the strength to do anything more.

"This is not negotiable. Do this right now! Breathe!"

"I can't."

"All right, don't do it. You're dead. You're going to die if you don't do it. Can you get that into your mind?"

I didn't want to live, but something happened when he yelled at me.

I breathed.

Shortly after that, the staff figured out how to elevate my leg so I could sit up. Just to sit up was a great step forward. I didn't think I'd ever get to lie on my side or stomach again.

Once while I was still in the ICU, it seemed as if every time I opened my eyes and blinked, within seconds someone thrust a spoon filled with food about six inches from my mouth.

"Just open up."

One time it was a man's voice.

I opened my eyes and stared. Holding the spoon was a burly man. He lifted my oxygen mask and gently poked the spoon into my mouth. "That's it, just take a bite."

I obeyed and swallowed while my drugged mind tried to figure out what was going on.

Slowly I realized that the voice belonged to Stan Mauldin, head football coach and athletic director of the Alvin High School Yellow Jackets. Our daughter would live with Stan and Suzan and their two children during my convalescence. Coach Mauldin had heard that because I wouldn't eat, I was losing weight at an alarming rate. (Although I had lost only a few pounds then, within my first six weeks in the hospital I lost nearly fifty pounds.)

As soon as Stan heard about the situation, he made time in his demanding schedule to show up at Hermann Hospital. He didn't just drop in to visit. He asked the nurses to give him my food, and he sat beside my bed until I awakened.

As soon as he realized I was fully awake, Stan shoveled in the food and talked while I did my best to chew and listen. That gentle act of sacrifice by a bear of a man was one of the most thoughtful acts I witnessed during my days of recovery. Stan epitomizes strength and tenderness combined in one exceptional person.

I've referred to the Ilizarov frame, which may have sounded like a common procedure. It was far from that. Eva had to make a decision no one should have to make alone. She had to decide whether to allow the then-experimental Ilizarov process.

Initially this device was used to stretch legs. Its invention came about to help individuals who have a congenital condition where one leg is shorter than the other—some as much as twelve inches—and have to rely on wheelchairs, calipers, or crutches. The Ilizarov frame forces the bone in the leg to grow while keeping the surrounding tissue intact. The body can form new bone between gaps in response to the mechanical force of the Ilizarov frame.

The Ilizarov bone growth device is what they call an external fixator. A Siberian doctor named Ilizarov invented it.

Dr. Ilizarov experimented on sheep to develop a way to grow missing bones or lengthen congenitally short bones. For missing bone cases like mine, the application involves breaking a limb with a clean break. Wires about the size of piano wire are placed through the skin and bone, and they exit out the other side.

The femur Ilizarov device is anchored in the hip by rods about the size of pencils. The doctors drilled holes for four large rods from my groin to the side of my left hip. After they did that, I had at least thirty holes in my left leg. Many of them went completely through my leg and out the other side. The larger ones just went into the flesh, and rods were embedded in the pelvis. After about six months passed, I could actually see down inside my leg as the pinholes stretched out.

Every day someone would come in and turn the screws on the Ilizarov device to stretch the bones. Most of the time the nursing staff took on this task. After I came home, Eva did it. For nearly a year, my left femur bone would regrow and replace the missing piece. It's an ingenious device, although terribly painful, requiring an arduous, lengthy recovery. I called it "hideously wonderful."

Six rods also went through the top of my left arm and came out the other side. Big stainless steel bars were placed above and below the arm to stabilize it, because both forearm bones were missing. The rods were the size of a pencil and allowed Dr. Greider to harvest bones from my right pelvis and place them in my left forearm. The doctor explained that this was like taking core samples when drilling an oil well. They also harvested about thirty-two square inches of skin from my right leg to place over the enormous wound in my left arm. Then they embedded a Teflon strip between the newly constructed bones in my forearm in order to prevent the new bones from adhering to each other—that is, attaching themselves and growing together.

Unfortunately for me, that part of the technique didn't work—the bones healed, but they attached themselves to each other. Consequently, I have no pronation or supination in my left arm—my arm does not straighten out at the elbow, and I can't turn palms up or palms down. When I extend my arm, my hand is always in a hand-shaking position. My hand cannot twist either right or left. I know all this seems barbaric, and at the time it felt like it. But like the Ilizarov, it works.

Yes, the Ilizarov device worked—and it was also the most painful process I endured as part of my recovery.

The stainless steel Ilizarov on my leg weighed about thirty pounds, and the external fixator on my arm probably weighed another twenty. Whether I was in my wheelchair (about eight months), on my rolling walker (three more months), or eventually my crutches (four more months), I carried that extra weight around for nearly a year.

Can you imagine the strange stares I received everywhere I went? People gasped and gawked at a man in a wheelchair with steel rods sticking out all over his body.

Virtually every time I made my routine visit to Dr. Greider's office in my wheelchair, the reaction of the other patients was universal. Though each wore casts or braces or walked on crutches, all of them would stare at me and my rods and halos. Then without fail, someone would say somewhat sardonically, "Wow, and I thought I was bad off." Occasionally, someone would even add, "After seeing you, I feel better." For a long time, I became the standard by which painful injury was judged.

I've often kidded others that because of all this "metalwork," if archaeologists discover my body years from now, they'll think they've found a new species! My anatomy has been completely rearranged.

Never again will I take simple physical ability for granted. During my recovery, even the tiniest movement was a miracle. Every time I relearned how to do something, it felt like an achievement.

Only later did I understand how hard Dr. Greider had worked to find a way to save my left leg and arm. I'll always be grateful that he didn't just give up on me.

My right knee was crushed, and I wore a cast on it for quite some time. They put a small, mesh basket around the kneecap so it would heal. My right arm was the only limb that didn't break.

Even with the success of the Ilizarov frame, however, the pain didn't leave—not for one minute.

I wonder how many times I asked, "How long?" I wanted to know how long I'd have to endure the device, how long before I'd know if it worked, how long before I'd walk again.

No one would—or could—give me an answer, but I kept asking anyway.

"A few months," was the usual answer.

"How few?" I persisted.

One of the doctors finally said, "Many months. Maybe longer."

"You mean possibly a few years?"

"Yes, perhaps years."

"And there's no guarantee that I'm going to be able to keep these limbs?"

71

"There's no guarantee. An infection could come on suddenly, and we'd be forced to remove your leg."

"You mean I could endure this for months and still end up with no leg?"

He nodded.

Obviously, that wasn't what I wanted to hear. Even though Eva had told me the same thing, denial must have set in. I kept seeking a guarantee that I would fully recover.

I wanted answers, but perhaps even more than that, I wanted assurance that I would be well. I wanted to be normal again. I wanted to be able to walk out of the hospital on my own two legs and go back to my former way of life. No one was willing—or able—to give me those assurances.

Many months passed, but one day I did walk back into that hospital and hug all those nurses.

During the months after I received the Ilizarov frame, I had other problems. I developed infections—several times. Each time, I faced the reality that it might rage through my body and I would wake up without my leg.

I also had infections after they released me. Three times I had to be rehospitalized, put in isolation, and receive massive amounts of antibiotics to cure the infections.

Even then, many nights I prayed, *God, take me back to heaven. I don't know why you brought me back to earth. Please don't leave me here.*

God's answer to that prayer was still "no."

I still don't know all the reasons, but in the months and years ahead, I slowly understood at least some of the reasons I had returned to earth.

The healing process had begun. As I lay in that hospital bed day after day, I slowly acknowledged that God had sent me back to earth. I couldn't figure out why I had to endure the physical suffering, but I kept thinking of the words of David Gentiles. He and others had cried out in prayer for me to live. Because God had answered them, there had to be a purpose in my staying alive.

Through days of intense agony, I would remember David's words. Sometimes the sense that God had a purpose in my being alive was all that kept me going.

I was in Hermann ICU for twelve days. Then I stayed four to five days in Hermann Hospital before they transferred me down the street to St. Luke's Hospital. Both hospitals are part of the world's largest medical center. I remained in St. Luke's for 105 days. Once I was home, I lay in bed for thirteen months and endured thirty-four surgeries. Without question, I am still alive because people prayed for me, beginning with Dick Onerecker and other people around the country, many of whom I've never met.

That's perhaps the biggest miracle: *People prayed and God honored their prayers.*

As I look back, I see how many people God used to save me. Dick Onerecker saved my life by his continued praying. Dr. Greider saved my leg and my arm and got me through that initial surgery. Dr. Houchins saved my life after the surgery because of his bulldog determination to keep me alive. The courageous nurses of the orthopedic floor of St. Luke's Hospital cared for me day and night. Each of them played a vital role.

I attribute leaving ICU alive to the prayers of David Gentiles and the others. "We're taking over from here. You don't have to do a thing to survive. We're going to pray you through this."

I knew I wasn't going to die.

God's people wouldn't let me.

# 8
# PAIN AND ADJUSTMENTS

Don't be afraid, for I am with you. Do not be dismayed, for I am your God. I will strengthen you. I will help you. I will uphold you with my victorious right hand.

ISAIAH 41:10

Even though they didn't realize it, visitors made my situation worse. They cared for me and wanted to express that concern. Because they cared, they did the most natural thing in the world—they visited my hospital room. That was the problem.

The constant flow in and out of my room exhausted me. I couldn't just lie there and allow them to sit with me or talk at me. Maybe I needed to function in my role as pastor or felt some kind of obligation to entertain them. I didn't want to hurt anyone's feelings by asking him or her to leave or not to come.

Many days, I smiled and chatted with them when all I really wanted to do was collapse. Sometimes the intense pain made it almost impossible for me to be a good host, but I still tried to be gracious. I kept reminding myself that they cared and had made an effort to see me.

Between friends, relatives, and church members, I felt as if a line stretched from the front door of the hospital to my room. Eva came in one afternoon and realized how much the visitors disturbed me. She chided me for allowing it.

I think she figured out that I wouldn't tell anyone not to come back, so she asked the nursing staff to cut back on the number of visitors they allowed. It didn't stop everyone from coming, but it did cut down the traffic in and out of the room.

Besides the pain and the flow of people in and out of my room, I lived in depression. A large part of it may have been the natural result of the trauma to my body and some of it may have been my reaction to the many drugs. I believe, however, that because I faced an unknown outcome and the pain never let up, I kept feeling I had little future to look forward to. Most of the time I didn't want to live.

Why was I brought back from a perfect heaven to live a pain-filled life on earth? No matter how hard I tried, I couldn't enjoy living again; I wanted to go back to heaven.

Pain has become a way of life for me since the accident, as I am sure it has for many. It's curious that we can learn to live with such conditions. Even now, on rare occasions when I am lying in bed after a good night's sleep, I will suddenly notice that I don't hurt anywhere. Only then am I reminded that I live in continuous pain the other twenty-three hours and fifty-five minutes of each day.

It took a while for me to realize how profoundly my condition affected my emotions.

I prayed and others prayed with me, but a sense of despair began to set in. "Is it worth all this?" I asked several times every day.

The doctors and nurses kept trying to push medications on me for my depression, but I refused. I'm not sure why. Perhaps because I had so much medicine in me, I didn't want any more. Besides, I didn't think more medicine would do any good.

I wanted to be free from my miserable existence and die. Obviously, I felt wholly unequipped to deal with that turn of events. I now know that I was a textbook depression case.

Soon everyone else knew it too.

"Would you like to talk to a psychiatrist?" my doctor asked.

"No," I said.

A few days later, one of the nurses asked, "Would you like me to call in a therapist? Someone you could talk to?"

My answer was the same.

Because I didn't want to talk to anyone, what I called "stealth shrinks" began to creep into my room.

"I see you've been in a very severe accident," one undercover psychiatrist said after reading my chart. He tried to get me to talk about how I felt.

"I don't want to talk about the accident," I said. The truth is, I couldn't. How could I possibly explain to anyone what had happened to me during the ninety minutes I was gone from this earth? How could I find words to express the inexpressible? I didn't know how to explain that I had literally gone to heaven. I was sure that if I started talking that way, he'd know I was crazy.

He'd think something had gone dreadfully wrong with my mind, that I had hallucinated, or that I needed stronger drugs to take away my delusions. How could I put into words that I had had the most joyful, powerful experience of my life? How could I sound rational by saying I preferred to die? I knew what was waiting, but he didn't.

I had no intention of talking to a psychiatrist (or anyone else) about what had happened to me. I saw that experience as something too intimate, too intense to share. As close as Eva and I are, I couldn't even tell her at that time.

Going to heaven had been too sacred, too special. I felt that talking about my ninety minutes in heaven would defile those precious moments. I never doubted or questioned whether my trip to heaven had been real. That never troubled me. Everything had been so vivid and real, I couldn't possibly deny it. No, the problem was I didn't want to share that powerful experience with anyone.

That didn't stop the psychiatrists from coming into my room and trying to help me. After a few times, they didn't tell me they were psychiatrists. It's humorous now, but the hospital psychiatrists were determined to help me. After I refused to talk to them, they would sneak into my room and observe me. Sometimes they came in while a nurse was working on me. Other times they came in and studied my chart and said nothing, and I assumed they expected me to start a conversation.

Often they'd walk in and say something like, "I'm Dr. Jones," but nothing else. The doctor might check my pulse and ask, "How's your stomach?" He'd examine my chart and ask pertinent questions. Eventually, he'd give himself away with a simple question such as "How do you feel today?"

"About the same."

"How do you really feel about all of this?" No matter how they varied the routine, they always asked how I *really* felt.

"You're a psychiatrist, aren't you?" I'd ask.

"Well, uh, actually, yes."

"Okay, what do you want to know? You want to know if I'm depressed? The answer is I'm very depressed. And I don't want to talk about it."

The conversations went on, but I've blotted most of them from my mind. Even though I knew Dr. Jones and the others were trying to help me, I didn't believe there was any hope. I hated being depressed, but I didn't know what to do about it.

The longer I lay in bed, the more convinced I became that I had nothing to look forward to. Heaven had been perfect—so beautiful and joyful. I wanted to be released from pain and go back.

"Why would anyone want to stay here after experiencing heaven?" I asked God. "Please, please take me back."

I didn't die, and I didn't get over my depression.

I didn't just refuse to talk to psychiatrists; I didn't want to talk to anyone about anything. I didn't want to see anyone. I would have been fine if no one visited me—or so I told myself.

In my depression, I just wanted to be left alone so I could die alone, without anyone trying to resuscitate me.

I also had enough pride as a professional and as a pastor that I didn't want anyone to see how bad off I was. I don't mean just the physical problems; I didn't want them to know about my low emotional state either.

When people did get into the room to see me, of course, their words and gazes made me feel as if they were saying, "You're the most pitiful thing I've ever seen."

I guess I was.

And so the depression continued. It would be a long time before God would give me another miracle.

I was the father of three children, the husband of a wonderful wife, and until the accident, a man with a great future. I was thirty-eight years old when the accident happened and until then, the picture of health and in great physical shape. Within days after my accident, I knew I would never be that virile, healthy man again. Now I was utterly helpless. I couldn't do anything for myself, not even lift my hand. Deep inside, I feared I would be helpless for the rest of my life.

As an example of my helplessness, I had not had a bowel movement for the first twelve days in the hospital. Knowing my system would turn septic, they gave me an enema, but that didn't do much good.

I say "not much good" because I would pass a tiny amount and the nurse or nursing assistant would smile with delight.

One day I managed to squeeze out a tiny bit. "Oh, that's so good. We're so happy for you. Let's wait. Maybe there'll be more."

In my depression, I'd think, *This is the most pitiful experience in my life. I'm like a baby and everybody gets excited over a tiny bowel movement.*

I don't remember what I said to the nursing assistant, but I'm sure I wasn't pleasant.

She left the room. That was one of those rare times when no one was visiting. I was totally alone and glad for the peace and quiet.

Within minutes after the nurse left, the enema took effect.

I exploded. I had the biggest bowel movement I've ever had in my life. The odor overwhelmed me.

In my panic, I clawed through the sheet and my fingers finally found the call button. Seconds later, the young nursing assistant raced into the room.

"I'm so sorry, I didn't mean to do this," I said. "I'll help you clean it up." The words had no sooner left my mouth before I realized I couldn't help her. I felt terrible, helpless, and loathsome.

I started to cry.

"No, no, no, don't worry about a thing. We're just so happy that you did it. This is good because it means your system is beginning to work again."

In humiliation, I could only lie there and watch the poor young woman change everything. It must have taken her at least half an hour to clean up and then at least twice that long for the odor to vanish.

My embarrassment didn't leave me, even though my mind tried to tell me differently. I had barely taken in any food for twelve days and this was a real breakthrough. I, however, could only think that this was one of the most embarrassing events in my life.

As awful as it seemed to me, more embarrassing, helpless experiences caught up with me. I had to have a urinal; I couldn't wipe myself; I couldn't shave. I couldn't even wash my hair. They had to bring special devices to lay my head in and pour water over my hair and then drain it down a tube to a garbage can. In yet another act of incredible kindness, Carol Benefield, who had cut my hair for years, came to trim my hair several times while I was confined to my bed. For these sixty-mile round-trips, Carol would accept no money whatsoever.

Friends, family, and medical personnel found ways of providing for all of my physical needs, but I could only think of myself as being completely, utterly helpless. My right arm, the one that hadn't been broken, had so many IVs in it that they had a piece of wood taped to me so I couldn't bend the arm.

I had IVs everywhere. They ran into my chest and entered the tops of my feet. They lined up in a major tube that went directly to my heart through my chest. Many of my veins collapsed. I was so completely incapacitated they had to lift me off the bed with chains to change my bedding or do anything else that required moving me.

I was losing weight at an alarming rate, which scared the doctors. I just couldn't eat anything and atrophy had set in. During the nearly four months I stayed in the hospital, I lost about sixty pounds. Before the accident I had weighed 210, and I got down to less than 150. The only way they could determine my weight was to put me in a sling like a baby to lift me up off the bed and weigh me. They tried to coax me into eating and tempted me by preparing my favorite foods, but nothing tasted good. Just the smell of food nauseated me. I had no appetite. I tried to eat, I really did, but I couldn't handle more than a few bites.

I assumed that depression stopped me from eating, although I don't know if that was the cause. I do know that when I tried, I couldn't force myself to chew anything. I didn't even want to swallow.

They attached me to a morphine pump they called a PC. Whenever the pain was really bad, I pushed a button to give myself a shot. I had to have pain medication constantly. At first I tried to resist taking more painkillers, but the doctor rebuked me for that. He said that my body was tensing from the pain and that retarded my healing.

At night they gave me additional medication to try to make me sleep. I write *try* because the additional medicine didn't work. Nothing they did put me to sleep—not sleeping pills, pain shots, or additional morphine. I had no way to get comfortable or even to feel relieved enough from pain to relax.

I've tried to explain it by saying it this way: "Imagine yourself lying in bed, and you've got rods through your arms, wires through your legs, and you're on your back. You can't turn over. In fact, just to move your shoulder a quarter of an inch is impossible unless you reach up and grab what looks like a trapeze bar that hangs above your bed. Even the exertion to move a fraction of an inch sends daggers of pain all through your body. You are completely immobile."

Because I began to break out with bedsores on my back due to being in one position too long, the hospital finally provided a special waterbed that constantly moved. That did take care of the bedsores.

The only time I ever left the room was when they wheeled me down to X-ray, which was always an adventure. Because of all the metal parts and equipment on me, they had trouble figuring out how to x-ray me. Three or four men wore lead suits in the X-ray room and held the lens and plates behind my steel-encased limbs, because no machine was designed to x-ray those types of things.

That also meant that some days I spent two or three hours in X-ray while the technicians tried to figure out how to take a picture so the doctors could see whether the bones were knitting. They had no precedent for a case such as mine.

When someone came to wheel me to X-ray, he'd always say, "We're taking a trip down the hall."

That was all they had to say, because I knew what they meant. To distract myself as the gurney cruised down the long hallways, I played a game of connect-the-dots with the ceiling tiles. I started that the day I came back from the first surgery. I was probably hallucinating, but I remember the ICU unit was brand-new, and I was the only patient. When they brought me in, I was moaning and couldn't stop. Then I saw the ceiling tiles, and as I stared at them, it seemed as if they were running together and forming some kind of pattern that I couldn't figure out. In my mind, I began making pictures and designs out of them. As I did that, I'd also think, *I'm going completely crazy.* But I did it anyway. Eventually, connecting the dots became a form of distraction allowing me to focus, if only momentarily, on something other than my pain.

The worst daily torment took place when a nurse cleaned the pinholes where the wires went into my skin. All the nurses that treated me on the orthopedic floor, the twenty-first floor of St. Luke's Hospital, had to be taught how to clean those pinholes. Because they didn't want the skin to adhere to the wire, they had to keep breaking the skin when it attached itself—as it did occasionally. Then the nurse forced hydrogen peroxide down each pinhole to prevent infection. I could think of nothing worse to endure, and it happened every day.

That wasn't all. Four times a day, every six hours, they'd take an Allen wrench and turn screws on the device. The idea was that this would stretch the ends of the bones inside the leg and eventually cause the growing bone to replace the missing bone. The turn hurt beyond description, even though each turn was very slight, less than half a millimeter. It didn't matter whether it was day or night, every six hours someone came into my room to turn the screws.

As a pastor, I had visited many hospital rooms, including trips to the ICU. I had seen agony on many faces, and I had frequently winced in sympathy. Even so, I couldn't imagine anything on a day-to-day basis that could be more painful.

Perhaps the worst part for me was that I never slept. For eleven and a half months I never went to sleep—I just passed out. Even with megadoses of morphine, I was never pain free. When they decided it was time for me to go to sleep, a nurse injected me with three or four shots of either morphine or another sleeping medicine. I'd lie in bed, and no matter how much I told myself to relax, I couldn't. I fought the pain and then, apparently, I passed out. My next conscious moment would be an awareness of intense pain. I felt nothing else in between.

Eventually, family members and even hospital personnel left me alone because they knew I didn't have a functioning body clock. I had no sense of time, and I couldn't relax, because I was under such tension. If I made the slightest effort to move, a wire embedded in my flesh would tear my skin at the point of entry. I could move, but the wires didn't. With even the tiniest movement, excruciating pain slashed through my entire body.

After a while, I learned to live with that situation, but I never got used to it.

The first person I "met" (we never saw each other in person) for whom the Ilizarov frame was used for its original purpose was Christy. The Ilizarov procedure was created to lengthen bones for people born with congenital birth defects. However, the device could not be attached until the bones had stopped growing. Especially during adolescence, bones grow at a very rapid pace, so doctors must carefully choose the right time for the procedure.

Christy, a teenage girl, was in the room next to mine. She had been born with one leg shorter than the other. Once her bones had matured, she had chosen surgery to attach the Ilizarov frame to have her bones lengthened so that both legs would be of normal size.

Because Christy's surgery was elective, she had some idea about the pain and the length of recovery she would have to go through. For months, she had gone through extensive counseling, and her family knew how to take care of the wounds. They also knew approximately how long it would take and the commitment they had to make to care for her.

The difference between Christy and me was that she knew what she was getting into—at least to the extent that anyone can. I woke up with the device already attached. In my depressed state, that made me feel even worse. Even though I knew they had put the Ilizarov frame on me to save my leg, I could only see it as the major source of my agony.

Another problem arose, although a minor one. Even though we had different doctors, the same staff people came into Christy's room and mine to turn the screws. Sometimes the wrenches got misplaced, and the attendant couldn't find them in my room so they'd rush over to Christy's for hers. Or they'd come and borrow mine. Fortunately for both of us, our fixators were interchangeable and someone could borrow wrenches from one room to adjust screws in the other room.

That's how I first learned about Christy—the borrowing of wrenches. We never saw each other face-to-face, but we did see each other's doctor, and somehow that, plus our common problem, created a bond between us.

Christy and I shared something else—pain. Many times I heard her crying. I don't mean weeping, but a cry, or a scream, and sometimes just a low moan. She probably heard similar sounds from my room as well. I wasn't as likely to cry because that's not my nature. One of the nurses suggested it might be better if I did let go and scream. Even though she may have been right, I never did—at least not consciously.

When I was in control of my faculties, I never cried out. I had heard others scream from their pain and their cries disturbed me greatly. Also, I had learned to keep my hurts and emotions to myself. I believed at that time that moans, wails, and screams did no good. The only times I screamed, I was either unconscious or heavily medicated. I learned about those outbursts because other people told me.

Although Christy and I never met during the twelve weeks we lived next door to each other, we corresponded by sending letters back and forth, and the nurses willingly acted as our mail carriers.

I tried to encourage Christy. She told me her story and was very sympathetic to my accident. She was also a believer. We corresponded on that level as well.

In some of my worst moments of self-pity, however, I would think that when all the pain was over, Christy would be a normal young woman; I would never be normal again. She could play and run and do everything a normal teen did. Even then I knew I would never run again.

I had many, many times of self-pity, reminding myself that she chose her pain, while I had no warning and no options. She knew in advance what she was getting into; I had no idea. She was doing something that positively impacted the rest of her life;

I was doing something just to save my life. Yes, self-pity filled my mind many, many days.

Always, however, I came back to one thing: God had chosen to keep me alive. Even in my worst moments of depression and self-pity, I never forgot that.

Christy and I shared similar pain. We also shared a faith that reminded us that our loving God was with us in the most terrible moments of suffering. Just having her in the next room comforted me, because I'd think, *I'm not the only one; somebody else understands how I feel.*

That's when I began to think of being part of an exclusive fraternity. In the years since my release, I've met other members of this reluctant and small fellowship. Because I knew what it felt like to suffer, I could understand their pain, just as Christy had felt mine and I had understood hers.

More than enduring, eventually I was able to do something doctors said I would never be able to do: I learned to walk again. I can stand on my own feet, put one foot in front of the other, and move.

They had warned me that because of the broken knee in my right leg, and the loss of the femur in my left (even with a replaced-and-stretched bone in place), I would not walk again, and if I did, I would be wearing heavy braces. More than once, I came close to losing my left leg, but somehow God took me through each crisis.

Therapy began on my arm about four weeks after the initial operation and on my legs two weeks after that.

About the same time, they put me in what I referred to as a Frankenstein bed. They strapped me to a large board and turned the bed so that my feet were on the floor and I was in a standing position, although still strapped to the bed. Two physical therapists placed a large belt around my waist and walked on either side of me. My legs had atrophied and grown extremely weak, so they helped me take my first steps. It took me days to learn to stand again so that I could put weight on my own legs. My equilibrium had changed because I had grown used to a horizontal position. I became incredibly nauseous each time they raised me into a vertical position. Days passed before I was used to that position enough to take my first step.

I didn't really learn to walk until after the hospital discharged me. A physical therapist came in every other day to help me. Six months would pass before I learned to walk on my own more than a few steps.

My doctor removed the Ilizarov device eleven and a half months after the accident. After that, I could use a walker and eventually a cane. I didn't walk without leg braces and a cane for a year and a half after the accident.

My accident occurred in January 1989. They removed the external metal work from my arm fixator in May, but they put internal metal plates down both of the bones of the forearm. Those metal plates stayed there for several more months.

In late November, they removed the fixator from my leg, but that wasn't the end. After that, I remained in a cast for a long time, and they inserted a plate in my leg—which stayed there for nine years. I was content to leave it there, but they said they had to take it out. My doctor explained that as I aged, the bones, relying on the plate for strength, would become brittle. As I learned, our bones become and remain strong only as a result of tension and use.

During those years with the fixator and the subsequent metal plates, whenever I had to fly, I set off metal detectors from Ohio to California. Rather than go through the customary walk-through detector, I would say to the security people, "I have more stainless steel in me than your silverware drawer at home."

They would wand me and smile. "You sure do."

My children took pride in referring to me as "Robopreacher" after the title character in the movie *Robocop*. After a horrible incident, doctors used high technology and metal plates to restore the policeman so he could fight crime.

Regardless of how barbaric all these rods and wires and plates might have seemed, they worked. People gasped when they saw them embedded in my flesh. Those same people are now awed at my mobility. But under this thin veneer of normalcy, I'm still a work in progress, always adjusting.

# 9
# ENDLESS ADJUSTMENTS

A friend is always loyal, and a brother is born to help in time
of need.

PROVERBS 17:17

I t's amazing how differently people responded after the accident. Several friends and members of South Park Church
saw me during those first five days after my accident. Many
of those same people saw me after the all-night prayer vigil that
David Gentiles instigated. As they watched each tiny step of my
recovery, they rejoiced. I saw everything in my recovery happening so slowly that acute depression continually gripped me.
After the ICU, I stayed in the hospital 105 days the first time. I
suppose depression would strike anyone who has been confined
that long.

During the months of my recovery, the church worked hard to make me feel useful. They brought vanloads of kids to the hospital to see me. Sometimes committees met in my hospital room—as if I could make any decisions. They knew I couldn't say or do much, but it was their way to affirm and encourage me. They did everything they could to make me feel worthwhile and useful.

Much of that time, however, I was depressed and filled with self-pity. I yearned to go back to heaven.

Beyond the depression, I had another problem: I didn't want anybody to do anything for me. That's my nature.

One day Jay B. Perkins, a retired minister, came to visit me. He had served as pastor of several south Texas churches before his retirement and had become a powerful father figure in the ministry for me. South Park hired him as the interim while I was incapacitated.

Jay visited me faithfully. That meant he had to drive more than forty miles each way. He came often to see me, sometimes two or three times a week. I wasn't fit company, but I smiled each time anyway. I'd lie in bed and feel sorry for myself. He'd speak kindly, always trying to find words to encourage me, but nothing he said helped—although that wasn't his fault. No one could help me. Not only was I miserable but, as I learned later, I made everyone else miserable.

My visitors tried to help me, and many wanted to do whatever they could for me. "Can I get you a magazine?" someone would ask.

"Would you like a milkshake? There's a McDonald's in the lobby. Or I could get you a hamburger or . . ."

"Would you like me to read the Bible to you? Or maybe some other book?"

"Are there any errands I can run for you?"

My answer was always the same: "No, thanks."

I don't think I was mean, but I wasn't friendly or cooperative, although I wasn't aware of how negatively I treated everyone. I didn't want to see anyone; I didn't want to talk to anyone; I wanted my pain and disfigurement to go away. If I had to stay on earth, then I wanted to get well and get back to living my life again.

Because Jay visited often, he noticed how detached I was from friends and family. One day he was sitting beside me when one of the South Park deacons came for a visit. After ten minutes, the man got up and said, "I just wanted to come by and check on you." Then he asked the inevitable question, "Is there anything I can get for you before I leave?"

"Thank you, no. I appreciate it, but—"

"Well, can I get you something to eat? Can I go downstairs and—"

"No, really. Thanks for coming."

He said good-bye and left.

Jay sat silently and stared out the window for several minutes after the deacon left. Finally he walked over to the bed and got close to my face and said, "You really need to get your act together."

"Sir?" I said like anyone would say respectfully to an eighty-year-old preacher.

"You need to get your act together," he repeated. "You're just not doing a very good job."

"I don't understand what—"

"Besides that," he said and moved even closer so that I couldn't look away. "Besides that, you're a raging hypocrite."

"I don't know what you're talking about."

"These people care about you so much, and you just can't imagine how deeply they love you."

"I know they love me."

"Really? Well, you're not doing a very good job of letting them know you're aware. You're not treating them right. They can't heal you. If they could heal you, they would do it. If they could change places with you, many of them would. If you ask them to do anything—anything—they would do it without hesitating."

"I know—"

"But you won't let them do anything for you."

"I don't *want* them to do anything." Without holding anything back, I said as loudly as I could, "The truth is I don't even want them to be here. I'd just as soon they didn't come. I know it's inconvenient. They must have better things to do. I know that—why would I want anybody to come and see me like this? It's just awful. I'm pathetic."

"It's not your call."

I stared back, shocked at his words.

"You've spent the better part of your life trying to minister to other people, to meet their needs, to help them during times of difficulty and tragedy and—"

"I . . . I've tried to—"

"And now you're doing a terrible job of letting these people do the same thing for you." I'll never forget the next sentence. *"Don, it's the only thing they have to offer you, and you're taking that gift away from them."*

94

Not ready to surrender, I protested and tried to explain. He interrupted me again.

"You're not letting them minister to you. It's what they want to do. Why can't you understand that?"

I really didn't get the impact of his words, but I said, "I appreciate them, and I know they want to help. I think that's very fine and everything but—"

"But nothing! You're cheating them out of an opportunity to express their love to you."

His words shocked me. In my thinking, I was trying to be selfless and not impose on them or cause them any trouble. Just then, his words penetrated my consciousness. In reality, I was being selfish. There was also an element of pride there—which I couldn't admit then. I knew how to give generously to others, but pride wouldn't let me receive others' generosity.

Jay didn't let up on me. After all, I was a completely captive audience. He stayed at me until he forced me to see how badly I distanced myself from everyone. Even then I found additional excuses, but Jay wore me down.

"I want you to let them help you. Did you hear me? You will allow them to help!"

"I can't—I just can't let—"

"Okay, Don, then if you don't do it for yourself, do this for *me*," he said.

He knew I'd do anything for him, so I nodded.

"The next time anyone comes in here and offers to do something—anything, no matter what it is—I want you to say yes. You probably can't do that with everyone, but you can start with just one or two people. Let a few of the people express their love by helping you. Promise me you'll do that."

"I'm not sure I can."

"Yes, you can."

"I'll try, but that's just not me."

"Then make it you." His gaze bored into me. "Do it!"

I'm amazed now as I think of Jay's patience with me. His voice softened, and he said, "Just try it for me, would you? You have to get better at this. Right now you're not doing very well. This is one of the lessons God wants you to learn. You're going to be hurting a long time. It'll feel longer if you keep on refusing help."

"Okay," I said, unable to resist any longer.

I promised. I didn't think he would leave until I did.

My first reaction had been irritation, maybe even anger. I thought he had stepped over the line, but I didn't say that. After he left, I thought about all the things he had said. Once I overcame my anger, my pride, and my selfishness, I realized he had spoken the truth—truth I needed to hear.

Two days passed, and I still couldn't do what he asked.

On the third day, a church member popped into my room, greeted me, and spent about five minutes with me before he got up to leave. "I just wanted to come by and check on you and see how you were doing," he said. "You're looking good."

I smiled; I looked terrible, but I didn't argue with him.

He stood up to leave. "Is there anything I can do for you before I go?"

I had my mouth poised to say the words, "No, thank you," and an image of Jay popped into my mind. "Well, I wish I had a magazine to read."

"You do?" He had the biggest grin on his face. "Really?"

"I think so. I haven't read one in a while—"

"I'll be right back!" Before I could tell him what kind, he dashed out the door so fast it was like a human blur. He had to go down twenty-one floors, but it seemed as if he were gone less than a minute. When he returned, he had an armload of magazines. He was still grinning as he showed me the covers of all of them.

I thanked him. "I'll read them a little later," I said.

He put them on the table and smiled. "Is there anything else?"

"No, no, that's all I need. Thank you."

Once I had opened the door and allowed someone to do something kind for me, I realized it wasn't so hard after all. After he left, I began skimming through the magazines. I wasn't really reading, because I kept thinking about what had happened.

Jay was right. I had cheated them out of the opportunity to express their love and concern.

About forty minutes later, a woman from the singles group came to see me, and we went through the regular ritual of chatting. "How are you doing?"

"Fine."

"Well, can I get you anything?"

"No, I . . . I—" Again, Jay's words popped into my head. "Well, maybe a strawberry milkshake."

"Strawberry milkshake? I'd love to get one for you." I don't think I had ever seen her smile so beautifully before. "Anything else? Some fries, maybe?"

"No."

She dashed out the door and came back with the strawberry milkshake. "Oh, pastor, I hope you enjoy this."

"I will," I said. "As a matter of fact, I love strawberry milkshakes."

Later, I imagined members of the congregation standing outside my door comparing notes. "He asked me to get a strawberry milkshake."

"Yes, and he let me run an errand for him."

Just then I realized how badly I had missed the whole idea. I had failed them and myself. In trying to be strong for them, I had cheated them out of opportunities to strengthen me. Guilt overwhelmed me, because I could—at last—see their gifts to me.

The shame flowed all over me, and I began to cry. *This is their ministry,* I thought, *and I've been spoiling it.* I felt such intense shame over not letting them help. When I finally did open up, I witnessed a drastic change in their facial expressions and in their movements. They loved it. All they had wanted was a chance to do something, and I was finally giving that to them.

*You need to get your act together.* For the next several hours those words of loving rebuke from Jay wouldn't go away. Tears flowed. I have no idea how much time passed, but it seemed hours before I finally realized God had forgiven me. I had learned a lesson.

In spite of my condition, not many people could have pulled off what Jay did. That experience changed my attitude. Even now, years later, I still fight with allowing others to help, but at least the door is now ajar instead of locked shut.

Sometimes when I'm emotionally low or physically down, I tend to brush people off or assert that I don't need anything. Yet when I can open up and allow others to exercise their gifts and help me, it makes such a difference. Their faces light up as if they're asking, "Will you really let me do that for you?"

I had seen my refusal as not wanting to impose; they saw my change as giving them an opportunity to help.

I'm eternally grateful for that lesson of allowing people to meet my needs. I'm also grateful because that lesson was learned in a hospital bed when I was helpless.

Someone brought a plaque to me in the hospital. At first, I thought it was supposed to be some kind of joke because it contained the words of Psalm 46:10: "Be still, and know that I am God" (NIV). Perhaps it was meant to console me. I'm not sure the person who gave it to me (and I don't remember who it was) realized that I couldn't do anything *but* be still.

Yet that plaque contained the message I needed; it just took me a long time to understand.

Weeks lapsed before I realized that part of what I needed was to be still—inwardly—and to trust that God knew what he was doing through all of this. Yes, it was a verse for me, even though it wasn't one I would have chosen.

God forced me to be still. By nature I'm not particularly introspective, but I became increasingly so; I had no choice. I could do little else—other than feel sorry for myself. The longer I lay immobile, the more open I became to God's quietness and to inner silence.

Eva found a beautiful version of that same verse engraved in gold and gave it to me as a gift. The plaque is now in my church office; I see it every time I look up from my desk.

Day after day I lay in bed, unable to move. I lay on my back a total of thirteen months before I could turn over on my side. Just that simple action made it one of the best days of recovery. "Oh, I had forgotten how good this feels," I said aloud.

During that long recovery, I learned a lot about myself, about my attitude, and my nature. I didn't like many things I saw in

Don Piper. In the midst of that inactivity, however, the depression persisted.

I began to wonder if that depression would ever go away.

Then God provided another miracle.

# 10

# MORE MIRACLES

I will praise the LORD at all times.
   I will constantly speak his praises.
I will boast only in the LORD;
   let all who are discouraged take heart.
Come, let us tell of the LORD's greatness;
   let us exalt his name together.
I prayed to the LORD, and he answered me,
   freeing me from all my fears.

PSALM 34:1–4

Sometimes the depression became so bad I didn't think I could breathe. It carried me back to the days in the ICU when I received breathing treatments because my lungs had collapsed. Except now my lungs weren't collapsed, only my spirit. Few things sap the human spirit like lack of hope. For weeks and months, no one could tell me when or even if I would ever be normal again. As a result, I went into a full-scale depression.

As my horribly mangled body mended, I needed spiritual mending as well. I began to think of it this way: The Greek word for "spirit" is *pneuma*. The word can also mean "wind" or "breath." That Greek word is the root for what we call *pneumonia*. Just as it was necessary to reinflate my lungs to overcome pneumonia, I needed the breath of God to help me overcome the depression of my spirit.

I don't know when I became aware of that depression. In the first few weeks of my recovery, I was in such constant physical pain I couldn't hold any thoughts in my mind for more than a second or two.

I also battled a lot of anger during those first weeks. I wasn't angry with God, though I often wondered why God had sent me back to earth and why I had to go through such intense physical agony. But even being in pain was not the issue for me. From my first day in the hospital, pain has always been present. Like many others, I've learned to live with that reality. My struggle is that I had experienced the glory and majesty of heaven only to return to earth. In my weaker moments, I didn't understand why God would return me to earth in such awful condition. Many live in greater pain, but few—if any—have experienced heaven.

Instead, my anger focused primarily on the medical staff. I suppose it was because they were there all the time. Deep inside, I seethed with an inner rage, perhaps at myself as much as the medical staff. Why wasn't I recuperating faster? I blamed them for the slowness of my recovery. In my rational moments, I knew they did the best they could. Despite my antagonism and irritation—which I'm sure they sensed—they stayed right with me and constantly encouraged me.

I didn't want encouragement—I wanted results. I wanted to be healthy again. Why couldn't my life be the way it used to be? I wanted to walk by myself, and I didn't want to depend on others all the time.

The medical staff wouldn't give me any definite answers, and that sent fresh waves of rage through my system. In retrospect, I'm sure they told me what they could, but I was anything but a typical case. No one knew my prognosis. In fact, for several weeks, they weren't even sure if I would live, let alone make a significant recovery.

I became paranoid—I knew I wasn't rational even when I complained and demanded more attention or additional medication to alleviate the pain. Nothing suited me. The pace was too slow. They made me wait too long before responding to my bell. No one wanted to answer questions.

"How long will I have to wear this Ilizarov frame?" I asked almost every medical person who came into my room.

"I don't know," was the most common answer.

"But I want to know something," I finally said.

"A long time, a very long time," was the only other answer a nurse or doctor would give me.

A couple of times I just had to have an answer, so I kept pressing the doctor.

"Weeks. Months," he said. "We can't tell you because we don't know. If I knew, I'd tell you."

Common sense said they were doing their best, but in those days, I didn't have much common sense. Part of it was the pain, and perhaps the mammoth doses of medications affected me as well, but I wasn't a good patient. Instead of being satisfied, I kept asking myself, *Why won't they tell me? What do they know that they're hiding? There are things they're not telling me, and I have a right to know what's going on.*

During many sleepless nights, I would lie in bed, convinced that the nurses conspired against me. It never occurred to me to wonder why they would want to do that.

*Then why don't they tell me anything?* I'd rail as I lay there. *What can they possibly do that will hurt more than this?*

The answer was *nothing.* I endured additional pain that resulted not from the accident itself but from the process of healing. For instance, when they harvested bones out of my right hip and put them in my left arm, they made an incision six inches long—and closed it up with metal staples. When the day came for them to take out the staples, they pulled them out of my skin. As they pulled each one, I winced in pain and steeled myself so that I wouldn't scream at the top of my lungs. I couldn't remember hurting that excruciatingly. I had, of course, but I had forgotten how much torture my body could take.

The poor nurse who was extracting the staples stopped after each one. Sadness filled her eyes, and I knew she sensed how deeply the procedure hurt me. She was a large woman and always treated me as gently as she could. "I'm so sorry, Reverend," she said softly.

"I know," I mumbled. "You can't help it." Momentarily, I lapsed into my pastoral role of trying to console her. I didn't want her to feel bad for the torture I felt.

"Reverend, why don't you just haul off and yell?"

"It wouldn't do any good."

"If it was me, I'd be yelling."

"Yeah, I bet you would." I offered a faint sense of humor. "And you'd wake up every patient in the hospital."

I just never could yell voluntarily. Maybe it was a fear of losing control. Perhaps I feared that if I did scream, she and others would consider me as weak. I'm not sure of the reasons, even now. I know only that I couldn't scream like others on my floor. From several other rooms, every day I heard patients scream out in agony. I just couldn't let go like that. Instead, I'd hold my breath and sometimes break out in a cold sweat, but I wouldn't scream purposely.

Though I know I wasn't the easiest of patients in demeanor or medical requirements, the nurses of the orthopedic floor treated me with kindness and much compassion. I learned to care a great deal for them and admire their dedication. I guess they must have seen something in me as well. I know the nursing staff often bent the rules when well-wishers showed up to see me, no matter what time of day or night they came. But the sweetest moment came when I was discharged from my 105-day stay at St. Luke's. Apparently, arrangements were made with nursing staffs of other hospital floors to cover for them as the nurses from my floor all accompanied me down the elevator and to my waiting ambulance on the day of my discharge. Being surrounded by nurses that fed me, medicated me, bathed me, and did only the Lord knows what else, made my going home that day so wonderful. It was as if they were saying, "We've done our best. Now you've got to get better and come back and see us." I can only imagine how different I must have seemed to them that going-home day from the day I had arrived wavering between life and death.

In spite of my stubborn resistance to showing emotion, before I left St. Luke's, the months of intense pain finally crumbled my resolve. I broke down and cried. I felt worthless, beaten down, and useless. I was convinced I would never get any better.

"God, God, why is it like this? Why am I going through this constant pain that never seems to get any better?" Again I prayed for God to take me. I didn't want to live any longer. I wanted to go back home, and now for me, home meant heaven.

I prayed that way for days, and usually, I'd fall asleep from exhaustion. When I'd awaken, a cloak of hopelessness would spread over me again. Nothing helped.

Just before the accident, I had ordered several cassette tapes of popular Christian songs originally recorded during the 1960s and '70s by people like the Imperials and David Meese. Eva had brought them to the hospital along with a tape player, but I had no interest in listening to them.

Instead, I watched TV. I once told a friend, "I've watched every *Brady Bunch* episode at least eight times, and I know all of the dialogue by heart."

One morning between three and five o'clock, I couldn't bear to watch another TV rerun, so I decided to play the cassettes. A nurse came in and helped me set up the first cassette to play.

The first song had been recorded by the Imperials, and it was called "Praise the Lord." The lyrics suggest that when we're up against a struggle and we think we can't go on, we need to praise God. As preposterous as that prospect seemed at three o'clock in the morning in a hospital bed, I continued to listen for any help to bring me out of my deep heartache. There was a phrase in the next verse about the chains that seem to bind us falling away when we turn ourselves over to praise. The whole song centered on praising God in spite of our circumstances.

The instant the Imperials sang the second chorus about the chains, I looked down at my chains—pounds of stainless steel encasing my arm and leg. Before my accident, I'm sure I'd heard and sung that song hundreds of times. I had even played it myself. Just then, those words became a message from God—a direct hit from on high.

Before they had finished singing the song, I lay there and heard my own voice say, "Praise the Lord!"

No sooner had that song ended than David Meese sang, "We Are the Reason." His words reminded me that we are the reason Jesus Christ wept, suffered, and died on the cross. Meese sang about how he finally found that the real purpose in living was in giving every part of his life to Christ. That wasn't a new song to me, but something happened during those predawn hours. Other than music, I heard nothing else—no moaning from other rooms or footsteps of nurses in the hallway. I felt totally isolated from the world around me.

Then the dam broke. Tears slid down my cheeks, and I couldn't wipe them away—and I didn't even want to try. They just flowed. The tears wouldn't stop, and I cried as I had never wept before. I'm not sure, but I think the crying lasted for about an hour.

Slowly the sobbing subsided. Calmness swept over me, and I lay relaxed and very much at peace. That's when I realized another miracle had taken place: My depression had lifted. Vanished.

I had been healed. Again.

Stark reminders from some simple songs had changed me. The Imperials reminded me that Satan is a liar. He wants to steal our joy and replace it with hopelessness. When we're up against a struggle and we think we can't keep going, we can change that by praising God. Our chains will fall from us.

Meese encouraged me by reminding me of the real reason we have for fully living this life. It's to give everything we have to God—even the heartbreaks and pain. God is our reason to live.

That morning I determined to get on with living the rest of my life, no matter what. I made that decision with no psychiatric help, no drugs, and no counseling. As I listened to those two songs, God had healed me. The despair lifted. My mental chains had broken. I also knew that nothing I had gone through—or would endure—was as horrific as what Jesus suffered.

I'm not trying to imply that I'm against psychological help. Before and since my accident, I've sent many people for counseling. But because I wasn't open to help of any kind, God healed me in a dramatic and unexplainable way.

As I lay there, my attitude changed. I had no idea when my physical pain would end or how long I'd have to wear the Ilizarov frame, but I knew Jesus Christ was with me. I still didn't understand why God had sent me back to live with all of this agony, but that no longer mattered.

Now I was free. He had healed my mind. My body would mend slowly, but I had experienced the major victory. Never again would depression afflict me. It was just one more miracle from heaven.

# 11
# BACK TO CHURCH

So humble yourselves under the mighty power of God, and in his good time he will honor you. Give all your worries and cares to God, for he cares about what happens to you.

1 PETER 5:6–7

Some people who have known me for a long time see me as some kind of courageous figure. I certainly haven't seen myself that way—not for an instant—because I know too much about the real me. I also know how little I did to get through my ordeal.

Despite my own perceptions, friends and church members say they received encouragement by watching me as I progressed from a totally helpless state and gradually moved toward a fairly normal lifestyle. A number of individuals have said to me in the midst of their own difficult times, "If you could go through all you endured, I can go through this."

I'm glad they've been heartened by my example, but I've had a great deal of difficulty accepting myself as a source of inspiration and courage. I don't know how to cope with their admiration and praise, because I didn't do anything. I wanted to die. How uplifting can that be?

When people tell me how inspiring I've been, I don't argue with them, of course, but I remember only too well the time David Gentiles told me that he and others would pray me back to health. I lived because others wouldn't let me die. Those praying friends are the ones who deserve the admiration.

Most of the time when people have that if-you-can-do-it attitude, I nod, acknowledge what they're saying, and add, "I'm just doing the best I can." And really, that's all I did during the worst days. Sometimes "the best I can" was nothing but to endure. Even when I struggled with depression, it was still the best I could do. Maybe that's what God honors. I don't know.

By nature, I'm a determined individual, which I admit can sometimes be a first cousin to stubbornness. Yet many times I felt terribly alone and was convinced that no one else understood. And I still think that's true. When our pain becomes intense and endures for weeks without relief, no one else really knows. I'm not sure it's worthwhile for them to know what it's like.

They care. That's what I think is important.

After I came home from the hospital in the middle of May, I still had to sleep in a hospital bed until February 1990—a total of thirteen months. Even after sleeping in my own house, I had setbacks of various kinds or developed infections. Back to the hospital I'd go, and some of those trips, especially in the early days, were for life-threatening infections. Sometimes I stayed two weeks and other times three. On most occasions Eva drove me there, but I always came home in an ambulance.

After they initially released me from the hospital, church members kept telling me how good I looked "considering all that's happened." No one actually said the words, but I imagined them saying, "We prayed for Don. We can't believe how well it turned out. We asked for him to live, and we asked for him to be better." That is, I was a pitiful mess, but I was alive and that's what they had asked for.

My twin sons, Joe and Christopher, were only eight at the time of the accident, and our daughter, Nicole, was twelve. One of the things that hurt me most during my recovery was the sense of pain my children had to cope with. They didn't say a great deal, but I knew how they felt.

This is a handmade card from my son Joe, written to me in February 1989 while he was living with his grandparents. (I didn't correct the spelling.)

hi dad,

You are the best. I love you and I hope you like the cards. I whish this never hapined
I love you Dad,

Joe

Months later when I finally came home, most afternoons, Joe's twin, Chris, came in from school and into the large living room where my bed was. Without saying a word, Chris would walk over and lay his head on my chest. I don't know how long his head lay there, probably not more than a full minute.

He never said a word.

He didn't need to. That simple gesture was enough. I felt so loved by my son.

After a minute or so, Chris would go into his room, get out of his school clothes, change into his play clothes, and then go outside and play. That's the way he greeted me almost every day.

I know it was hard on him—really hard on him—and he expressed his grief in the only way he knew how.

Just six months after the accident, I was able to participate in a very special moment for Nicole.

Southern Baptists have mission organizations for young people. The most well-known are the Royal Ambassadors for boys and Girls in Action (GAs) and Acteens for girls. As soon as she was old enough, Nicole participated in GAs and Acteens. She fulfilled all the requirements, such as Scripture memorization, various service projects, and mission trips. When she was fourteen, she learned she would be awarded the honor of Queen with Scepter at a coronation ceremony at South Park Baptist Church in June 1989.

This award is the pinnacle of Acteen participation and is presented during a church ceremony. Her receiving the award was a tribute to her own utter determination. During the time she threw herself into those activities, she wasn't able to live at home. Our friends Suzan and Stan Mauldin had opened their home to her, and she lived with them. Nicole received no emotional or physical support from me, because I was barely surviving in the hospital. She received little support from her mother, because Eva's

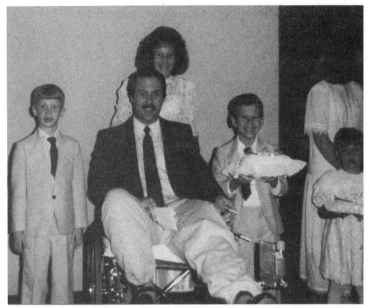

*Don attends Nicole's Girls in Action coronation.*

life consisted of leaving school every afternoon and rushing to the hospital, where she stayed with me until she went home to bed.

The challenges made us all the more proud of Nicole.

One of the traditions associated with the coronation is that fathers escort their daughters down the aisle. Brothers, if the girls have any, follow and carry the crown and scepter.

Because of the timing of South Park's annual coronation, there was great doubt about my being able to be present, much less escort her down the aisle.

I'm grateful that my doctors discharged me from the hospital in time to be present for the coronation. I really wanted to be there. This wasn't her wedding, but it was the biggest thing so far in her young life, and I wanted to share the moment with her.

I was in a wheelchair, and Nicole held my arm as I rolled down the aisle. Chris and Joe walked behind us, carrying her crown and scepter on pillows. They also helped roll my chair down the aisle. I wore a suit coat and tie (my first time since the accident) along with my warm-ups split down the sides to allow for my Ilizarov.

Not only was Nicole absolutely elated that her daddy could be present for her extremely important occasion, she was thrilled that her father could "walk" her down the aisle.

Tears filled my eyes as I maneuvered down the aisle. I heard others sniffling. But I also knew that we wept tears of joy over this wonderful moment in Nicole's life.

The doctors sent me home initially, I believe, because they thought I'd recover faster in an environment with family around me. It may also have cost a lot less for me to be home. I'm not sure, but I was glad to be out of the hospital. Insurance didn't pay for any of my treatment. The bill was covered at first by workmen's compensation, and ultimately the State of Texas, because a federal court found them at fault.

Still, being in my own home wasn't much easier for me or my family, especially Eva. Every day someone had to give me shots. I had to have physical therapy treatments—all done to me and for me at home. Our living room looked like a hospital room. I did feel better being out of that sterile environment. Just being around familiar things lifted my spirit. I enjoyed being able to look out the window at my neighborhood or having people drop in to see me who didn't wear white uniforms.

The medical team sent my bed and a trapeze contraption—just like what I had used at the hospital. Nurses visited every day; physical therapists came every other day.

Some of the sweetest memories I have are of the kind people who simply spent each day with me while Eva went back to work. When church members heard that she had to return to teaching or lose her job, they decided to do what they could.

Ginny Foster, the senior pastor's wife, organized a group of people to stay with me each day. Ginny organized what she laughingly called the "Don Patrol"—mostly women from the church, along with a few retired men.

It was about seven hours from the time Eva left in the morning until she returned. My sleep habits depended on when I could fight the pain no more and would pass out. But gradually, a pattern began to emerge. I would generally go to sleep about two or three o'clock in the morning and wake up around ten. The Don Patrol arrived about nine o'clock while I was still asleep. They either prepared lunch for me or brought it with them.

Often I would awake to find a charming woman knitting at the end of my bed. Or perhaps an older man would be reading the *Houston Chronicle.* He'd lower the newspaper and grin at me, "Good morning. Do you need anything?"

The parade of sweet faces changed every day. Although the volunteers were different, the goals remained the same: Take care of Don and keep him company.

As I lay in bed day after day, I realized how much others had done for us. While I was still hospitalized, friends from the Alvin church had packed up our furniture and moved us to a new house, where I could be on the ground level with no stairs to worry about.

During the day, I would look through the patio window from my "hospital room." Often I spotted high schoolers Brandon and Matt Mealer and their buddy Chris Alston mowing our lawn. Chris arranged to borrow our van one night and surprise me by taking me to a movie. I don't even remember what the movie was, but I will never forget his thoughtfulness. Once when our fence blew down during a windstorm, it was back up before we could call anyone to help. Only God knows all the kindnesses shown to us during my recovery.

As I began to stir in my bed each morning, my "keeper" would get up and bring me a toothbrush and a pan to brush my teeth and wash my face. I'd have a glass of juice held to my lips and later a huge lunch ready for me.

After feeding me, washing up, and making sure I was as comfortable as my physical condition would allow, they all asked the same question: "Is there anything else I can get for you before I leave?"

My answer was always the same: "No, thanks." I would muster what I hoped was my best smile. It probably wasn't, but they always smiled back.

"It's all right. I'll be fine."

The capacity for sacrifice and service that human beings have for one another knows no bounds. With all our faults, surely God must have meant that the kindnesses shown to me during my injury and recovery were paramount examples of us being created in his image.

Within an hour or so after my daily Don Patrol angel quietly exited, the door would open, and Eva would enter from a long day at school. She always gave me a big smile and kissed me.

"Are you all right?" she would ask.

"I'm fine," I would say, meaning it.

I couldn't put my feelings into words then, but the assurance that I had been visited by an angel from the Don Patrol caused my spirit to soar.

For months after I came home, good-hearted members of the Don Patrol transported me back and forth for water therapy, which was done near our home in Alvin. During the first thirteen months, if I wasn't inside the hospital, I was lying in the hospital bed at the house. For months, I probably wasn't out of the bed more than five minutes a day except for therapy. Some days I didn't even get out of bed.

The worst part is that once I was in the hospital bed, I was completely incapacitated. I couldn't get up or do anything for myself. Without the help of the therapist, I never would have sat up or been able to move on my own again.

Slowly, gradually, I learned to walk again. The first day I got out of bed on my own, I took three steps. I slumped back onto the bed, feeling a wave of exhaustion overwhelm me. But I smiled. *I had walked.* Three steps sounds like so little, and yet I felt a powerful sense of accomplishment.

So much of recovery from a trauma of this magnitude has a striking similarity to training a child in infancy. I had been helpless for such a long time that when I could finally go to the bathroom by myself, it felt like a remarkable accomplishment. Walking again was a stark reminder of what we all take for granted every day as we talk, move, and live.

When I could walk again, it was not only a singular accomplishment but a tribute to hundreds of medical people who worked tirelessly to help me. It was also a tribute to my friends and family who believed in me, although they couldn't have known just how difficult it would be for me to put one foot in front of the other.

While I suppose walking represented a certain triumph of will, it also meant I could begin to live in relative normalcy. I often thought of the last night at Trinity Pines when J. V. Thomas and I took our walk around the camp. That was my last normal walk ever. For many months no one was sure I'd ever walk again. For a long time, taking just three shaky steps seemed like climbing Mount Everest.

"I did it!" I shouted to the silent room. "I walked! I walked."

Taking those first steps at home on my own remains one of the best moments of my recovery. Those few steps convinced me that I was getting better. Now I had goals to work toward. I had gone through the worst part of the recovery. I knew I would continue to improve. Each day I took a few more steps. By the end of the week, I had made a complete circle of the living room.

When Eva came home and watched me demonstrate my daily progress, her smile made me feel as if I had won a marathon. She reacted with absolute joyful delight the afternoon I showed her that I could walk throughout the house all by myself.

A week after I came home from the hospital, I had decided I wanted to go to church on a Sunday morning.

In retrospect, it was premature, but I felt a burning desire to be back with people I loved and to worship with them. With the help of a small group, we planned for them to help me get there. In case I couldn't make it, we didn't want to disappoint anyone, so we decided not to announce it to the congregation.

By then I could sit in a wheelchair—as long as someone was there to lift me out of bed and into it—but I still couldn't stand up. Six friends from church came to our house and took the seats out of one of the church vans. At the church, they had constructed a ramp so they could roll me up to its doors.

I kept thinking of all the work I had laid on them, and several times I started to apologize, but they assured me it was their pleasure.

Then I remembered Jay's words. My family and friends saw me the first day of the accident. I never saw what I looked like. They endured the shock and the fear. They had to come to grips with the possibility of my death or my long-term disability. In some respects, this ordeal was more difficult for my family and friends than it was for me. They loved being able to help me. In a way, this was part of their own recovery, and they were glad to be able to do something special for me.

Yet, as much as I wanted to attend the worship service that morning, it was still hard to let them do everything for me. I felt totally helpless and absolutely dependent on them. As I realized that once again, I smiled.

"Thank you," I said and then allowed them to take care of me.

They carefully put me into the van, drove me to the church, and pulled up at the side door. When one of the men in the van opened the door, church members on their way into the sanctuary saw me.

"Look! It's Pastor Don!" someone yelled.

I heard cheering and clapping as people stood around and made way for the men to wheel me up the ramp.

Just then, everything turned chaotic. People rushed toward me. Several cheered. It seemed as if everyone wanted to touch me or shake my hand. I could hardly believe the fuss they made over me.

Finally someone wheeled me inside and stopped my chair in front of the platform near the church organ. It wasn't possible to lift me up.

By then the entire congregation had become aware that I was in front of the sanctuary. I smiled as I thought, *It's only taken me five months to get from the conference at Trinity Pines back to church. I may be slow, but I'm faithful.*

Just then someone whispered in my ear, "We want you to say something to the congregation." He got behind me and steered me toward the center of the sanctuary, right in front of the pulpit.

By then exhaustion had begun to seep in. It had probably nagged at me all along, but I had been so determined to get back to church, I refused to admit how tired I felt. I had been out of bed more than two hours. That was the longest time I had been out of bed up to that point, and also the longest time I had spent in a wheelchair.

In that moment I realized I had been foolish in wanting to come, because I wasn't up to the physical demands on my body. My stubbornness had overestimated my endurance.

Perhaps just as bad, I became completely overwhelmed at the congregation's loving response. I didn't know if I could speak. What could I say after all those weeks of absence and all I'd been through?

While I was still trying to figure that out, someone thrust a microphone in my hand. As I clutched it, I kept thinking, *You people really have no idea how little I contributed to my recovery. You see it as a triumph. I see it merely as survival.*

Just then spontaneous applause broke out. I had expected them to be glad to see me; I had not been prepared for the avalanche of praise to God. Every person in that building stood, and the applause began—and it kept on for a long time. I finally waved them to stop.

As I stared at them, I felt guilty about their applause and excitement. I couldn't believe those people were applauding me. *If they only knew*, I thought. *If they only knew.*

Then God spoke to me. This was one of the few times in my life when I heard a very clear voice inside my head.

*They're not applauding for you.*

Just those words, but it made a difference and I could speak. Finally, I had it straight. They were giving thanks to God for what he had done for me. God had brought me back from death to life once again. I relaxed. This was a moment to glorify God. This wasn't praise for me.

I still had to wait for what seemed like a long time until the applause ceased. I spoke only four words. Anyone who was there that glorious day can tell you what they were: "You prayed. I'm here."

The congregation erupted in spontaneous applause again. If I had said anything else, I'm sure they wouldn't have heard it anyway.

I couldn't say it, but I believed then—and still do—that I survived only because a number of people wanted me to. They were relentless, passionate, and desperate, and they believed God would hear them. People prayed for me who had never seriously prayed before; some who hadn't uttered a word of petition in years cried out to God to spare me. My experience brought people to their knees, and many of them had changed in the process of praying for me to live.

When I did live, those same people—especially those who hadn't been in the habit of praying—said the experience revolutionized their lives. In some instances, individuals I had never met—from Cottonwood, Arizona, to Buffalo, New York—heard my story second-, third-, and fourthhand. Over the next three years, people would approach me and say, "I saw you on a video interview. You're the man! I prayed for you." Or they heard one of the audiotapes of my testimony distributed by my church and would say, "You just don't know what it means. God heard *our* prayers, and we're so happy you lived."

To some individuals, I'm not really a person but a symbol. For them, I represent answered prayer. They may remember my ministry at South Park Church or even some of the messages I preached, but what they remember most is that they sought God's face in deep, sincere, earnest prayer. They pleaded for me to survive, and I did. I don't know what to make of it, except to say that this is something outside of and beyond me.

I think I'm also a human response to some of the questions people wanted answered. Since I began to tell others about my experience in heaven, I can't begin to count the people who have come to me and asked such questions as, Is heaven real? What is heaven really like? Or they'll ask specific questions about the praise or the streets of gold. Someone seems to always mention a recently departed loved one.

Just to know that I've been there and come back to earth and am able to talk to them seems to bring deep comfort to many. Sometimes it amazes me.

Others look at the marks on my body even today and say, "You're a miracle because of all you went through. You're a walking miracle."

# 12
# OPENING UP

For we know that when this earthly tent we live in is taken down—
when we die and leave these bodies—we will have a home in heaven,
an eternal body made for us by God himself and not by human
hands. We grow weary in our present bodies, and we long for the
day when we will put on our heavenly bodies like new clothing.
For we will not be spirits without bodies, but we will put on new
heavenly bodies. Our dying bodies make us groan and sigh, but it's
not that we want to die and have no bodies at all. We want to slip
into our new bodies so that these dying bodies will be swallowed
up by everlasting life.

2 CORINTHIANS 5:1–4

God used my closest friend, David Gentiles, to keep me
alive, and I'm grateful. He also used David again in my
life nearly two years after the accident.

Until then I had never talked to anyone about my heavenly
experience. In a general sense, I had talked to Eva, but I always
closed off the conversation before she asked questions. She tacitly
understood that part of my experience was off-limits. To her
credit, she never pressured me to say anything more.

It wasn't that I wanted to withhold anything from Eva; I just couldn't talk about the experience. At times I felt that it had been too sacred and that to try to explain it would diminish the incident.

Nearly a year and a half after my release from the hospital, David came to the Houston area for a discipleship weekend. He used that as an excuse to come to the house and spend time with me.

When the two of us were alone, I had a flashback to the time when I had been lying in ICU and had told him that I couldn't go on. That's when he had told me that he would pray me through. We talked about that day, and I thanked him again for his friendship and relentless commitment to prayer.

"How are you feeling now?" he asked.

"I'm in pain." I tried to laugh and added, "I'm always in pain, but that's not the worst part for me right now."

He leaned closer. "What is the worst part?"

"I just don't know where I'm going. I lack any clear direction about my future."

David listened as I talked about the things I would like to do, the things I couldn't physically do, and how I wasn't sure that God wanted me to continue at South Park. I felt loved and needed there, but I wasn't sure that was where I should be.

He listened for a long time and then asked gently, "What did you learn from your accident and recovery experience?"

For three or four minutes I shared several things, especially about letting other people inside and allowing them to help me. Then I said, "But in the midst of all this suffering and despondency, I have learned that heaven is real."

He raised his eyebrows. "What do you mean by that?"

Slowly, hesitantly, I shared a little—very little—about my brief visit to heaven. "Tell me more," he said, and I didn't hear it as prying. He was my friend and wanted to know. I also sensed that I could speak about heaven to David and that, as much as any human being was able, he would understand.

"I died in that accident. The next moment I stood in heaven," I said.

He leaned forward, and although he waited silently for me to continue, I saw the excitement in his eyes.

The more I shared, the more animated he became. In retrospect, I believe David's exuberance was a combination of my personal confirmation of heaven's reality and his relief in knowing something good had come out of my long nightmare.

After I had shared my experience in heaven, he said nothing, and a peaceful silence filled the room. Our friendship was such that we didn't have to fill the gap with words.

David finally nodded slowly and asked, "Why haven't you talked about this before?"

"I have two very good reasons. Number one, if I go around talking about having been in heaven, people will think I'm nuts."

"Why would you think that? I heard you, and I didn't—"

"Number two," I said, interrupting him, "I don't want to go over that experience again. It's . . . well, it's just too personal. Too special. This is something I haven't even processed enough to understand it myself. It's not that I don't want to share it, but I don't think I can."

"Why do you think you experienced heaven if you're not supposed to share it?"

"I don't have an answer for that question."

"Why?"

"I'll tell you a better question I've asked myself—Why did I experience it and have it taken away from me? What was that all about?" Months of pent-up anger burst forth, and all the interior pain spewed out. "Okay, why did I have to go through this? I saw the glory and the beauty—the most powerful, over-whelming experiences in my life—and then I had to come back. Why? For this?" I pointed to my arm and leg. "Listen. I was in an accident that took my life. Immediately I went to heaven, and it was greater and more wonderful than anything I've ever imagined. I had a magnificent taste of heaven, and then I was pulled back to this life again. My body is a mess. I'm constantly in pain. I'll never be healthy or strong again. I'm still processing this because—because, frankly it all seems cruel to me."

David stared at me and asked again, "Why do you think you experienced it if you're not supposed to share it?"

"Like I said, I don't have an answer for that question."

"Is it possible that God took you to heaven and brought you back for you to share what happened to you? Don't you realize what a powerful encouragement you can be to others?"

His words shocked me. I had been so focused on myself, I hadn't thought about anyone else.

I broke down as I tried to relate to him how I felt and to explain it to myself. I cried in his presence, and I knew it was all right.

For perhaps twenty minutes we discussed it. David nudged me, and although I knew he was right, it still wasn't easy for me to share my experience.

Finally David said, "I want you to make a covenant with me."

"What kind of covenant?"

"Simple. Pick two people you trust. Just tell them a little of your experience and gauge their response." He went on to explain that if they thought I was crazy or that I had hallucinated, then I would never have to speak about it again.

"But if they rejoice with you," he said, "and if they urge you to tell them more, I want you to take this as a sign—a sign that God wants you to talk about those ninety minutes you spent in heaven."

After considering the matter carefully, I covenanted with him. "I can do that much."

"When?"

"I promise to do it soon."

"Very soon, right?"

"Okay, I promise I won't put it off."

David prayed for me, and as I listened to him speak, the certainty came over me. It was no longer a choice—I had to speak out—but I would do it my way.

First, I decided on those I could trust with my holy secret. Once I had narrowed it down to a handful, I still took a cautious approach. I made sure it was a one-to-one conversation. I'd wait until the matter of my health came up—and it always did—and then I'd say something simple such as, "You know, I died that day. And I woke up in heaven."

The reaction was the same each time: "Tell me more." They didn't always say those words, but that's what they wanted. I could see their eyes widen, and they wanted to know more.

As I shared a little more, no one questioned my sanity. No one told me I had hallucinated.

"You have to tell people about this," one of them said.

"That experience wasn't just for you," another friend said. "It's for us as well. It's for me."

127

As I listened to each one over the next two weeks, I realized I was right back where I had been in the hospital the time Jay had rebuked me. That time I wouldn't let anyone help me, and it was selfish. This time I wouldn't share what had happened to me—and it was also selfish.

"Okay, I'll talk about it," I vowed to myself.

Since virtually everyone already knew about my tragic auto accident, I used the occasion as the natural catalyst to speak about my time in heaven—cautiously at first. As people responded with overwhelming support, I became more open and less careful about the people with whom I shared my story.

I want to make it clear that even though I knew it was what I was supposed to do, it wasn't easy for me. Even now, years later, it's just against my nature to talk deeply and personally about things in my life. Today, I only discuss my glimpse of heaven when someone asks, and then only because I feel that person really wants to know. Otherwise, I still wouldn't talk about it.

That's part of the reason it's taken me so many years to write this book. I didn't want my experience in heaven and my return to earth to be my sole reason for being alive. On the contrary, it was such an extraordinarily personal and intimate experience that going back over it repeatedly isn't something I feel comfortable doing.

I talk about my experience both publicly and to individuals. I'm writing about what happened because my story seems to mean so much to people for many different reasons. For example, when I speak to any large crowd, at least one person will be present who has recently lost a loved one and needs assurance of that person's destination.

When I finish speaking, it still amazes me to see how quickly the line forms of those who want to talk to me. They come with tears in their eyes and grief written all over their faces. I feel so grateful that I can offer them peace and assurance.

I've accepted that my words do bring comfort, but it was never something I thought about doing. If it hadn't been for David Gentiles pushing me, I'm sure that even to this day I wouldn't have told anyone.

I'm also grateful for his urging me, because I've seen the effect not only in worship services but also when I've conducted funerals. In fact, my experience has changed many things about the way I look at life. I've changed the way I do funerals. Now I can speak authoritatively about heaven from firsthand knowledge.

Besides my own miraculous experience, four things stand out from my heavenly journey. First, I'm thoroughly convinced that God answers prayer. Answered prayer is why I'm still alive. Second, I have an unquestionable belief that God still is in the miracle business. Too many people read about the supernatural in the Bible and think, *That's the way it was in biblical times.* I'm convinced that God continues to do the more-than-ordinary. Every day I thank God that I'm a living, walking, talking miracle.

Third, I want as many people as possible to go to heaven. I've always believed Christian theology that declares heaven is real and a place for God's people. Since my own experience of having been there, I've felt a stronger sense of responsibility to make the way absolutely clear. Not only do I want people to go to heaven, I now feel an urgency about helping them open their lives so they can be assured that's where they'll go when they die.

I've actually thought about the people who get killed on the highways. In evangelistic services, some have used such stories as a scare tactic to manipulate people into making commitments to Jesus Christ. But because of my experience, I see such accidents as definite possibilities of death at any moment in our lives. I don't want to see others die without Jesus Christ.

Finally, one time, Dick Onerecker and I talked about this urgency. He understood why I felt that way. Then I told him, "Again, Dick, I want to thank you for saving my life. I obviously can't thank you enough for your faithfulness in obeying God that rainy day."

"It was what anybody would have done," he said, and then he started crying.

"I didn't mean to upset you," I said, feeling bad that I had said something to make him cry like that. "That's the last thing on earth I'd ever want to do."

"That's not what I'm crying about."

Several minutes lapsed before he finally pulled himself back together again.

"What were you crying about?" I asked.

"I was thinking that I came upon the scene of the accident and I asked the officer if I could pray for you—and I thought of it as just something any Christian would do. Although he said you were dead, I knew—I just knew—I had to pray for you. I could only think that you were hurt, and I wanted to make you feel better. I didn't do anything unusual."

"But you did. When the officer told you I was already dead—"

"Listen to me, Don. If you saw a little kid run out in the street, you'd dash out there and try to save the child's life. Human nature is like that. We try to preserve life, and I will do that any time I get the opportunity. So would you."

We were sitting in a restaurant, and he paused to look around. "Yet here we are sitting in this place, surrounded by people, many of whom are probably lost and going to hell, and we won't say a word about how they can have eternal life. Something is wrong with us."

"You're absolutely right," I said. "We're willing to save someone in a visible crisis, but a lot of folks are in spiritual crisis and we don't say a word about how they can get out of it."

"That's why I was crying. I've been convicted about my silence, my fear of speaking to people, my reluctance to speak up."

Dick said then, and again later, that hearing my experience and his role in my coming back to earth had set him free. After that he felt a boldness to talk about Jesus Christ that he hadn't had before.

# THE CLASPING HAND

## 13

He is your God, the one who is worthy of your praise, the one who has done mighty miracles that you yourself have seen.

DEUTERONOMY 10:21

I was privileged to share my story in Dick's church, Klein First Baptist, a little more than a year after the accident. His wife, Anita, was there, and so was my own family. Because I still wore leg braces, two people had to help me walk up on the platform.

I told everyone about the accident and about Dick's part in bringing me back. "I believe I'm alive today because Dick prayed me back to earth," I said. "In my first moments of consciousness, two things stand out. First, I was singing 'What a Friend We Have in Jesus.' The second was that Dick's hand gripped mine and held it tight."

After the morning worship, many of us went out to lunch together at a Chinese restaurant. Anita sat across from me. I remember sipping my wonton soup and having a delightful time with the church members.

When there was a lull in the conversation, Anita leaned across the table and said in a low voice, "I appreciated everything you said this morning."

"Thank you—"

"There's just one thing—one thing I need to correct about what you said in your message."

"Really?" Her words shocked me. "I tried to be as accurate as possible in everything I said. I certainly didn't intend to exaggerate anything. What did I say that was incorrect?"

"You were talking about Dick getting into the car with you. Then you said he prayed for you while he was holding your hand."

"Yes, I remember that part very distinctly. I have a number of memory gaps, and most of the things I don't remember." That morning I had readily admitted that some of the information I gave came secondhand. "The one thing that's totally clear was Dick being in the car and praying with me."

"That's true. He did get in the car and pray with you." She leaned closer. "But, Don, he never held your hand."

"I distinctly remember holding his hand."

"That didn't happen. It was physically impossible."

"But I remember that so clearly. It's one of the most vivid—"

"Think about it. Dick leaned over from the rear of the trunk over the backseat and put his hand on your *shoulder* and touched you. You were facing forward and your left arm was barely hanging together."

"Yes, that's true."

134

"Dick said you were slumped over on the seat toward the passenger side."

I closed my eyes, visualizing what she had just said. I nodded.

"Your right hand was on the floor of the passenger side of the car. Although the tarp covered the car, there was enough light for him to see your hand down there. There was no way Dick could have reached your right hand."

"But . . . but . . ." I sputtered.

"Someone was holding your hand. But it wasn't Dick."

"If it wasn't Dick's hand, whose was it?"

She smiled and said, "I think you know."

I put down my spoon and stared at her for several seconds. I had no doubt whatsoever that someone had held my hand. Then I understood. "Yes, I think I know too."

Immediately I thought of the verse in Hebrews about entertaining angels unaware. As I pondered for a moment, I also remembered other incidents where there was nothing but a spiritual explanation. For instance, many times in the hospital room in the middle of the night, I would be at my worst. I never saw or heard anyone, but I felt a presence—something—someone—sustaining and encouraging me. That also was something I hadn't talked about. I couldn't explain it, so I assumed others wouldn't understand.

This was another miracle, and I wouldn't have known about it if Anita hadn't corrected me.

Five years after my accident, Dick and I both appeared on Pat Robertson's *700 Club*. A camera crew came to Texas to re-enact the accident and then asked me to talk about my visit to heaven's gates. The *700 Club* aired that segment many times over the next two years.

In one of life's great ironic twists, Dick died of a heart attack in 2001. I confess that I was saddened to hear of his passing, but delighted that he is in glory. Dick saved my life, and God took him to heaven first. I was glad he heard me share about my journey to heaven before he made his own trip.

Since that experience with Anita a little more than a year after my accident, I've been more convinced than ever that God brought me back to this earth for a purpose. The angel gripping my hand was God's way of sustaining me and letting me know that he would not let go of me no matter how hard things became.

I may not feel that hand each day, but I know it's there.

# THE NEW NORMAL

14

"I will give you back your health and heal your wounds, says the Lord. Now you are called an outcast—'Jerusalem for whom nobody cares.'"

JEREMIAH 30:17

Some things happen to us from which we never recover, and they disrupt the normalcy of our lives. That's how life is.

Human nature has a tendency to try to reconstruct old ways and pick up where we left off. If we're wise, we won't continue to go back to the way things were (we can't anyway). We must instead forget the old standard and accept a "new normal."

I wasted a lot of time thinking about how I used to be healthy and had no physical limitations. In my mind, I'd reconstruct how life *ought* to be, but in reality, I knew my life would never be the same. I had to adjust and accept my physical limits as part of my new normal.

As a child I'd sit on a big brown rug in my great-grandparents' living room and listen to them talk about the good old days. After hearing several stories, I thought, *Those days weren't that good*—at least the recollections they shared didn't seem so great. Maybe for them they truly were the good old days, or perhaps they forgot the negative parts of those days. At some points in our lives, most of us want to go back to a simpler, healthier, or happier time. We can't, but we still keep dreaming about how it once was.

In my twenties, when I was a disc jockey, we used to play oldies, and people who called in to request those songs often commented that music used to be better than it is now. The reality is that in the old days we played good and bad records, but the bad ones faded quickly from memory just like bad ones do now. No one ever asked us to play the music that bombed. The good songs make the former times seem great, as if all the music was outstanding. In reality, there was bad music thirty years ago or fifty years ago—in fact, a lot of bad music. The same is true with experiences. We tend to forget the negative and go back to recapture pleasant events. The reality is, we have selectively remembered—and just as selectively forgotten.

Once that idea got through to me, I decided I couldn't recapture the past. No matter how much I tried to idealize it, that part of my life was over and I would never be healthy or strong again. The only thing for me to do was to discover a new normal.

*Yes,* I said to myself, *there are things I will never be able to do again. I don't like that and may even hate it, but that doesn't change the way things are. The sooner I make peace with that fact and accept the way things are, the sooner I'll be able to live in peace and enjoy my new normalcy.*

Here's an example of what I mean.

In early 2000, I took a group of college kids on a ski trip from Houston to Colorado. Skiing is one of the things I'd always loved doing. Unable to participate, I sat in a clubhouse at the bottom of the hill, gazed out the window, and watched them glide down. Sadness came over me, and I thought, *I made a big mistake. I should never have come here.* As happy as I was for them, I mourned over my inability ever to ski again.

Then I thought for the thousandth time of other things I would never do again. When I was a senior pastor, most of the adults greeted me at the door following each morning service. "Enjoyed your sermon," they'd said. "Great service."

Kids, however, behaved differently. They'd race up with a picture they'd colored for me. Before my accident, I loved the kids flocking around me; I'd kneel down and talk with them. After my recovery, I couldn't squat down and stare at their smiling faces the way I used to before as I said, "Thank you very much. I really like this picture. This is very nice."

After my accident, the best I could do was lean forward and talk to them. Perhaps that doesn't seem like a big thing, but it is for me. I'll never squat again; I'll never be able to kneel so that I can be at a child's level again, because my legs won't give me the ability to do that.

Here's another example: When I go to a drive-through fast-food restaurant, I can't reach for the change with my left arm. The best I can do is reach out across my body with my right arm. It must look strange, and I get a few odd looks, but it's the best I can do.

While neither of these examples is particularly dramatic, they are nonetheless reminders that sometimes things we take for granted every day can be taken from us permanently and suddenly, and we're changed forever.

During my long hospitalization, somebody gave me a magazine article about a young man who lost his sight. He went through an incredibly bitter, depressive time. He wrote that he got so demoralized that a friend who cared enough about him to tell him the truth said, "You just need to get past this."

I paused from reading and thought, *Yes, that sounds like the way I was after my accident.* The article went on, however, to tell the practical instructions the blind man's friend gave him: "I want you to make a list of all the stuff you can still do."

"Now what kind of a list would that be?" the angry blind man asked.

"Just do it for me. You can't write it, obviously, but you can get a tape recorder and dictate it. Just make a list of all the things you can still do. And I'm talking about simple things like 'I can still smell flowers.' Make the list as extensive as you can. When you're finished, I want to hear that list."

The blind man finally agreed and made the list. I don't know how much time passed, but when the friend returned, the blind man was smiling and peaceful.

"You seem like you're in a much better frame of mind than the last time I saw you," the friend said.

"I am. I really am, and that's because I've been working on my list."

"How many things are on your list?"

"About a thousand so far."

"That's fantastic."

"Some of them are very simple. None of them are big, but there are thousands of things I can still do."

The blind man had changed so radically that his friend asked, "Tell me what made you change."

"I've decided to do all the stuff I can. The more I thought about it, the fewer limitations I saw. There are thousands of things I can do—and I'm going to do them for the rest of my life."

After I read that article, I thought, *That's exactly what I need—not mourning, pining, and going back over the way things used to be or what I used to have that I don't have anymore. Instead, I need to discover what I have now, not only to celebrate but also to recognize I'm not helpless.*

As I continued to ponder that idea, I realized I had more going for me than I thought. I had focused so heavily on my losses that I had forgotten what I had left. And I hadn't realized the opportunities I might never have tried otherwise.

In the article, the blind man said something like, "I'm not going to worry about what I can't do. I'm going to do what I can do well." Those words seemed simple.

I read that article at just the right time, and the words seemed incredibly profound. God had sent the message I needed when I needed it. It was one of those powerful moments that caused me to say, "I've got to get on with my life. Whatever I have, I'm going to use it and magnify it to the max."

*I'm running out of time,* I thought, *but so is everyone else.* I suppose I'm more conscious of time than some people are for two reasons: First, I lost a big chunk of my life because of the accident. Second, I know we don't get to stay long on this earth. As many of the old hymns say, we're really like strangers passing through. It's something we all know from reading the Bible and other books, but those realizations became a wake-up call for me.

141

I also know that my loved ones are waiting for me at the gate. Some days I can't wait to get back there.

I also realize that I have to wait until God sends me back.

Members of South Park Baptist Church moved our family while I was hospitalized. We had been living in a town called Friendswood, about ten miles from the church. We had needed a place nearer the church but hadn't found one. While I was in the hospital, the church leaders found a house, rented it, packed up everything for us, and moved us. When I got out of the hospital, I entered a house I had never seen before. After the ambulance backed up and unloaded me from a gurney to my home hospital bed, I stared at our house for the first time.

I soon adjusted to the new living quarters, because for a long time I could only see the living room, where they set up my hospital bed.

In some ways the move into the rented house was more difficult on the family than on me. I sensed some of the adjustments and difficulties my wife went through with my illness. Eva almost lost her job because she had spent so much time with me that she ran out of conference days, vacation days, and sick days. Other teachers donated their own sick days to her so she could come and be with me in the hospital. Eventually, she ran out of those donated days and had to go back to work. She was our primary source of income.

Eva's colleagues at Robert Louis Stevenson Primary School in Alvin often graded her papers for her, wrote her lesson plans, and covered her classes when she left early to come see me in the hospital. Her fellow teachers even made little gifts to give our kids each day so they would have something to look forward to. They called them "surprise boxes." Fellow teachers also came to our home, along with church members, to clean our house and bring meals. Had it not been for the teachers and the church, Eva would have certainly lost her job and so would I. Yet even with all these incredibly sacrificial gifts and assistance, how she and our children got through that spring semester of 1989 remains a miracle.

One time when Eva inquired about my long-term prognosis, a nurse told her, "Honey, you don't need to know all of that, you're just a wife."

To that nurse, she may have been "just a wife," but Eva took over and functioned for both of us after my accident. I had always taken care of the bills, bank accounts, insurance, and most family matters. She had no choice but to handle them herself, and she did everything well. Eva found strength and a new level of confidence. God provided her with the wisdom to help her take care of family matters. She also learned to remain calm during my complaints and grumbling throughout my lengthy recovery.

The church didn't stop paying me, but we realized that they might, and they were entitled to because I wasn't working. We never talked about the money, but it was always a possibility that hung over our heads.

When the State of Texas was found at fault for the accident, the law limited their liability to $250,000. All the money went to hospital bills, and a quarter of a million dollars didn't make much of a dent.

Ironically, the attorney general of Texas defended the man who drove the truck that hit me, because the defendant was an indigent inmate. Therefore my tax dollars went to defend the state and the man who caused the accident. Isn't life strange sometimes?

During the 105 days I spent in the hospital, Eva had the most strain. Not only did she take on the burden of everything in our home, she got up at 6:00 every morning and did everything she had to do around the house and hurried to school. As soon as school was over, she rushed to my bedside, where she stayed until 10:30 every night. Day after day was the same stressful routine.

One of the most challenging experiences for her—by herself—was to buy a van to replace my wrecked car. By then, I was home and able to walk with my Ilizarov still attached. That meant, however, that if I wanted to go anywhere, we had to have a van to transport me. We had no idea how long it would be before I could sit in a normal sedan.

Eva had never bought a vehicle in her life, but she didn't complain. She went to a dealer, test-drove a van, picked out one, and brought it home. "Here's our van," she said.

She made me proud of her—and I felt very grateful.

I learned to drive again in that van. One day as the family was washing it, I walked outside still wearing my Ilizarov. As I lumbered around the van, I noticed that the driver's side door was open. Peering inside, I calculated what it would take for me and my thirty pounds of stainless steel to get behind the wheel. While the family wasn't looking, I maneuvered myself into the seat and started the engine. My family was stunned.

Eva came around to the door and asked, "What are you doing?"

I smiled and said, "I'm going for a drive!"

Incredulous, she stammered, "But you can't."

However, something told me that not having driven for nearly a year, and having had my last drive end in my death, it was now or never for taking the wheel and driving again.

I backed out slowly and drove around the block. It wasn't a long drive, but it was another milestone in my recovery. I'm still not very fond of eighteen-wheelers or long two-lane bridges, but so far I manage to get where I'm going.

Of course, it fell on Eva to make all my appointments and to see that I got to my doctor's office twice a week. And I must add that I wasn't the easiest person to look after. In fact, I was difficult. As my health improved, I became demanding and curt (I wasn't aware of that), and Eva agonized over trying to please me, although she handled it well.

The fact is that I was very unhappy. Many of my problems stemmed from my feeling completely helpless. For a long time I couldn't even get myself a glass of water. Even if I could have poured one for myself, I couldn't have drunk it without help. Even the simplest tasks made me feel useless.

Eva often had to make decisions on the spot without talking to me. She did the best she could. At times, when Eva related what she had done, I was quick to let her know how I would have done it. Almost immediately, I'd realize I hurt her feelings when I did that, but the words had been said. I reminded myself, and her, "I'm sorry. You're doing the best you can." I also reminded myself that regardless of how I would have done things, I wasn't able to do them.

Although she said little during that period, she later allowed me to read what she wrote in her diary. One entry reads: "Don is critical of everything I do. He must be getting better."

That's both sad and funny to me. She knew I was getting better because I started to make decisions again. The desire to get active in doing things was her yardstick for my recovery. I seemed to want to get more involved in life and to question what was going on.

I just wish I had been a better patient and made it easier for her.

The worst part of my convalescence for the family was that we farmed out our three kids. They weren't orphans, but they lived with other people for about six months. Our twin sons stayed with Eva's parents in Louisiana. I know they weren't happy about having to move so far away. The distance made the boys feel detached and separated, but they handled it quite well. They were still in elementary school and, at that age, it probably wasn't too difficult relocating. Nicole, who was five years older and thirteen at the time, moved in with her girlfriend's family and was able to stay in her middle school. It would have been much more traumatic for her to move away.

The accident happened in January, and the kids didn't come home permanently until June. I felt terrible that we couldn't provide for our children.

The kids came to see me on weekends during my hospital stays, which was tough on them. When they made their first visit to the hospital, a staff psychologist did a kind thing for them. He took all three kids into a room and showed them a life-size dummy with devices attached to it, similar to what was on my body. This way he could explain what they would see when they entered my room.

I'm glad he did that for them, because even many adults, not having that kind of preparation, showed obvious shock when they first saw me. In my condition, I interpreted their reactions as horror.

When the children came into my room the first time, all three of them stepped as close as they could to hug me. They loved me and wanted to see for themselves that I was okay. Of course, I was barely alive, but it still did me a lot of good just to see them. The staff didn't let them stay long. As awful as I looked, the children believed me when I said I would get well.

After they left, Eva came back into ICU. I don't remember this—I don't remember much from those days. She said I looked at her through my oxygen mask and said, "We have the best kids in the world."

I've never gotten the impression that our children felt as if they had missed anything, but I sometimes felt they were cheated out of experiences with their father.

When I finally was out and could walk, I remember trying to play pitch with the boys, even though I knew I couldn't take more than a step or two. If one of them hit a ball that went out of my immediate range, I couldn't chase it. They felt terrible about that.

I sensed my limitation kept them from enjoying the game, so we stopped doing it. Although they didn't say so, I knew they didn't want to see me try to run or risk falling down—though many times I did fall.

Also, both boys like to surf, and before the accident, I went surfing with them. After I was able to walk and drive, on several occasions I loaded them and their boards in the van and drove them to the Gulf, but I couldn't do anything with them. I could only watch. They seemed to understand, but it was still hard on me.

I have no doubt that there are things my sons probably wanted to do, but they never mentioned them for fear of putting me in a situation where I'd have to decide whether I might hurt myself. So I do feel that my boys were cheated out of normal boy things in their growing up years.

Nicole, being a girl, had that "Daddy thing." She was our oldest child. She expressed her feelings very differently from Joe, who is a very emotional kid. Chris is the cool one, although deeply sensitive, and doesn't show his feelings as easily as his twin.

While writing this book, I asked my kids to tell me how the accident affected them and our family and how it changed their perception of me. When the accident happened in 1989, Nicole was thirteen years old. Here is her response:

> The biggest impact on my life was living away from my parents for several months. I lived with the Mauldin family from our church during that time. The accident taught me to appreciate my own family. I'm very close to all of them, because I realize how fortunate I was to be a part of such a wonderful family. I also feel that I am able to help people in crisis situations because I learned at a young age how to use prayer and friends to help me get through difficult times. It caused me to look at life in a different way. At a young age I was able to realize that life is precious, and that we have to seize every moment.
>
> I feel that our family is very close because of the accident. I also feel we really look after one another, and that we would do anything for our family members. The boys and I have a special bond that we don't always see between brothers and sisters. Daddy's accident and recovery taught us to be there for each

other. Mom became a lot stronger and independent, because Dad couldn't take care of the things he always had. I only wish Daddy didn't have to go through this to bring us so close together.

After Dad was hurt so bad, I saw for the first time that he was a vulnerable person. Before the accident, he had seemed indestructible. Over the years since, I have seen that the accident has made him even stronger. He may have been hurt physically, but he is the strongest person I know spiritually and emotionally. To have gone through what he did and still be such a loving and devoted servant of God is amazing to me.

For a long time I was angry about the accident, but I grew up and realized how fortunate we are to still have him and how the accident brought us closer. If he had died in that accident I don't know how I would have made it through some of the toughest times in my life. There is something very special about getting advice from someone who has been to heaven, survived countless surgeries, and lived to tell about it. I tend to listen a little harder to him now.

Joe was eight years old at the time of the accident, and this is how he responded:

My first memory was being picked up by a teacher friend of my mother's. When I saw my mom crying, I knew something was very wrong.

I remember going to the hospital to see Dad. They showed us a doll made up to look like Dad's injuries, so when we went in we would be prepared. It was really hard to see Dad like that. We didn't stay long, which was fine with me because I did not like seeing him that way. Chris and I had to move in with our grandparents in Louisiana. I thought it was cool at first, but then I started to miss my family. I'm really glad I had my twin brother with me. Every weekend we drove from Bossier City to Houston. That got old very fast.

The worst thing about the accident was that while other kids were going camping and fishing with their dads, I never got to experience those things. I still think about that a lot even today. Sometimes I feel kind of angry and cheated or depressed. But in the past few years, I've gotten to go camping and fishing with Dad. I'm not sure that he realizes how happy that makes me. Through this experience I realized how many people loved and cared about our family. If we hadn't had God in our lives, I don't know how we would have gotten through this.

This is Chris's response:

When you're an eight-year-old, your father is a superhero. He's invincible. When I first heard about Dad's accident, I didn't think it was nearly as serious as it turned out to be. Mom was upset when she told me the news and couldn't hide the tears. But Dad was strong, and I'd never seen him cry. Even when I saw him surrounded by monitors in the ICU, hooked up to oxygen, and barely able to speak, I fully expected him to be home in a week.

I wasn't present for most of the major surgeries. I went to live with my grandparents only days after the accident and saw my dad only on weekends. During those brief encounters, I began to understand just how bad he hurt—both his body and his spirit.

I was fascinated by the metal contraptions that surrounded his left arm and leg, but I knew they caused him immense pain. He looked so worn out as if he had just woken up, or maybe could never quite fall asleep. Sometimes I got the impression he didn't want me or anyone else in the room. Even as little as I understood about depression, I knew he was suffering from it.

The first thing I did each time I visited him was to approach slowly and put my arms around him. I hugged him gently. For the first time in my life, he seemed fragile. Even when he returned home from the hospital, I continued the same routine—come home from school and hug Dad. It was as much to reassure me as it was to comfort him. I hope it served both purposes.

As my brother, Joe, and I grew older, and Dad's recovery continued, we became more interested in sports and the outdoors. Dad would do his best to join us. I remember feeling terrible when I threw the football too far for Dad's reach. He'd stumble and sometimes he'd fall. I choked back tears on a number of occasions. I'm sure he did the same. But from an emotional standpoint, Dad was always there for me. He is vitally interested in what his kids do. After all, I suppose we make his return from Paradise worthwhile in some regard.

The family grew closer as a result of Dad's accident. We all took different roles out of sheer necessity. Mom became the decision maker and disciplinarian during Dad's recovery. I tried my best to be the man of the house. Sometimes I was really just a bully, but I grew out of it. I learned to lean on the others as they leaned on me. Nicole mothered Joe and me as best she could.

Dad suffered from depression for years after the accident—still does to some extent. Maybe he struggled with it before the accident, but if he did, I never noticed. Dad is fiercely independent and seldom lets his family into his darkest corners. I guess I'm the same way.

Here is Eva's response to how her perception of me has changed:

I was most surprised by Don's lack of determination during the initial days following the wreck. He had always been a fighter, one who was constantly pushing himself and others to do more. When he wouldn't try to breathe it was almost as if I didn't know him. The depression had also been a new aspect. I learned to recognize the sign of a "bad time" approaching. It is harder when the pain is worse; he doesn't sleep and the stress builds.

Through the years I've learned that if I leave Don alone he eventually returns to a more even keel. When I wanted to tell him something he really needed to hear but didn't want to know, I had to bite my tongue—and on a few occasions I didn't succeed.

Today, I don't think of him as injured, even though I know he is and always will be. Don goes at such a pace that it is easy for me to forget his pain and handicaps. My husband is truly a remarkable person.

My kids were probably more confident about my recovery than I was. They never saw me receiving therapy, agonizing, or throwing up because I'd gotten so sick, or seen me when I tried to stand up too fast. As much as possible, we tried to insulate them. Eva saw me at my worst, but she protected the children as much as possible.

Although they don't admit it, there probably is a "Dad gap" for my children, especially the twins. Because they were eight years old, they missed my being there for an important developmental time to help them learn to do things such as play team sports and go camping.

Looking back, I think the accident affected my parents more permanently than anybody. In fact, they were devastated. I'm the oldest of three sons, and all of us had been healthy. Then, suddenly, when I reached the age of thirty-eight, they were heartbroken and felt helpless to do anything for me. For a long time, they thought I would probably die.

My dad had been a career military man, and my mother had to learn to handle just about everything. Yet when they came to see me during the first week in the hospital, Mom fainted. Dad grabbed her and helped her out of the room. She wasn't prepared to see me in such bad shape. I'm not sure anyone would have been.

Even now, I'm not sure my mother has fully recovered from my accident. But here are two of many very beautiful memories of my parents' devotion to me.

First, during the summer following the accident, as if Eva didn't have enough to concern herself with, she decided to take the South Park youth to summer camp. That would have been my job had I been physically able. But she tackled it with gusto. That meant someone would have to stay with me while she was away.

My mother cheerfully agreed to do so. The week of the church youth camp came, and Eva left me with Mom. Each day Mother prepared meals for me, and I was so glad to have her there. But I did dread one daily occurrence—my mother would be required to empty my urinals and bedpans. Now, I know she had diapered me when I was a baby, but a lot of time had passed between infant powderings and the present.

I remember the first time I had to go when she was caring for me, and I asked for the bedpan. She acted as if it were the most natural thing ever. After I had finished, I agonized over having to tell her.

She saved me the embarrassment by asking if I was through. I just nodded. She took the bedpan into the bathroom, and then I heard one of the most remarkable sounds I have ever heard in my life. After she entered the bathroom and flushed the commode, I could hear my mother singing. In spite of the most lowly of tasks one human can perform for another, she sang as she washed out the bedpan. It was as if her whole motherhood was wrapped up in that moment. She was again doing something for her son that he could not do for himself, and she was happy and fulfilled. I will cherish that memory, for it defines the devotion that only a mother could have.

Second, I remember one private moment I had with my father, equally poignant and dramatic. One day, following yet another 250-mile trip to see me for an afternoon at St. Luke's, my parents were preparing for the return trip to their home near Bossier City.

For some reason I don't recall, Mom had stepped out of the room. Alone now, my father came close to my bed and took my only unbroken limb, my right hand, in his gnarled hand. He leaned close to me and with great emotion and absolute honesty said, "I would give anything to trade places with you and take this on me."

He's my dad, and more than at any other time, I realized how much he loves me.

Repeatedly, my doctor has told me, "Everything we did for you is the best we can do. Don't count on being able to live a long, productive life. Because of arthritis and a lot of other complications that will set in, you're going to have an uphill battle to be even as mobile as you are now."

He knew what he was talking about. It's been fifteen years since my accident. I've already felt the beginning of arthritis. Weather changes affect me; I grow tired faster. Some of it may be age, but I think it's a reflection of the fact that I have to use my legs and knees in ways God didn't design them to be used.

Even today, my left knee hyperextends, so if someone comes from behind and inadvertently slaps me on the back, I have to catch myself or I'll keep going forward. I can't lock my knee into place to keep from losing my balance and pitching forward.

I've tried to make light of this, quipping, "I've fallen in some of the best places in Texas." Or, "I've considered commissioning some little plaques that say, 'Don Piper fell here.'"

One time I led an outdoor conference in the Texas hill country. The ground was uneven and I'd walk along and all of a sudden, I'd fall. I wasn't hurt, but I fell three times the first day.

Despite everything they did for me, one of my legs is an inch and a half shorter than the other. That alone makes my backbone curve. The backbone is beginning to show wear and tear, as are my hip joints. My left elbow is so messed up I can't straighten it out. Doctors did everything they could, including operating on it several times. The elbow was fractured on the inside, and when it knitted back together, it wouldn't allow me to straighten it. To use the doctor's expression, "It's a very gimpy joint."

An injury like that, he pointed out, is not forgiving. Once it gets messed up, it's hard to fix it again.

This is part of my new normal.

Once after a visit to Dr. Tom Greider's office, he asked me back into his private suite. Despite his busy caseload, I felt he was genuinely interested in me, and we talked about a lot of things.

On a whim I asked, "Tom, just how bad was I when they brought me in that night of the accident?"

He didn't flinch. "I've seen worse." He paused for a moment, leaned over his desk, and then continued, "but none of them lived."

I've had to find different ways to do things. I am alive, however, and I intend to serve Jesus Christ as long as I remain alive. But I already know what's ahead, waiting for me.

I'm ready to leave this earth anytime.

# 15
# TOUCHING LIVES

> All praise to the God and Father of our Lord Jesus Christ. He
> is the source of every mercy and the God who comforts us. He
> comforts us in all our troubles so that we can comfort others.
> When others are troubled, we will be able to give them the same
> comfort God has given us.
>
> 2 CORINTHIANS 1:3–4

Sometimes I still ask God why I wasn't allowed to stay in heaven. I have no answer to that question. I have learned, however, that God brings people into my life who need me or need to hear my message, giving me the opportunity to touch their lives.

One of the first times I was able to minister to someone as a result of my accident was when I was the guest preacher in a large church. They invited me specifically to talk about my trip to heaven. A woman who sat near the front and to my left began to weep shortly after I began to speak. I could see the tears sliding down her cheeks. As soon as we closed the meeting, she rushed up to me and clasped my hand.

"My mother died last week."

"I'm so sorry for your loss—"

"No, no, you don't understand. God sent you here tonight. I needed this kind of reassurance. Not that I didn't believe—I did, but my heart has been so heavy because of the loss. I feel so much better. She *is* in a better place. Oh, Reverend Piper, I needed to hear that tonight."

Before I could say anything more, she hugged me and added, "God also sent *me* here tonight because I needed this reassurance. Not that I didn't believe and didn't know—because I'm a believer and so was she—but I needed to hear those words tonight. I needed to know about heaven from someone who had been there."

So far as I recall, she was the first to talk to me that way, but certainly not the last. I've heard this kind of response hundreds of times. It still amazes me that I can be a blessing to so many just by sharing my experience.

For those who already believe, my testimony has been reassuring; for skeptics, it's opened them up to think more seriously about God.

Two years after the accident, when I still wore leg braces and walked with crutches, I took a group of our young people to a conference at Houston's First Baptist Church. Dawson McAllister, a great teacher to youth, was the speaker. He's so popular he fills up the place.

As happens when you work with teens, we were late in leaving South Park Church. I didn't say anything, but I felt extremely irritated with the delay. I had wanted to arrive early because I knew the best seats would be taken if we didn't get there at least an hour before starting time.

I tried not to let it show, but I was still upset by the time we reached First Baptist Church in Houston. Once we went inside the huge building, we realized—as I had expected—that all the seats on the lower floor were filled. We'd have to climb the stairs.

I groaned at the thought of having to do more walking. Even though I was mobile, wearing those braces and the pressure of the crutches under my armpits tired me out. To make it worse, the elevator wasn't working. *If that person hadn't been late,* I kept thinking, *I wouldn't have to hobble up all those stairs.*

It wasn't just clumping up the stairs, but the auditorium was so full that the only places left to sit were in the top rows. Our young people, naturally, raced ahead to claim those seats. They promised to save one for me on the end. I counted 150 steps as I painfully made my way up.

By the time I finally reached the top, exhaustion had overcome me. I could hardly walk the last flight and across the back of the auditorium to the seat the kids had saved for me. Before I sat down—which also demanded a lot of effort—I rested by leaning against the wall. As I tried to catch my breath, I asked myself, *What am I doing here?*

I could have gotten other adults to take the kids, but I really wanted to be with them. I wanted to feel useful again. I also knew this would be an exciting event for the youth, and I wanted to be part of it. Boisterous laughter and shouting back and forth filled the place. The youth were ready to be blessed and challenged, but at that moment, I didn't think about the kids or how much they would get out of the meeting. I thought only of being worn out.

At that moment self-pity took over. As I continued to lean against the wall, my gaze swept the auditorium. Two sections over I spotted a teenage boy in a wheelchair. He was sitting with his head in his hands, his back to me. As I stared at him, I *knew* I had to go over and talk to him. Suddenly I didn't question my actions and I forgot about being tired.

I leaned my crutches against the wall and then slowly, painfully made my way across to his section and down the steps. He was a large, good-looking kid, maybe sixteen years old. When I got closer, I realized why I needed to talk to him. He was wearing an Ilizarov frame—which I hadn't been able to see from where I had stood. My tiredness vanished, along with my anger and self-pity. It was as if I saw myself in that wheelchair and reexperienced all the pain of those days.

He was looking away from me when I laid my hand on his shoulder. His head spun around and he glared at me.

"That really hurts doesn't it?" I asked.

He looked at me as if to say, *What kind of fool are you?* Instead he said, "Yeah. It hurts very much."

"I know." I patted his shoulder. "Believe me, I know."

His eyes widened. "You do?"

"I do. I had one too."

"It's horrible."

"I know that. It's just horrible. I wore one on my left leg for eleven months."

"Nobody ever understands," he said plaintively.

"They can't. It's not something you can talk about and have anyone understand your pain."

For the first time I saw something in his eyes. Maybe it was hope, or maybe just a sense of peace because at long last he had found someone who knew what he was going through. We had connected, and I felt privileged to be standing next to him.

"My name is Don," I said, "and you've just met somebody who understands the pain and the discouragement you're going through."

He stared at me, and then his eyes moistened. "I don't know if I'm going to make it."

"You're going to make it. Trust me, you'll make it."

"Maybe," he said.

"What happened?" By then I'd realized it hadn't been a voluntary surgery.

"I had a ski accident."

I noticed that he was wearing a letter jacket. I asked, "You a football player?"

"Yes, sir."

Briefly I told him about my accident, and he told me more about what had happened to him. "I'm going to tell you something," I said. "One day you will walk again."

His face registered skepticism.

"You might not play football again, but you'll walk." I handed him my business card. "My number is on the card, and you can call me anytime, day or night, twenty-four hours a day."

He took the card and stared at it.

"I'm going to walk back up there to my kids." I pointed to where they sat. "I want you to watch me. And as you watch, I want you to know that one day you will walk too." I laughed. "And I'll bet you'll walk better than I do."

He reached up, grabbed me, and hugged me. He held me tight for a long time. I could feel his constricted breathing as he fought back tears. Finally he released me and mumbled his thanks.

161

"You've found somebody who understands," I said. "Please call me."

That boy needed somebody who understood. I don't know that I had much to offer, but I had my experience and I could talk to him about pain. Had I not gone through it myself, I'd just be telling him, "I hope you feel better. You're going to be okay"—well-meaning words that most people used.

When I reached the top row, perspiration drenched my body from all the effort, but I didn't care. I turned around. He still stared at me. I smiled and waved, and he waved back. The dejection and despair had left his face.

Over the next six months, I received three calls from him, two just to talk and one late at night when he was really discouraged. They were phone calls I will always cherish, one struggling pilgrim to another.

One time, a Houston TV station scheduled me to appear on a live talk show. While I was waiting in their greenroom, the producer came in and began to explain how the show worked and some of the questions I could expect to be asked.

"That's fine," I said. "Who else is a guest on the show?"

"You're it."

"Wait a minute. You're going to do an hour-long show and I'm the only guest?"

"That's right."

I wondered what I would talk about for an hour. It was fairly early in my recovery, and at the time I had no idea how interested people were in my story. By then the doctor had removed the Ilizarov frame and I was wearing braces and using crutches. I had brought pictures of me in the hospital, which they televised that day. And I brought the Ilizarov device itself.

Once the TV interview started, I told my story, and then the host asked me questions. The hour passed quickly. While we were still live on the show, a woman called the TV station and insisted, "I need to talk to Reverend Piper immediately."

They wouldn't interrupt the program, but as soon as the program ended, someone handed me a slip of paper with her telephone number. I called her.

"You've got to talk to my brother," she said.

"What's the matter with him?"

"He was involved in a fight in a bar, and another man pulled out a shotgun and blew his leg off. He's wearing one of those things like you used to have on your leg."

"Of course I'll talk to him," I said. "Where is he?"

"He's home in bed."

"Give me the address and I'll go—"

"Oh no, you can't go over there. He's angry and mean. And he's violent. He won't talk to anybody who comes to see him." She gave me his telephone number. "Please call him, but he's so mean right now, I guarantee that he'll cuss you out." Then she added, "And he may just hang up on you, but try him anyway. Please."

As soon as I got home, I called her brother and introduced myself. Before I had spoken more than three sentences, he did just what she had predicted. He yelled at me. He screamed and let me have it with just about every swear word I'd ever heard, and he repeated them several times.

When he paused I said quietly, "I had one of those things on my leg that you have—that fixator."

He didn't say anything for a few seconds, so I said, "I wore one of those Ilizarov devices on my left leg. I know what you must be going through."

"Oh, man, this is killing me. It hurts all the time. It's just—" and he went off again as if he hadn't heard me, peppering his anger with a lot of profanity.

When he paused again, I said, "I understand what it feels like to have one of them."

"You don't have it anymore?"

"No, I finally got it off. If you do what you're supposed to do, you can get yours off one day." That didn't sound like much, but it was the only thing I could think to say.

"If I had some wrenches I'd take it off right now."

"If you take it off, you might as well cut your leg off, because it's the only thing that's holding your leg on."

"I know that, but it's just killing me. I can't sleep—" Then he went on again, telling me how miserable he was and how much he hated everything.

Then something occurred to me, and I interrupted him. "What does your leg look like? Does it seem to be hot near the pinholes? Is it the same color up and down your skin? Are there certain holes that hurt more than others?"

"Yeah, that's right. One of them especially—man, it hurts real bad."

"Is your sister there yet?" When he said she was, I ordered him, "Put her on the phone."

He didn't argue and she picked up the phone. "Thank you," she said. "I appreciate so—"

"Listen to me," I said, interrupting her. "I want you to call an ambulance *right now.* Take your brother to the hospital as fast

164

as you can get there. He has a serious infection in that leg. If he doesn't get there soon, he's going to lose his leg."

"You think so?"

"I'm telling you. He has all the symptoms. He's probably got a fever too. Have you checked?"

"Yes, that's right. He's running a fever."

"Get him to the hospital immediately. Call me afterward."

The next day she called. "Oh, you were right! He has an infection, and he was in terrible shape. They gave him all those antibiotics. They said he got there just in time, and he's doing better today."

"I assume he's still in the isolation unit." When she said he was, I added, "I'm going to come and see him."

As a minister I could get in to see him. I went to the hospital, talked to him, and prayed with him. Eventually that young man turned to Jesus Christ.

If I hadn't been on that TV show and his sister hadn't watched it, he might not have only lost a leg; there is a strong possibility that he would have died. Not only had God used me to save the young man's physical life but I had been an instrument in his salvation. That was just one more instance of my beginning to see that God still has things for me to do here on earth.

I had immediately recognized the problem because it had happened to me when I was still in the hospital. I had gotten an infection and began hurting badly. I thought it was just part of the pain I'd have to go through. Then a nurse discovered that I had infection in one of those pinholes.

I remembered then how days before, one of the nurses apparently had cross-contaminated the pinholes. She was a surly type and never showed me compassion like the others. She came in and did her work, but she acted as if she resented having to work with me.

They used Q-tips, and they had been instructed to use a new one to clean each hole. I had noticed that this time, the nurse didn't get a fresh Q-tip each time, probably because it was faster not to reach for a new one. I didn't think anything about that until after the hole became infected. My added pain had come about because of her laziness. Once they discovered the infection and my elevated temperature, they rushed me into the isolation unit, where I stayed for two weeks. While I was there, no one could visit me.

Eva complained and told the doctor what happened. I never saw that nurse again, so I don't know if they fired her or transferred her.

As much as I enjoy public speaking, few opportunities excite me more than speaking at my alma mater, Louisiana State University (LSU). My wife and I met at LSU, and two of our three children also studied there.

One of the on-campus organizations where I have spoken on several occasions is the Baptist Collegiate Ministry (BCM). While Nicole was a student at LSU and served as one of the officers in that group, the BCM invited me to speak. Knowing she would be in the audience made the experience even more delightful.

Among the many campus activities the BCM sponsored was a Thursday night praise and worship service called TNT. The committee asked me to speak to them about my accident.

The students advertised my talk all over campus as "Dead Man Talking." Because so many showed up, they scheduled two back-to-back services. As I spoke, the audience seemed mesmerized by the story of a man who died and came back to life. I spoke of heaven, answered prayer, and miracles. I told them about singing "What a Friend We Have in Jesus" in the car with Dick Onerecker.

As each service ended, the praise band led us in a chorus of that meaningful song. I didn't know they were going to do it. While I have no doubt they were led by the Spirit to do so, "What a Friend We Have in Jesus" remains a difficult song for me to hear or sing.

Afterward a large number of students waited around to ask questions. Among them was an African-American student named Walter Foster. He asked many questions himself and stayed and listened to the other students' questions as well. When I left the auditorium, Walter followed me. Although I didn't mind, I felt as if he pursued me with dogged determination—as if he couldn't get enough details about heaven or hear enough about my experience.

A few months later, Nicole called me. "Do you remember Walter Foster?" Her voice broke and she started to cry. As soon as I said I remembered him, she said, "He . . . he died. He suffered a heart attack! Just like that—and he was gone."

Apparently Walter had known about his serious heart condition and was under medical care; everyone assumed he was doing all right. Obviously his death shocked all the students who knew him.

"Twenty-year-old students aren't supposed to die," one of his friends had said.

After I hung up the phone, I thought back to the day when Walter and I met. I wondered if he had had a premonition about his death. The fact that he followed me the whole time I was at LSU and plied me with endless questions about heaven caused me to wonder. His questions seemed more than just curiosity. *Maybe,* I thought, *even then God was preparing him for his homeward journey.*

His sudden death devastated his friends, especially those involved with the Baptist Collegiate Ministry. They were a close-knit group and mourned the loss of their dear member. The night following his death, they gathered at the BCM building—the place Walter loved most.

During an emotional meeting that night, a number of his friends spoke at length about how much it had meant to Walter that I had shared my experience about heaven. Many mentioned the excitement he expressed to them over what he had heard. He talked about it for days afterward.

"Several times during the day when Reverend Piper was here," one of them said, "Walter told me, 'One day I know I'm going to be in heaven myself!'"

Pressing church business kept me from being at Walter's memorial service at First Baptist Church of Baton Rouge. Nicole represented our family and reported that evening about the celebration of Walter's life. Two special requests from his friends were that the preacher would share the gospel message and that someone would sing one particular song. Of course, it was "What a Friend We Have in Jesus." The audience learned the special significance that hymn held for Walter.

Nicole, a music major at LSU and an excellent soloist, sang the song to the assembled mourners. They responded with both great sadness and glorious hope. Tears flowed and many smiled peacefully.

After the service, many students lingered to talk about how much Walter's unwavering belief in heaven had comforted and encouraged them.

One of the other bright things to emerge from my testimony at the BCM and Walter's later passing was the construction and dedication of a prayer garden at the LSU BCM. That seems appropriate to me, because each time I share my story, I stress the paramount importance of prayer. After all, I'm still alive because of answered prayer.

Like many others whose lives have divinely intersected with mine since my accident and my return from heaven, Walter represents those who will be waiting for me the next time God calls me home.

Sue Fayle's first husband died of cancer. His long torturous passing took a lot out of her. She assumed she would live the rest of her life as a widow. But her neighbor Charles, also without a spouse, changed that. They were not only neighbors, but in their common sense of loss, they became good friends. As time passed, they seemed to fulfill needs for each other in a way that only those who have loved and lost seem to understand. Their friendship evolved into love, and they cautiously considered marriage.

Sue had serious reservations about marrying Charles because he came from what she called a rough-and-tough working-class neighborhood. He had a history of hard drinking, and she said, "I can't live with that."

As their love continued to grow, however, Sue issued one simple condition for marriage: "I won't marry a man who gets drunk."

Charles not only stopped getting drunk, he quit drinking altogether. Now they were ready to talk of marriage.

One day they talked about the death of their spouses—both of whom had died of cancer. "If I'm ever diagnosed with cancer," he said, "I'll kill myself." He knew that not only did the person with the disease suffer but their loved ones went through deep agony as well. "I couldn't put anyone through that ordeal."

They did marry, had a good marriage, and Charles never drank again. Sue had already been active in our church, but after their marriage, Charles also became active.

One day, however, he received the one diagnosis he feared most of all: He had cancer. Now he had to face his deep-seated terror. He was afraid that his diagnosis would put Sue through the same terrible ordeal she had faced before.

He also faced another fear after he received the diagnosis: The news forced him to confront his own mortality. "I'm terrified of dying," he confessed. Although Charles was a church member and said he believed, he was one of those individuals who doubted his salvation. Sue assured him that while she was dedicated to seeing him through this crisis, she was concerned about his lack of assurance of his salvation. She had heard my testimony about heaven on several occasions and had retold my story to others.

"Can you talk to Charles?" she asked me one day. "He needs to hear your testimony from you."

By then I had become the single adult minister of Pasadena's First Baptist Church, where I am today. Sue and I had worked together on projects on many occasions.

"Please talk to him about salvation, but also tell him about what life is like after death. I believe that a man-to-man talk with Charles would do a lot for him."

I knew Charles, of course, and because of his past, I suspected he thought he wasn't good enough for God. I agreed to talk to him.

Charles and I hit it off right away. He was a great guy and easy to relate to. I made it a point to visit him on a regular basis. Whenever I came, Sue excused herself and stayed out of the room until I was ready to leave.

Even as Charles's health deteriorated, he never displayed the least bit of anger or depression. We even talked about how difficult it was to be dependent on others for even the most personal of functions—bedpans, urinals, and bathing.

About the fourth time I visited, Charles finally opened up. "I'm afraid. I want to go to heaven, but I need assurance—I want to be certain that when I die, I'll go to heaven."

As he talked about his life, it was obvious that his experience with God was authentic. As is often the case, for many years before he married Sue, he simply hadn't been a faithful follower of Christ. Several times I reminded him of the verses in the Bible that promise heaven as the ultimate destination for all believers.

"I know, I know," he said. "Before I was saved, I knew I wouldn't go to heaven. I was going to hell. Now I want to be sure about heaven."

My description of heaven encouraged him. "Yes, yes, that's what I want," he said.

On one visit as he talked, he smiled and said, "I'm ready. I'm at peace. I finally know that I'll go to heaven."

On both of the last two visits I made, Charles said, "Tell me again. Tell me once more what heaven is like."

I told him again, even though he had already heard everything I had to say. It was as if his assurance grew each time I talked about heaven.

A short time before he died, Sue put Charles in hospice at the Houston Medical Center, just a few doors away from where I had been hospitalized for such a long time.

On the last day of his life on earth, Charles told Sue, "It's going to be all right. I'm going from pain to peace. Someday we'll be together again."

When Sue called and told me, she added, "He died absolutely without fear."

Charles's calm assurance and acceptance gave Sue peace as she worked through her own grief and loss. She told me that only weeks before his death, he'd said listening to my experience and seeing the positive glow in my life made the difference. "It's settled," he'd said. "I know I'm going to a better place."

As Sue shared her memories of Charles, she laughed and said, "Won't I be the lucky one? I've got two men waiting for me. One day, when my time comes, I'll have one on each arm, former husbands who are also brothers in Christ, and they can escort me down the streets of gold."

When Joe, one of my twins, reached his teens, we decided to look for a used car for him. He wanted a truck, so we searched until we found one he liked, a 1993 Ford Ranger.

The dealer's name was Gary Emmons; he owned a longtime automobile dealership in our area. Once we settled on the truck Joe wanted, we went inside to make the deal. Mr. Emmons gave us an excellent price, and Joe bought the truck.

Because of that experience, a good relationship formed between Gary Emmons and my family. We bought three or four more cars from him after that.

Gary knew a little about what had happened to me, but no details. He was a race-car driver as well as a car dealer. He seemed fascinated with my story. He had said he'd like to hear the whole story one day, but either he was too busy or I had to rush on.

One day Joe went to the dealership to make a payment. Gary waved him over. "You'll never believe this." The man grinned. "An amazing thing happened yesterday."

"What?"

"I went to check out a car that we had just bought. I got inside the car to do the things I usually do—you know, punch all the buttons to see if everything works—things like listen to the engine for any defects, check the air conditioner, and see if the radio works. I noticed a tape inside the cassette deck. I pushed the eject button."

He paused and smiled. "Bet you'll never guess what was on that tape."

"I have no idea," Joe said.

"It was your dad's story. We had bought the car in an auction, so there was no owner to give the tape back to. I took the tape and listened to it. The only thing I could think of when I heard it was one word—*awesome*."

As I look back, it's amazing. Gary had wanted to hear my story, but we just had not gotten together.

"What are the odds of my going to an automobile auction with thousands of cars for sale," Gary asked Joe, "then I sit inside one, push a button, and hear your dad talking?"

For days after that, I think Gary must have told everybody he talked to about my accident.

Of course, that testimony thrilled me. I've also heard many other stories of the way God has used my story.

I had made a tape about my experience while preaching in my church, Pasadena's First Baptist, and had it duplicated. I must have distributed thousands of them. I also know people took the tape and copied it for their friends. I know people who ordered as many as twenty tapes over a period of months.

That testimonial tape just keeps going on and on. Many people who heard my story duplicated it for people going through physical trauma themselves or those who are dealing with the loss of a loved one.

I can only conclude that God had a plan for Gary Emmons to hear that tape and made sure he did.

One day while I was walking down the hallway of First Baptist Church of Pasadena, a woman stopped me. That's not unusual, of course. In fact, my wife jokes that it takes me thirty minutes to walk twenty feet because everyone has something he or she needs to ask me or tell me. We have over ten thousand members; that's a lot of folks to get around to.

"Oh, Reverend Piper, I came by just to see you. I want to tell you something—something that I think you need to hear."

Usually when someone starts out that way, he usually adds, "It's for your own good," and it's usually not something I want to hear. Several other people were with me, and I wasn't sure how to react. As I stared at her, however, I sensed an urgency in her face and a deep intensity. I turned to the others and asked, "Would you mind?"

They were gracious, of course.

"I'm a registered nurse, and you will never believe what happened."

"I've had a lot of unbelievable things happen. Just try me."

"This happened at the hospital. A woman whose mother was very ill and hospitalized was able to hear your tape, and it changed her life."

I had heard that before, but I never minded hearing new stories, so I said, "Tell me more."

"Somebody brought her this tape and she wasn't a believer. But the person wanted her to listen to the tape anyway. Her friends had tried to talk to her about God. They had given her Bibles, all kinds of books and pamphlets, but nothing affected her. She said, 'I don't want to talk about God, religion, or salvation.' Even though she was terminally ill, she wasn't open to any message about eternity."

She paused to wipe a tear from her eyes before she continued, "Somebody brought her a tape—your tape about your experience in heaven—and asked her if she would listen to it. The friend didn't press it, but said something casual like, 'You might find this helpful. It's about a man who died, went to heaven, and came back to life again.'"

The nurse told me that the woman said that she might listen to it if she thought about it. The friend left. The tape lay on the stand next to her bed, unheard. Her health soon deteriorated so badly that doctors told her daughter that it was only a matter of a week, two at the most.

The daughter, who was a believer, desperately wanted her mother to hear the tape of my testimony. The tape contains two messages. The first side tells of the miracles that had to happen for me to live, and recounts the answered prayer that took place for me to live—as I've written about earlier in this book. The second side of the tape tells about what heaven is like. I called it "The Cure for Heart Trouble." That's the part the daughter wanted her mother to listen to.

175

But the woman refused. "I don't want to listen to all that stuff," she said.

Days went by, and the older woman's condition grew more desperate. The nurse who was talking to me, and who was a Christian, realized what was going on. After she talked with the daughter, the nurse decided to talk to the patient herself about her soul—something she had not done before. She reasoned that sometimes it's easier for a stranger or someone less known to give a positive witness than it is for a family member.

After working her shift, the nurse walked into the room and asked, "May I sit down and talk to you a few minutes?"

The dying woman nodded.

Gently and discreetly the nurse talked about faith and God's peace and how much of a difference Jesus Christ had made in her own life.

The whole time, the woman said nothing.

The nurse mentioned the tape. "I've heard it, and I think it's something you would like to know. Would you like to listen to the tape?"

The old woman nodded, so the nurse put the tape in the cassette recorder and left.

The next day the dying woman told her daughter and the nurse that she had listened to the tape. "I found it very interesting. I'm seriously thinking about becoming a Christian."

Even though the nurse and the daughter rejoiced, they didn't try to pressure the dying woman. Two days passed before the woman said, "I have become a believer." She told her daughter first and then the nurse. After that, no matter who came into the room to see her, the dying woman would say, "I have become a Christian. I've accepted Jesus Christ as my Savior and I'm going to heaven."

Within hours after her publicly telling others about her conversion, the woman's condition deteriorated. She drifted in and out of consciousness. The next day when the nurse came on duty, she learned that the old woman had died only minutes earlier.

The nurse told me all of that and then said, "You won't believe what was happening during those final moments while she was dying."

Before I could ask, she said, "The tape recorder was on the bed beside her, and her daughter had put in the second side of your tape where you describe heaven. As her life drifted away, she was listening to your account of what heaven is like. The last thing she heard before she left this world to join God in heaven was a description of heaven."

Despite my trying to remain stoic, tears seeped from the corners of my eyes.

"I just thought you'd like to know that."

"Yes," I said. "Thank you for telling me. That's great encouragement for me."

As she retold some of the story to those with me, I thanked God for bringing me back to earth. "Oh, God, I do see some purpose in my staying here. Thank you for allowing me to hear this story."

One time I preached at the Chocolate Bayou Baptist Church, south of Houston. They had asked me to share my death-and-heaven experience.

I was getting my final thoughts together. Typically, in Baptist churches, they have a soloist or some kind of special music just before the guest speaker comes to the pulpit. A woman, who had not been in the service and apparently didn't know what I was going to talk about, came in from a side door to sing.

She had a lovely voice and began to sing a song called "Broken and Spilled Out" about the alabaster jar the woman used when she washed Jesus' feet.

As soon as she sat down, I stood up and began to tell them about my accident. I didn't make any connection between her song and my message, but I noticed that several people kept frowning at the woman.

After the service, I heard someone say to the soloist, "That was an interesting song about being broken and spilled out for you to sing before Don talked." The way he said the word *interesting* really meant *tasteless*.

"Oh!" she said. The shock on her face made me aware that she hadn't known what I was going to speak about. Obviously, she hadn't made the connection either.

Our eyes met and she started to cry. "I'm sorry . . . I'm sorry."

"That's fine," I said. "Really, it's all right." I started to walk on.

"Broken and spilled," someone said. "That's what happened to you, wasn't it?" At least a dozen people made similar comments. A few assumed we had planned for her to sing that particular song.

I stopped and looked back. The soloist stood next to the piano, and she was crying. I excused myself and walked back to her. "That's a beautiful song about a wonderful experience. You didn't know what I was going to talk about, but that's all right, because I can't think of a better song."

178

She smiled in gratefulness and started to apologize again. "It's fine. Really, it's fine," I assured her.

As I walked away, I thought maybe I had been broken and spilled out. But I smiled at another idea: *I'm also being put back together again.*

# 16
# FINDING PURPOSE

I am convinced of this, so I will continue with you so that you
will grow and experience the joy of your faith.

PHILIPPIANS 1:25

Brad Turpin, a motorcycle police officer from the Houston suburb of Pasadena, almost lost a leg. His police motorcycle crashed into the back of a flatbed truck. He would have bled out on the concrete if the EMTs hadn't applied a tourniquet to his leg.

Sonny Steed, the former minister of education at our church, knew Brad personally and asked me to go see him. "Absolutely," I said, especially after I heard that he would be wearing a fixator. I called and made sure he'd let me come. I don't know why, but just before we left, I picked up pictures showing my accident and my recovery.

Sonny drove me to the officer's house. Once we had walked inside, it was almost like seeing the way my living room had looked for months. Brad was lying in a hospital bed with the trapeze bar above him. His device was similar, but not quite the same as mine, because in the dozen years since my accident, technology had improved.

Other people were there, so I sat down and joined in casual conversation. He was nice enough, but I knew he'd seen so many people he was tired of visitors. As soon as the last visitor left, I said, "You really are tired of talking to people aren't you?"

Brad nodded.

"I understand. You almost feel like you're on display here. The phone never stops ringing. Everybody wants to come by to see you."

He nodded again. "I appreciate them coming, but I need some peace and quiet."

"I apologize for interrupting you, but Sonny brought me by to see you because I wanted to talk to you about what to expect. I pointed to the Ilizarov and said, "I had one of these external fixators."

"Oh, you did?"

I showed him my pictures, beginning with those taken the day after they put on the Ilizarov frame. Each one showed progression to the next step. He stared at each one closely and saw that I had been worse off than he was.

"And you recovered, didn't you?"

"Yes, I did, and so will you."

"That's good that you made it all right, but I don't think I'm going to make it. They can't give me any guarantee that I'm going to keep this leg. The doctors are pessimistic, so that makes it harder for me."

"Well, that's just the way they are," I said, remembering so well my feelings in those early days. "They try to err on the side of being conservative and try not to get your hopes up. Months from now, they know, you could have this fixator and everything could be working fine and then your leg could get infected and you could still lose it."

"That's what I mean. I'm just not sure it's worth all this pain."

"The good news is that the pain will ease up as you get better."

His wife had walked in during the conversation and listened. "I'm just so tired at the lack of progress, and nobody will tell us anything," she said. "We're about ready to change doctors."

"You might find a better doctor," I said, "but wait a bit. Be patient. I'm sure your doctor is doing his best."

Then I told them about the time I reached the end of my patience:

"When my doctor came in to see me I was fuming.

"'Sit down,' I yelled.

"He did, and for maybe five minutes I complained about everything that bothered and upset me. As I watched his face, I realized I had hurt his feelings. I hadn't been thinking about him, of course. I was hurting, never pain free, couldn't sleep, and I wanted answers. 'I get tired of all this not knowing. I ask you how long I have to wear this, and you say, "Maybe another month, maybe two months, maybe three months."' I wasn't through yet, and my anger really burst out with another round of complaints. I ended with, 'Why can't you give me a straight answer?'

"He dropped his head and said softly, 'I'm doing the best I can. I don't know the answers. That's why I can't tell you.'

"'I'm just looking for—'

"'I know you are, but this isn't an exact science. We're re-inventing the wheel. We don't have that much experience in this area, and this is all new technology for us. We're doing the best we can.'"

After I told Brad and his wife about that incident, I added, "Please be patient with your doctor. He can't give you answers he doesn't have. He'll also tell you things to do and load you down with prescriptions. He's going to put you in a lot of therapy, and you're just going to have to learn how to deal with it—with all of it."

"Yeah, I know," he said, "but I just can't control my emotions anymore. I'm a cop. I've seen a lot of hard, bad, difficult stuff. I find myself just breaking down—I mean, real emotional. Know what I mean?"

"Absolutely. Just go ahead and break down. It'll happen again."

"I feel out of control."

"You are out of control!"

Brad stared at me.

"Think about it. What can you control? Nothing."

"I can't even wipe myself."

"That's right. You're totally helpless. There's nothing you can do or control."

"Before this I was a weight lifter and a bodybuilder," he said. "I had a physique you wouldn't believe."

"I have no doubt about that." I could see that he had once been muscular and strong. "But you don't have that now. You may have a great body again someday, but the inability to get up and do the things that you used to do will cause you to change. Be prepared to change. You're going to lose weight; muscles will atrophy. You can't control your body the way you did before."

His wife was obviously feeling all the stress as well, and she was on the verge of tears. "He just feels so bad, even with medication. I just don't know what to do."

"I can suggest a few things. First of all, manage the visits and phone calls. You don't have to let everyone come whenever they want," I said. "Be firm. If you allow everyone to come, you'll wear yourself out trying to be nice. Your friends will understand."

Then I turned to Brad. "Be prepared for all your therapy, because you're going to have to do all kinds of difficult things. Do them if you want to learn to walk again. Be patient, because it will take a long time. Probably one of the best things I can tell you is this: Don't try to act like the Lone Ranger." I paused briefly and almost smiled, because I remembered how I had been. "Let people know where you hurt and how they can help—especially the people you trust. Let them know so they can do things for you. Let them pray for you. You've got a lot of nice folks coming by here, and they want to bring you a cake, cook a meal, or do something for you. Let them express their friendship and love."

After I had talked a few minutes, I got up to leave. I wrote down my phone number. "Call me. If you're struggling to go to sleep at three o'clock in the morning or you're angry, call me. I'll listen. I'll understand because I *can* understand. It's a small fraternity, and none of us joined it by choice."

Before I left, Brad said, "I can't tell you how much I appreciate your coming by. Just visiting with somebody who knows about the pain helps me a lot. You're the first person I've met who understands what it's like to live with pain twenty-four hours a day."

"It's not something I set out to do—visiting people who are where I was," I said, "but I'm willing to do it. I want to help, but you're going to have to make the effort to call me. Remember—don't try to tough it out alone."

Brad's wife followed me out to the car and said, "He needed this. In public he tries to be the source of strength and sound positive. In quiet moments he's frustrated and emotional, and he falls apart. I've been really worried about him. Never in our lives together have I seen him this way."

"I remember my wife working hard all day teaching school and then coming to spend the evening with me," I said. "Just hang in with him. He will get better."

I told her that one time when I was at my worst, Eva had tried to encourage me and had said something like, "Just give it time. You're going to be fine."

I had exploded with frustration and rage—"What makes you think I'm going to be fine? What are the odds of my ever being fine? Nobody can ever tell me that. Nobody can promise me that."

To her credit, Eva hadn't argued. She'd wrapped her arms around me. I had wept. I had never done that before in her presence.

After I told that story to Brad's wife, I said, "Be prepared for changes in your life and his. He can't control his emotions, but don't take it as a personal attack when he yells or screams. It's the pain and the frustration, not you." I shook her hand and said, "And for goodness' sake, call me if you need me. Push Brad to call me."

After that, I saw Brad four or five times. Weeks later when he was able to get out of the house with his walker, I spotted him in a restaurant. I went over to his table and sat down. "How are you doing?" I asked.

"I'm doing okay. Really okay." He thanked me again for coming at one of his lowest moments. He still wasn't in top shape, but he was getting healthy again. When he clasped my hand and held it a long time, I knew it was his way of expressing his appreciation in ways he couldn't put into words.

I felt grateful to God for being able to help Brad in his dark time.

About two years after my accident, I heard that Chad Vowell had been in a serious car accident. He had been a member of our youth ministry at South Park, and his parents were among the most supportive parents I had at the church. His mother, Carol, was on the committee that came to my hospital room with others to plan youth retreats. I hadn't been very helpful, but it had been their way of making me feel useful and needed.

Chad had been an outstanding soccer player and was with our youth group about a year before he went to college.

When I called his mother, she told me they had helicoptered Chad to John Sealy Hospital in Galveston. I had no idea just how serious he was until she added, "The report is that he has mangled his lower leg and is in a fixator."

When I heard the word *fixator,* I knew I had to see him. I would have gone anyway, because he was a member of South Park. But the word *fixator* gave extra urgency.

When I walked into his room, Chad lay there depressed, and he obviously didn't want to talk. This wasn't the Chad I knew. Before that, he'd always been glad to see me, and his face would light up in recognition. This time he acknowledged my presence but made no effort to engage in conversation.

"Are you okay? Are you going to be all right?" I asked and then looked at his leg. "I see they gave you a fixator."

"Yeah, they did," he said.

"Chad, you remember when I had my accident? That's the same thing they put on me."

"Really?" he asked. For the first time he looked at me with interest. I don't know if he'd never seen me with mine or if he just didn't remember. I leaned closer and said, "Just remember this: I know what it feels like to have one of them."

His injury was on the lower leg. Because there are two bones in the lower leg it's less difficult to heal. As I learned before I left, his prognosis was very good.

I was able to talk to that boy, hold his hand, and pray with him in a way that made him realize I identified with his plight. For the first time, he had a sense of what he had to look forward to in his treatment. Until then, like me after my accident, no one would give Chad any specific information. Like me, he felt angry and depressed.

"The pain will last a long time, and the recovery will seem to last forever, but you'll get better. Just remember that: You will get better."

And he did.

Cancer claimed Joyce Pentecost one week before her thirty-ninth birthday. I loved her very much. She was married to Eva's brother Eddie and left behind two beautiful redheaded kids, Jordan and Colton.

Not only was Joyce one of the liveliest people I've ever met, and a fireball of a singer, but she could also light up a room by merely entering it. She rarely just sang a song; she belted it in the great tradition of Ethel Merman.

I felt honored to speak at her memorial service at First Baptist Church of Forrest City, Arkansas. More than six hundred people packed the auditorium. Because Joyce had recorded several CDs of Christian music, she left a legacy for the rest of us. On that sunny afternoon, we heard Joyce sing her own benediction.

Following her recorded music, her father, Reverend Charles Bradley, delivered a message of hope and salvation. He told the crowd, "Years ago Joyce and I made a covenant. If I went first, she would sing at my funeral. And if she went first, I would speak at hers. Today I am fulfilling that promise to my baby girl."

That moment still stays with me. Melancholy smiles broke out, tears flowed, but I don't think anyone felt anger or hopelessness.

After Joyce's father concluded his message, it was my turn to speak.

"Some may ask today, 'How could Joyce die?'" I said. "But I would say to you the better question is, how did she live? She lived well, beloved. She lived very well."

I told the hurting throng that Joyce was a redheaded comet streaking across the stage of life, that she lived and loved to make people happy, that she was a devoted friend, an ideal daughter, a doting aunt, a sweet sister, a loving mother, and a wonderful wife. I admitted freely that I didn't have the answer to the question that must have penetrated many hearts in the room: Why?

"There is comfort when there are no answers," I said. "Joyce firmly believed that if she died, she would instantly be with God. She believed that if she lived, God would be with her. That was her reason for living. That can be our reason for carrying on."

I concluded by sharing one personal moment. The last extended conversation I had with Joyce before she returned home from the hospital was about heaven. She never tired of hearing me describe my trip to heaven, so we "visited" there one final time. We talked of the angels, the gate, and our loved ones. (Joyce's own mother had died of cancer.) Joyce always wanted me to describe the music, and our final conversation together was no different.

"Just a few days ago," I said to the congregation, "I believe God was sitting behind those gates, and he told the angels, 'What we need around here is a good redheaded soprano.'

"'That would be Joyce Pentecost!' the angels said.

"God sent for Joyce, and she answered the call. She is singing now with the angelic hosts. Joyce Pentecost is absent from the body but present with the Lord."

My final words at the service were a question: "Can you lose someone if you know where she is?"

I was thirty-eight years old when I was killed in that car wreck. Joyce was the same age when she was diagnosed with cancer. I survived the ordeal; Joyce did not. But I know this: Because I was able to experience heaven, I was able to prepare her and her loved ones for it. And now I am preparing you.

Many times since my accident I have wished someone who had already gone through the ordeal of wearing a fixator for months had visited me in the hospital. I know it would have relieved a lot of my anxiety.

Whenever I hear about people having a fixator, I try to contact them. When I talk to those facing long-term illness, I try to be totally honest. There is no easy way through that recovery process, and they need to know that. Because I have been there, I can tell them (and they listen) that although it will take a long time, eventually they will get better. I also talk to them about some of the short-term problems they'll face.

My visits with Chad and Brad and others also remind me that God still has a purpose for me on earth. During that long recovery period, I sometimes longed for heaven. Looking back, however, I can see how the personal experiences I have shared with others provided a gentle pull earthward when I was in heaven. "When God is ready to take me," I was finally able to say, "he'll release me." In the meantime, I try to offer as much comfort as possible to others.

Like me, when other victims first see the fixator attached to their leg, and especially when they begin to experience the pain and their inability to move, depression flows through them. They have no idea what's going to happen next. Even though doctors try to reassure them of recovery, they hurt too much to receive comfort from the doctors' words.

Sometimes, however, the patients may be inadvertently misled into saying to me, "I'll get over this soon."

"You may get over it, but it won't be soon," I say. "This is a long-term commitment, and there's no way to speed up the process. When you face injuries of this magnitude, there is no easy way out. You have to live with it for now."

I could share other stories, but these are the experiences that kept me going through some of my own dark periods. I found purpose again in being alive. I still long to return to heaven, but for now, this is where I belong. I am serving my purpose here on earth.

# 17
# LONGING FOR HOME

You do this because you are looking forward to the joys of heaven—as you have been ever since you first heard the truth of the Good News.

COLOSSIANS 1:5

One of my favorite stories is about a little girl who left her house and her mother didn't know where she had gone. Once the mother missed her, she worried that something might have happened to her child. She stood on the front porch and yelled her daughter's name several times.

Almost immediately the little girl ran from the house next door. The mother hugged her, said she was worried, and finally asked, "Where have you been?"

"I went next door to be with Mr. Smith."

"Why were you over there?"

"His wife died and he is very sad."

"Oh, I'm so sorry, I didn't know that," the mother said. "What did you do?"

"I just helped him cry."

In a way, that's what I do. Sharing my experiences is my way of crying with others in pain.

I've discovered one reason I can bring comfort to people who are facing death themselves or have suffered the loss of a loved one: I've been there. I can give them every assurance that heaven is a place of unparalleled and indescribable joy.

Without the slightest doubt, I know heaven *is* real. It's more real than anything I've ever experienced in my life. I sometimes say, "Think of the worst thing that's ever happened to you, the best thing that's ever happened to you, and everything in between; heaven is more real than any of those things."

Since my return to earth, I've been acutely aware that all of us are on a pilgrimage. At the end of this life, wherever we go—heaven or hell—life will be more real than this one we're now living.

I never thought of that before my accident, of course. Heaven was a concept, something I believed in, but I didn't think about it often.

In the years since my accident, I've repeatedly thought of the last night Jesus was with his disciples before his betrayal and crucifixion. Only hours before he began that journey to heaven, he sat with his disciples in the upper room. He begged them not to be troubled and to trust in him. Then he told them he was going away and added, "In my Father's house are many rooms; if it were not so, I would have told you. I am going there to prepare a place for you. And if I go and prepare a place for you,

I will come back and take you to be with me that you also may be where I am" (John 14:2–3 NIV).

I had never really noticed it before, but twice Jesus used the word *place*—a location. Perhaps that may not stir most people, but I think about it often. It is a literal place, and I can testify that I know that place. I've been there. I know heaven is real.

Since my accident, I've felt more intensely and deeply than ever before. A year in a hospital bed can do that for anyone, but it was more than just that. Those ninety minutes in heaven left such an impression on me that I can never be the same person I was. I can never again be totally content here, because I live in anticipation.

I experienced more pain than I thought a human could endure and still live to tell about it. In spite of all that happened to me during those months of unrelenting pain, I still feel the reality of heaven far, far more than the suffering I endured.

Because I am such a driven person and hardly ever slow down, I have often felt I needed to explain why I can't do certain things. When I'm fully dressed, most folks would never realize I have such debilitating injuries. However, when I face an activity that this reconstructed body just can't do (and people are sometimes surprised how simple some of those acts are), I often get strange responses.

"You look healthy," more than one person has said. "What's the matter with you?"

Occasionally, when I follow someone down a flight of stairs—a difficult experience for me—they hear my knees grinding and turn around. "Is that awful noise coming from you?" they ask.

"Yes." I smile and add, "Isn't it ridiculous!"

My relative mobility is quite deceptive. I get around better than anyone imagined I would. But I know—even if it doesn't show—that I'm quite limited in what I can do. I work hard to walk properly, because I don't want to attract attention to myself. I had enough stares and gawks when I wore my fixator.

Trying to act and look normal and to keep pushing myself is my way of dealing with my infirmities. I've learned that if I stay busy, especially by helping others, I don't think about my pain. In an odd way, my pain is its own therapy. I intend to go on until I can't go anymore.

We're such victims of our human invention of time that we have to think in temporal concepts—it's the way we're wired. That's an important point for me to make. My human inclination is to wonder what my welcoming committee is doing during these years while I'm back on earth.

As I ponder this, I don't believe my greeting committee said, "Oh no, he doesn't get to stay." They're still there at the gate. They're waiting. For them, time is not passing. Everything is in the eternal now—even if I can't put that into words. Even if ten more years pass, or thirty, in heaven it will be only an instant before I'm back there again.

Going to heaven that January morning wasn't my choice. The only choice in all of this is that one day I turned to Jesus Christ and accepted him as my Savior. Unworthy as I am, he allowed me to go to heaven, and I know the next time I go there, I'll stay.

I don't have a death wish. I'm not suicidal, but every day I think about going back. I long to return. In God's timing, I know with utter certainty that I will. Now I look forward to that time and eagerly await the moment. I have absolutely no fear of death. Why would I? There's nothing to fear—only joy to experience.

As I've pointed out before, when I became conscious again on earth, a bitter disappointment raged through me. I didn't want to return, but it wasn't my choice.

For a long time, I didn't accept that God had sent me back. But even in my disappointment, I knew that God had a purpose in everything that happened. There was a reason I went to heaven and a purpose in my returning. Eventually, I grasped that God had given me a special experience and a glimpse of what eternity will be.

Although I long for my heavenly home, I'm prepared to wait until the final summons comes for me.

Going through thirty-four surgeries and many years of pain has also helped me realize the truth of Paul's words to the Corinthians: "Praise be to the God and Father of our Lord Jesus Christ, the Father of compassion and the God of all comfort, who comforts us in all our troubles, so that we can comfort those in any trouble with the comfort we ourselves have received from God" (2 Cor. 1:3–4 NIV).

As long as I'm here on earth, God still has a purpose for me. Knowing that fact enables me to endure the pain and cope with my physical disabilities.

In my darkest moments, I remember a line from an old song: "It will be worth it all when we see Jesus."

I know it will.

# 18
# THE *WHY* QUESTIONS

Now we see things imperfectly as in a poor mirror, but then we
will see everything with perfect clarity. All that I know now is
partial and incomplete, but then I will know everything completely, just as God knows me now.

1 CORINTHIANS 13:12

Many times I've watched people on TV who say they've
had near-death experiences (NDE). I confess to being
fascinated, but I also admit to being skeptical. In
fact, I'm highly skeptical. Before and after those people spoke, I
thought, *They've probably had some kind of brain lapse. Or maybe
there was already something in their memory bank and they just
re-experienced it.* I didn't doubt their sincerity; they wanted to
believe what they talked about.

I've watched many talk shows and read about victims who
had died and been heroically resuscitated. Descriptions of their

ordeals often seemed too rehearsed and disturbingly similar, as if one person copied the story of the last. One person who claimed to have been dead for more than twenty-four hours wrote a book and said he had talked to Adam and Eve. Some of the things the first earthly couple purportedly told him don't measure up with the Bible.

Despite my skepticism—even today—of many of their testimonies, I have never questioned my own death. In fact, it was so powerful, so life-changing, that I couldn't talk about it to anyone until David Gentiles pried out the information almost two years after the accident.

I have looked at the research on NDE and thought about it often during the years.

In December 2001, *Lancet,* the journal of the British Medical Society, reported research on NDE. Most scientific and medical experts had previously dismissed these dramatic occurrences as wishful thinking or the misguided musings of oxygen-starved brains.

The study, conducted in the Netherlands, is one of the first scientific studies. Instead of interviewing those who reported they had once had a NDE, they followed hundreds of patients who had been resuscitated after suffering clinical death—that is, after their hearts stopped. They hoped that approach would provide more accurate accounts by documenting the experiences as they happened, rather than basing them on recollections long after the event of resuscitation.

Their results: About 18 percent of the patients in the study spoke of recollection of the time in which they had been clinically dead. Between 8 and 12 percent reported the commonly accepted NDE experiences, such as seeing bright lights, going through a tunnel, or even crossing over into heaven and speaking with dead relatives and friends. The researchers concluded that afterlife experiences or NDE are merely "something we would all desperately like to believe is true."[1]

Conversely, other scholars made conclusions based on their study of 344 people (ages twenty-six to ninety-two) who had been resuscitated. Most of them were interviewed within five days of the experience. The researchers contacted those same people two years later and then eight years after the event.

Researchers discovered that the experiences didn't correlate with any of the measured psychological, physiological, or medical parameters—that is, the experiences were unrelated to processes in the dying brain. Most patients had excellent recall of the events, which, the researchers said, undermined the idea that the memories were false.

The most important thing to me is that those who had such experiences reported marked changes in their personalities. They lost their fear of death. They became more compassionate, giving, and loving.

The study really proved nothing about the reality of NDE. As had been the case before the studies, one group believed NDE were merely the psychological states of those dying; the other group maintained that hard evidence supported the validity of near-death occurrences, suggesting that scientists rethink theories that dismiss out-of-body experiences.

I have no intention of trying to solve this debate. I can only relate what happened to me. No matter what researchers may or may not try to tell me, I *know* I went to heaven.

I've devoted an immense amount of time to considering *why* it happened rather than *what* happened. I have reached only one solid conclusion: Before being killed in a car accident, I remained skeptical of near-death experiences. I simply didn't see how a person could die, go to heaven, and return to tell about it. I never doubted dying, the reality of heaven, or life after death. I doubted descriptions of near-death stories. These stories all seemed too rehearsed and sounded alike. Then I died, went to heaven, and returned. I can only tell what happened to me. Not for an instant have I ever thought it was merely a vision, some case of mental wires crossing, or the result of stories I'd heard. I *know* heaven is real. I have been there and come back.

It comes down to this: Until some mere mortal is dead for a lengthy period and subsequently returns to life with irrefutable evidence of an afterlife, near-death experiences will continue to be a matter of faith, or at the very least, conjecture. But then, as one of my friends would say, "What else is new?"

One time I shared my experiences with a large congregation that included my wife's parents, Eldon and Ethel Pentecost. They've been consistently supportive and made great sacrifices during my accident and lengthy recovery.

After the service, we went to their home. At one point, Eldon and I were alone, and he told me, "I was angry the first time you shared your story of your trip to heaven."

I had no idea he felt that way.

"You finished by saying you never wanted to come back to earth."

I just nodded in affirmation, not knowing where this was going.

"I didn't understand it then, but I've changed. Now when I hear you talk about heaven's beauty, I understand a little better why you'd willingly be separated from my daughter and grandkids for a while. You know—you really do know, don't you—that they'll join you someday?"

"Without a doubt," I said.

Eldon's revelation caught me off guard. He was right, of course. I had the distinct privilege of baptizing my own children and seeing my wife baptized as well. I knew that their professions of faith were authentic. By faith, I knew that they would be residents of heaven someday. Being separated from them had never crossed my mind while I was in heaven. People in heaven simply don't have an awareness of who is *not* there. They do know who is coming.

Even today, I can say honestly that I wish I could have stayed in heaven, but my ultimate time had not yet come. After leaving heaven, if I had known that I would face two weeks in ICU, a year in a hospital bed, and thirty-four operations, I surely would have been even more disheartened from the outset. However, this was not my choice, and I returned to the sounds of one voice praying, boots crunching glass underfoot, and the Jaws of Life ripping through my shattered auto.

One question keeps troubling me: *Why?* It takes many forms.

Why did I die in that car wreck?

Why did I have the unique privilege of going to heaven?

Why did I glimpse heaven, only to be sent back?

Why did I nearly die in the hospital?

Why has God let me live in constant pain since January 18, 1989?

The short answer: I don't know. And yet that single word, *why*, remains the consummate human query. By nature, we're curious. We want to know.

All these years later, it's still not easy for me to relate what happened. Several times I tried to write this myself but couldn't. That's why I asked my friend Cec Murphey to help me with this book—if it were up to me, this book would never have been written. The emotional trauma of reliving all the events is too difficult. Only with someone else actually writing it has it finally been possible to go through this ordeal.

I still don't know why such things happen.

I do know God is with me in the darkest moments of life.

Besides asking why, there are other questions. I think they're even more important for me to ponder.

Did God want me to know how real pain could feel so that I could understand the pain of others?

Did God want me to know how real heaven is?

What did God want me to learn from all my experiences, my death, and the long period of recovery?

How can my experiences be of the most benefit to others?

After all these years, I don't have the answers to most of those questions either. I have learned a few things and realize that God still has reasons for keeping me alive on earth. I may never know his reasons, and God has no obligation to explain them to me.

Even though I don't have full answers to many of my questions, I do have peace. I know I am where God wants me to be. I know I'm doing the work God has given me.

I find comfort in a story recorded in John's Gospel. A man born blind meets Jesus and is healed. After that, he runs around praising God, but his healing is an embarrassment to the religious leaders who have been trying to turn the people against Jesus.

They interrogate the formerly blind man, trying to force him to admit that Jesus is a sinner (that is, a fraud).

The man wisely says, "Whether he is a sinner or not, I don't know. One thing I do know. I was blind but now I see!" (John 9:25 NIV). In the same way, some may not believe my account; they may think it was some kind of wish fulfillment during a point of severe trauma. I don't have to defend my experience.

I know what happened to me. For those of us whose faith is in the reality of heaven, no amount of evidence is necessary. *I know what I experienced.*

I believe God gave me a hint of what eternity in heaven will be like.

I also believe that part of the reason I am still alive, as I've already pointed out, is that people prayed. Dick Onerecker prayed me back to life—to live without brain damage. David Gentiles and others prayed so that God wouldn't take me back to heaven just yet.

I am here, I am alive, and it's because God's purposes have not yet been fulfilled in my life. When God is finished with me, I'll return to the place I yearn to be. I have made my final reservations for heaven and I'm going back someday—permanently.

Prayerfully, I'll see you there too.

# NOTES

## Chapter 4

1. Commonly called "Jaws of Life," this is a brand of tools trademarked by the Hurst Jaws of Life Company. The term refers to several types of piston-rod hydraulic tools known as cutters, spreaders, and rams that are used to pry trapped victims from crashed vehicles.

2. "What a Friend We Have in Jesus," words by Joseph Scriven, 1855.

## Chapter 18

1. Pim van Lommel, Ruud van Wees, Vincent Meyers, Ingrid Elffench, "Near-death Experience in Survivors of Cardiac Arrest: A Prospective Study in the Netherlands," *Lancet* 358, no. 9298 (December 15, 2001): 2039–45.

**Don Piper** has been an ordained minister since 1985 and has served in several capacities on church staffs, including six years as a senior pastor. He and his wife, Eva, are residents of Pasadena, Texas, and are the parents of three grown children. Don has appeared on numerous Christian and secular television and radio programs and has been the subject of countless newspaper and magazine features. He writes a weekly newspaper column, and every week you will find him preaching and leading conferences and retreats all over the United States and abroad. Don can be contacted at donpiperministries@yahoo.com.